P9-DCX-285

Company and Community

HD59
H59

Company and Community

CASE STUDIES IN INDUSTRY–CITY RELATIONSHIPS

JUL 1960

By Wayne Hodges

*Professor, New York State School of Industrial and
Labor Relations at Cornell University*

HARPER & BROTHERS, PUBLISHERS, NEW YORK

63377

COMPANY AND COMMUNITY

Copyright © 1958 by Wayne Hodges

Printed in the United States of America
All rights in this book are reserved.
No part of the book may be used or reproduced
in any manner whatsoever without written permission except in the case of brief quotations
embodied in critical articles and reviews. For
information address Harper & Brothers
49 East 33rd Street, New York 16, N. Y.

FIRST EDITION

K-H

Library of Congress catalog card number: 58–11041

Contents

1. Why Community Relations?   1
2. Community Leadership and Organization   13
3. The City and Its Problems   42
4. Financial Contributions   75
5. Industry-School Relationships   114
6. Air and Water Pollution   155
7. Strikes and Community Relations   187
8. Plant Sites and Plant Communities   242
9. Conclusions   295
   Appendix a–e   305
   Index   353

Preface

THIS book originated from discussions with community relations professionals who have attended one or another of Cornell's annual summer seminars in Community Relations for Business and Industry. Our consensus was that there ought to be a study of community relations ideas, principles and approaches based on an investigation of a variety of company-community problems in one city.

I selected Syracuse, N.Y., as the city to study for several reasons:

1. It is a diversified, middle-sized, industrial city far enough removed from other cities to supply an independent laboratory of company-community problems.

2. It has well-established company-community relationships, leadership, and community organizations.

3. Considerable community research of various kinds already had been done there, or was in prospect, to provide helpful bases on which to build. This research included a professionally conducted community survey of attitudes related to local business and industry.

Principally, I have tried in my investigations to find out how things get done in a community—why certain community projects fail while others succeed. More specifically, I have selected the community relations problem areas of greatest concern both to company managements and to industrial communities of my acquaintance. These areas, illustrated by rather detailed case studies, are: (1) financial contributions in the community, (2) public school relations, (3) pollution, (4) labor relations, and (5) attraction of new industry.

Most chapters, then, are introduced by "Syracuse Cases." Part Two of these chapters describes pertinent experiences and information got from other communities and other companies, to afford comparisons with the findings at Syracuse and to add to the usefulness of the book.

The conviction of the public relations executives of companies supporting this project is that there is more to industrial community relations than the collecting and localizing of standard public relations gimmicks from here and there. This book intends to present background information necessary to the intelligent management of any community relations program that goes beyond mere techniques.

There is hope, too, that this book may be helpful to local government bodies and agencies, to public schools, to health and welfare agencies, and to industrial development organizations, all of which might profit by knowing more than they generally do about the community interests, values and expectations of locally operating industry.

The study was financially supported by ten companies: Allied Chemical and Dye, American Airlines, Carrier Corporation, Ford Motor, General Electric, General Foods, Robert Gair Corporation, Grumman Aircraft, Fred Rudge, Inc., and New York Telephone.

I cannot list by name all the people who have helped me in this project. To the above companies and their officers I am grateful for sponsorship as well as for the advice and assistance of their able staffs. To all the alumni of all Cornell Community Relations management seminars, I am thankful for supplying me with more material than could be used in a whole series of books. To the many companies in Syracuse, and to people there in city and county government, to staffs of health and welfare agencies and the community chest, and to the officers of other organizations, who gave me collectively literally months of time, my thanks. To the executives of national or area organizations, both in industry and in welfare work, who wrote pages of informative letters, also my appreciation. To the librarians who remained tolerant of me under difficult conditions, including the librarians at various units of Cornell and Syracuse Universities, at the Syracuse Public Library, and at the American Management Association, and Public Relations Society of America offices in New York, my gratitude.

In Syracuse I had a helpful committee, known rather negatively to its membership as the "Keep Hodges Out of Trouble Committee"; to its members I am grateful for a job well done. The entire roll of the Central New York Chapter of the Public Relations Society of America, too, must be especially thanked. Several people in Syracuse deserve to be remembered by name and with particular gratitude; they are Gwyn Thomas, then Director of Public Relations for the Manufacturers Association and now with Associated Industries of New York; Robert Sloan, President of Crouse-Hinds Company; Howard Dirks, Vice President of Carrier Corporation; Arthur Grimm, district manager of the New York Telephone Company; and Stewart F. Hancock, attorney.

At Cornell, a faculty committee at the School of Industrial and Labor Relations afforded me invaluable early guidance; on it were Professors Alpheus Smith, Alice Cook, and Frank Miller. My thanks, too, to Professors William F. Whyte and Leonard P. Adams of Cornell for critically reading sections of the manuscript. And to Dean M. P. Catherwood my appreciation for additional backing, moral and financial, when I needed it.

To Mrs. Patricia Barry and to Miss Ruth Olmstead, my
assistants at Cornell, my thanks for their diligence in research
and preparation of the manuscript.

Finally to my wife and my children, who cheerfully resigned
themselves to months of living with cartons of notes, and
often with notes outside of cartons, many thanks.

Cornell University, August 1958

Company and Community

1-
Why Community Relations?

INDUSTRIAL Community Relations is Public Relations at the plant city level; and public relations I would define simply as an organization's relationships, good and bad, with groups important to its prestige and/or profit. Most definitions of public relations have two parts: The first part has to do with corporate responsibility and with policies and projects that are in the public good. The second part has to do with effective communication about those responsible policies and projects.

This book is concerned with both parts of public relations at the plant city level, but puts greater emphasis on the first. Public relations as a staff function is largely communication; but, more broadly viewed, public relations is a matter of establishing and improving corporate relationships, and of solving and, preferably, preventing problems that grow out of these relationships. Such concern gets us into management policy making; and in some companies, where the public relations executive is only a hired newspaperman, that means getting out of the public relations department altogether.

This book is about community relationships and community problems that affect locally operating companies.

Industrial community relations is expensive in management time. It involves executive time, first, to build a spirit of community within a plant, and, second, to provide community-centered leadership outside the plant. Most com-

I

munity-minded executives of well-thought-of companies I encountered in Syracuse were loath to count their hours given to achieve these two ends; yet to their way of thinking this contribution of management time was the most important part of their companies' community relations.

I found that ten to fourteen hours a week, more than half of that spent at luncheon and evening sessions, was about par for the most active executives; and six to ten hours a week was fairly common in these managements.

Without an expenditure of management time and honest concern, a community relations program will not succeed on any long-range basis. Some companies are skeptical about the possibility of returns on such an investment. Here are some realistic, and to them rhetorical questions which certain management men have asked:

Isn't it cheaper to concentrate exclusively on operations, and to pay wages that will attract the kind of workers needed? Isn't it true that all this emphasis on human relations, public relations, personnel relations, and community relations is leading American management close to paternalism on the one hand and to a surrender of its prerogatives on the other hand? Wasn't America built upon rugged competition and hard-headed business acumen rather than upon conciliation and giving-in to demands from employees and do-good groups? Isn't the old saying that "business is the business of business" still a valid assumption, even socially considered?

One of these questioners, a company president, still shaking with indignation, complained: "We opened the company's swimming pool to the community—and shortly after our workers walked out on strike. So this is community relations!"

All public relations, this executive is convinced, is a sort of random giving away of premiums, without any return in increased sales.

These objectors deserve an answer:

Companies which do not recognize any responsibility to their plant communities not covered by public law (and, numerically, more companies are in this category than not) are free riders on the good reputation of their betters. The managements of such companies consider themselves to be rugged individualists, and they are among the most vehement critics of enlarged government controls over business and society. The preservation of such corporate freedoms as they enjoy, however, is due to the community-minded companies, to companies which are offsetting the public disapproval of business engendered by their lack of social responsibility.

Although a company ought to evaluate every aspect of its operations as closely as possible, it is difficult to place a specific dollar value on a community relations program.[1] "Industry's responsibility to the community can be met practically and profitably," Board Chairman of the National Cash Register Company, Stanley C. Allyn, once said. "Delay in assuming this obligation is dangerous. We have a costly and formidable lesson in labor relations. The consequence of years of indecision is a Federal mandate to curb and control. History may repeat itself with the corporation in its relation to the community."

Just as most people are not disturbed by the federal labor law, or by the former Wagner Act, so most people would not be nearly so disturbed by such a community relations law as the managers of business might be. In this voting democracy, every business, and every aspect of every business, exists only by public permission.

Community relations has somewhat more immediate advantages as well:

Employee recruiting is encouraged by a local reputation as "The best place in town to work." Good communities, in turn, attract and keep not only wage earners but professional employees. Community activities serve a definite management function in the development of executives. Increasing product sales in plant cities is not an important item in the community relations thinking of most companies; but the connection between community relations and customer relations is a vital one to service-type operations, as utilities, public carriers, etc. Community-acceptance activities will build a reservoir of good will to stand the company in good stead in time of trouble, as during times of strikes or shortages. And, most important, the workman who is proud rather than ashamed of his company when he talks with his neighbors is, more than likely, a productive workman. A worker whose family is living in a pleasant, progressive town will not carry so many worries with him to his desk, bench or machine.

Since the subject of industrial community relations first began to receive serious management consideration following World War II, one paramount concept has been growing each year; now it has become almost a fundamental of community relations thinking:

The social aspects of a plant town, which make it a better or worse place to live, cannot be separated from the "business climate" aspects of the town which permit or hinder the profitability of locally operating companies.

That America got along without a publicly organized welfare policy almost up to the Great Depression, the famous Norwegian sociologist, Gunnar Myrdal, believes, was the result not only of our relative prosperity and rugged individualism, but also the result of "the world's most generous private charity." [2] Society since has grown complicated.

As the nation, and its communities and companies, have grown in size and complexity, inter-group relationships have become increasingly difficult. As companies got bigger, public suspicion of them grew, too. "You can't hide an elephant," Kennerly Woody, vice-president of New York Telephone Company, once dryly remarked to his fellow executives. "And even a friendly elephant is likely to be looked upon with suspicion."

Some journalistic and academic observers of the business scene are consistently cynical about management's motivation for entering community affairs. "Most management people," said one such in Syracuse, "are on committees out of self-interest, personal ambition, or company policy; not because they are really interested or believe in the project they are serving."

W. Lloyd Warner and James C. Abegglen believe that community activities "do not necessarily represent . . . a felt obligation to the community or an opportunity to participate with a broad social group." [3]

The editors of *Fortune*, in their book, *The Executive Life*, report they have found that executives do not really like civic work:

When they engage in it they do so more out of a sense of obligation, or on order from their company, than for any inward satisfaction they expect from the participation. Older executives are often heavily involved in good works, but the involvement, many confess, is more entrapment than free choice. [4]

I largely disagree with these observations, on the basis of many interviews with Syracuse industrialists. Certainly they joke rather ruefully that their problem is "not getting into community affairs, but rather getting out of them." Community service *is* work, and worrisome if undertaken at the sacrifice of other obligations. And motives may indeed be mixed, as are those of anyone giving time to charitable causes. Continued activity in community projects, nevertheless, invariably results in increased interest in the projects, whatever the initial motivation may have been. In actual truth, most businessmen active in their communities would be separated from these activities only with great reluctance.

Analysts of the business psyche sometimes infer that the American businessman has "guilt feelings" which cause him to preach about corporate responsibility and human relations, and occasionally even to behave in socially acceptable ways. That a business background—or, for that matter, an academic, labor, law or other background—somehow deprives people of honest concern for their communities or gives them guilt complexes, is a conclusion reached perhaps by supposition rather than research.

David Reisman's popular book, *The Lonely Crowd*, makes the related but perhaps more sensible point that industry, in trying to manipulate the public into thinking better of it, finds that actually it has manipulated itself into being socially responsible, and even into *feeling* socially responsible.[5]

Industrial plant managers and other company executives are neither more nor less virtuous and honest than the average American.

"Much has been said in recent years of the 'new type of businessman,' as if, by some process of sexless eugenics, the bull terriers and bloodhounds of the business past had been crossbred to produce a race of intelligent and kindly poodles," said Crawford H. Greenewalt, who as president of Du Pont has had some opportunity to observe the breed. "I have never been able to accept this concept. It seems to me that men will always reflect the society in which they live, will respond to its pressures, its ideals, and its customs."[6]

There is historical perception in that remark. The development of basic public relations—meaning the formulation of public-centered policies and the execution of projects in conformance with such policies—has grown with a changed society, changed outlooks, and changed corporate structure. Its evolution has been in close parallel with the development of managerial control of big business by salaried professional career men and with the public ownership of stock in most large corporations.

Salaried industrial leaders have achieved their positions by ability and effort in the stiffest kind of competition, and they are professional in every sense of the word. It is as important to the new business leader and his career as it is to the corporation which he manages that public respect shall result from his supervision.

Americans are not much frightened by industrialists any more. The "Organization Man" is more to be pitied than scorned. Industrialists with their hearts in their work may not consider this change in public attitudes, if it is a change, altogether for the better. Most Americans, including business-men themselves, have considerably more confidence in the free market economy and the civilization which it has given us than they have in the individuals who buy, sell and manu-facture under that system. Community citizens, when they understand it, are willing to accept the need for good "busi-ness climate," even if at the same time they may dislike a few of the industrialists in the community's leadership structure.

Is it possible, or even likely, that American industry will become too expert at public relations for the good of the country? Can industry become so powerful in prestige and influence within a community that it can manipulate the townspeople and their organizations at will?

Actually, most communities suffer from a lack of industrial management's abilities in civic affairs. Every segment of society ought, as a democratic obligation (a) to do all it can for those aspects of society with which it is connected, and

(b) to present its points of view, if it has such, as ably as it can for acceptance or rejection by the people.

Management's greatest contribution—personal contribution, that is—to its community is its organizing and administrative ability, precisely the talent it exercises to make plants profitable. Communities have hardly begun to capitalize on this potential of talent.

Among health agencies, as Aubrey Mallach of the New York State Citizens' Health Council puts it, "each has its own favorite way of not dying." It took years of persuading, Mr. Mallach reported, to get the tuberculosis people to look at the hearts photographed on their X-ray pictures of lungs.[7] Health agencies' opposition to multiple-analyses of clients' health problems is another example in point.

The industrialist or business executive, as a lay board member with an organizing turn of mind, can maintain his objectivity; he has less inclination to think of the agency as an end in itself. Diagnoses and procedures for such coordination are the province of professional social workers, or rather teams of specialized social workers. But board members from industry can initiate and push the plan of coordination to reduce the case loads of their community. A program reducing the burden of health and welfare costs must involve both professional knowledge and organizational know-how. There is too little of this kind of team work on the part of management men and agency professionals. The initiative in the matter will have to be management's.

The need for a similar management service exists in many other community areas, as later chapters will make clear. Organization is necessary both to community achievement and to industrial recognition in the community. But leadership—however efficient the organization which it leads—

ultimately is a personal matter. Management skills have more to offer society than has yet been given.

As with most activities of a service nature, which go beyond one's self or beyond the corporate entity, one finds two sets of reasons for performing them. This is true of community relations. So far, we have talked about the first set of reasons—the practical reasons, all of which relate to the fact that the industrial plant and its community mutually affect one another and, to a degree, will be happy and prosperous or unhappy and poor together.

The second set of reasons for community relations concerns the responsibility that each man of ability and influence has to mankind, to help people to stay individuals in the face of great pressures for conformity, and hence for social mediocrity.

Pressures toward mediocrity and conformity stem in part from our "least common denominator" public education system. In part, they stem from industry itself, as an evening of sponsored television or a reading of William H. Whyte's *The Organization Man*,[8] makes all too clear. "The great new term of reproach nowadays is 'controversial,' " says Dr. Robert Maynard Hutchins. "The dream of the public relations man is that all the people of America will discern in his clients the perfect combination of all the popular stereotypes of the day. Hence the tendency toward the flat conformity to what the public relations man discovers, through a series of careful polls, to be the prevalent opinion of the moment. . . . A civilization in which there is not continuous controversy about important issues, speculative and practical, is on the way to totalitarianism and death." [9]

There is, of course, some paradox in the two concepts: (1) that the establishment of "bridges of agreement" between the company and its publics is the essence of public relations; and (2) that public relations at the same time is an essence of the

American competitive economic system. But honest community relations does not seek for a "togetherness" to the point of developing a brand of community "Organization Man." The purpose of community relations is not town-wide conformity. The purpose of community relations, rather, is to improve a plant community in all aspects which directly or indirectly affect a business; and a surprising number of aspects of the community so classify.

Community activities, according to one public relations professional, can be classified roughly in two categories: *angelic* and *controversial*.

Angelic activities—that is, serving on the boards of well-established institutions devoted to building character in the young, or working on community chest committees—are *safe* contributions of executives' time. Some of the public good will shining upon these devoted citizens will be reflected upon their companies.

Controversial activities—participating in almost any sort of city planning, or serving on school boards—have a potential of trouble. Decisions on some issues are apt to be unpopular with a portion of the citizenry. Some of the ill will accruing to these equally devoted community leaders will rub off on their companies, or so it is feared.

Robert E. Wilson, board chairman of Standard Oil Co. (Indiana), believes that management has a "moral responsibility to take the lead in fighting for sound principles and opposing the bad," and deplores lack of courage in fighting political dishonesty and demagoguery. "Maybe we have become so obsessed with the desirability of making friends that we are unwilling to make any enemies, even the right kind."

Actually, a division between the angelic and the controversial is more academic than real. Even what seems to be the most innocent project may explode into controversy; likewise, it is quite possible to spend an entirely peaceful term on a planning commission. Public attitudes in the long run are bound to be favorable toward a company which selects activities for management participation on the basis of their benefit to employees, company and community, regardless of controversial implications.

A community, as one definition has it, is a place plus people plus organizations plus common interests. A community of interests ought not to be confused with conformity of opinions, even conformity with one's own opinions.

The businessman in his community finds himself in a position similar to the position forced upon the United States in the world of free nations. Both are surprised, and a little uncomfortable, to discover that now they are looked upon as more or less enlightened leaders. In their unaccustomed responsibility, both occasionally bumble; both usually profit from their mistakes. In both cases, and despite their protestations to the contrary, it is historically true that the respective parties, the United States and the American business executive, put in some pretty good licks to get where they are.

Often, the same people are the skeptics of the leadership abilities of both these parties. Can this industrialist and this nation, which have achieved productivity and profitability, achieve also as leaders in social matters?

I would not presume to advise the Department of State, but let the community-minded management man ponder these remarks by the philosopher Whitehead:

The essence of democratic leadership is that it shall be so exercised as to promote opportunities for the fitting initiative of those within the society. . . .
In any society, each member is to some degree a leader, whilst to a large extent he is directed by others or by the ways of life he finds about him. For leadership consists in obtaining the permis-

sion of a group to make an individual contribution, to give it a way of life somewhat different from what it would otherwise have had.[10]

FOOTNOTES

[1] *See* Appendix B for a discussion of evaluation techniques.

[2] *An American Dilemma*, New York: Harper & Brothers, 1944.

[3] W. Lloyd Warner and James C. Abegglen, *Big Business Leaders in America*. Harper & Brothers, New York, 1955, p. 97.

[4] Doubleday, Garden City, 1956, p. 71.

[5] Doubleday, Garden City (Anchor Books), 1956.

[6] An address before ANPA, New York, April 26, 1956.

[7] Address to central regional meeting of the Council for Local Public Health Services of New Jersey, Allentown, Oct. 1, 1952.

[8] Doubleday (Anchor Books), Garden City, 1957.

[9] Quoted in an editorial, *Public Relations Journal*, Dec. 1953, p. 2.

[10] T. N. Whitehead, *Leadership in a Free Society*, Harvard University Press, 1944, p. 258.

2-
Community Leadership and Organization

How local industry developed its present leadership, and how local company managements have organized to strengthen this leadership and improve their community relations makes an enlightening study.

Community leadership is by no means inheritable. Yet the dead leaders of previous generations do influence today's leaders in subtle ways. America's fabulous, last century generation of inspired tinkerers, of whom Syracuse had its share, were *personal* leaders for the most part. Herbert H. Franklin (automobiles with air-cooled engines), L. C. Smith (typewriters), and Rowland Hazard (industrial chemicals) were among other Syracusans in this classical American tradition of enterprise and individualism.

These men did not hitch rides to success on established industry; they first made their own industries, or contributed materially to them, then drove their companies to success. Those who succeeded became wealthy, and, for the most part, the companies they founded are operating today. As the industrial and community leaders of their time, they ran their businesses and gave their charity as they pleased. With palatial homes on fashionable James Street, they were the city's indus-

trial peerage. Their wives planned and organized the city's
charities, and the men financed them generously. Theirs was a
personal responsibility for the less fortunate. They understood
well the meanings of both "profit" and "charity"; but they
never heard of "public relations," much less of "community
relations."

Their successors to the leadership of Syracuse—still top executive officers of such older local companies as Smith-Corona,
Easy Washing Machine, Crouse Hinds, Onondaga Pottery,
Lipe Rollway—retained much of the classical tradition of personal leadership and personal responsibility. At the same time,
they founded such cooperative organizations as the Chamber
of Commerce and the early Manufacturers Association of Syracuse. These men of the city's second generation of industrial
leadership, some of whom are still living, also developed the
community relations concept of corporate (as well as personal) responsibility to the city.

Present managements of older, local companies maintain
this philosophy, and continue to serve in the community's
leadership structure. But no longer is the title of "Mister Syracuse" passed around among them as it once was.

Today, Stewart F. Hancock, a corporation attorney who has
been sitting on local company boards since 1909, is "Mr. Syracuse" to the officers of most locally-owned concerns. To them
he personifies the Syracuse tradition of leadership; and unquestionably, Mr. Hancock was the principal figure behind
the city's progress during the 1930's and 1940's.

Although his influence has not materially declined, his
energy, at age 70-plus, has. Perhaps he can be most aptly
described presently as the philosopher-guide of the Syracuse
leadership. A slender, gentle and quietly humorous man, he
has been at times very forceful indeed.[2]

But some younger Syracuse leaders would deny that there is

any longer a "Mr. Syracuse"—and claim that this mythical office itself is *passé*—disappearing from the American scene along with the centralized leadership it symbolizes. Yet the almost stereotyped answer to the question, "Who are the real community leaders in Syracuse?" is—revealingly—"Stewart Hancock and a half dozen top industrial men." Since Carrier Corporation moved to Syracuse in 1937, Cloud Wampler, now chairman of the board, has been acknowledged a top leader.

Of late, the upper pinnacle of the city's leadership triangle is becoming rounded instead of pointed; industrial decentralization has made for more management men, and the leadership base has broadened. The locally owned company is no longer the exclusive source of Syracuse leadership, although it continues to dominate.

Dispersion of American industry—which has increased the number of branch plants to about half of the total of the area's industry—is not significantly changing the conservative philosophy of Syracuse community leadership. The patriarchs among local managements confess to one another that the problem now is to educate branch plant managers to be as concerned for the community as they themselves are.

This concern is evident in the rule that the president of the Manufacturers Association of Syracuse shall always be selected from among presidents and board chairmen of companies, thus ruling out branch managers and other "newcomers" from its top position. The rationale behind this decision was verbalized by Mr. Hancock at the 1956 Cornell seminar in Industrial Community Relations when he said:

> Our local communities have lost support for their community institutions from locally owned corporations. They have lost the leadership of top executives who were also owners of their businesses . . . The duty of providing leadership for community activities and organizations which determine the character of the

community is so important that we in Syracuse are unwilling to admit that the president of a local company has any right to delegate concern for them to someone else . . . It is fundamental that there can be no successful organization without leadership.

Professional managers who run local branch plants may, it is true, have less sentimental attachment to the city; and they may be handicapped by headquarters policies. But as the concept of industrial community relations spreads, they increasingly take professional interest in their plant community just as they take professional interest in their industry. Theirs is a professional community relations program, but one no less honest, and perhaps no less beneficial to company and community. Inevitably they will achieve at least equal representation in city leadership structuring in the future.

The top leadership in Syracuse is industrial, as befits an industrial city.[3] Its membership (actually nearer two dozen than a "half dozen") is as varied in opinions, appearance, personality, and background as a like number of college professors would be. But they traditionally work together in community affairs with remarkable unanimity. Decisions concerning a particular community project, it would seem, must be nearly unanimous before the project will be undertaken.

Many categories of citizens not often found at the top level are leaders nevertheless: proprietors of leading stores, the mayor and the chairman of the county board of supervisors, the top officers of local banks, a few of the leading clergymen and at least one newspaper editor and one radio-television executive. But in this category these are outnumbered by heads of smaller companies, vice presidents of more important corporations, and executive heads of leading management organizations. At this level are the people who operate or "chair" the various community projects, whose names appear in the newspapers frequently. As the second tier of the leadership structure, they qualify as "captains."

Below them are the many people commonly referred to by the community relations specialist as "thought leaders," leaders of larger ethnic groups (the Poles and Italians in Syracuse), educators, lawyers, doctors, clergymen, departmental editors and columnists, executive heads of social agencies and professional societies, a few (very few in Syracuse) union leaders, plus a great many active middle management men from business and industry. A better term than "thought leaders" for this third level of leadership would be "communicators." They are the media for reaching, in a personal way, a fair proportion of the citizenry.

The Syracuse leadership structure, and that of most industrial cities, is somewhat fluid. Occasionally key people from the second and third levels of the structure will join the policy makers because of special knowledge and areas of influence. But this fluidity should not obscure the fact that leadership structure exists. Nameless, perhaps, not talked about, not formalized at all, but it is there. *And no major community project—particularly projects that involve large sums of money—can succeed without recognizing it and using it.*

It is easy to characterize community citizens, below the several levels of leadership, as quiescent, apathetic, and indifferent to improving their city. Quiescent they usually are, but not so apathetic or indifferent as their slowness to move might indicate. "The people" make their own decisions, albeit they most often are decisions of a thumbs-up or thumbs-down nature. They rarely originate important community projects, although their wants and prejudices may be sensed far up the leadership ladder, there to be considered when plans are formulated.

For example, inclusion of mental health programs in community chest financing came about in Syracuse, Detroit and perhaps other cities, only when the public was ready (or had been educated) to accept mental illness as a community problem. Leaders were convinced of the importance of mental health long before they dared to include it in chest drives. The people at large have taken a stubbornly conservative position, too, against fluoridation of water.

Wise leaders don't over-estimate their leadership; they never put it to a real test if they can avoid doing so. The citizens' democratic power is the power of final decision.

Syracusans are, characteristically, a vocal, meeting-holding, letter-writing lot, usually in active debate about something: fluoridation, hospital reorganization, public housing, the pigeon nuisance, the transit system, State Fair improvements or the high cost of haircuts. Organizations are fantastically numerous, each with at least one avowed purpose, regular meetings and a publicity chairman. Most are more than social avenues for expressing private opinions in public; they actually initiate many worthwhile community services.

Women's organizations busy themselves with supporting activities for the elderly, a nursery school for blind children, scholarships for delinquents and for student teachers, and investigations of local slums. Elks, Masons and service clubs work hard for health and safety education, the Kiwanians campaigning to rescue the city's trees from Dutch elm disease. The city's ethnic groups are collected into a multitude of societies, among them the Polish Citizens Club, a nice mixture of the civic, the political and the religious. The professionally managed Jewish organizations are among the most effective in the city, supporting a home for the aged, a community center and numerous welfare campaigns. Church groups in Syracuse have been involved in everything from inter-faith "tot lots," and migrant workers counselling, to sexy comics and higher teachers salaries.

Cataloguing of Syracuse's organizations and their interests could be extended for many pages (and has been by some authors), but this is sufficient to make the point that a city with as strong an industrial leadership structure as Syracuse's may also have plenty of widely dispersed community activities.[4] And these essentially democratic activities may add up to significant community contributions. Yet it is apparent that few such projects are large-scale.

Myriad, complicated organization is not peculiar to Syracuse. "In some American communities," writes Professor Robin Williams of Cornell, "the large number of formally organized groups and associations appear to have reached practically the upper limit in their demands for participation —a limit imposed by sheer paucity of time. . . . This is the familiar picture of so-called over-organization in many local areas, a condition which would have been unthinkable in the old-fashioned rural community."[5]

This situation, Professor Williams believes, is made possible by the "permissive power structure" and is encouraged by the diversity of interests and values, by the political weakness of organized groupings, and by organizational complexity. He thinks these organizations tend to proliferate because they find themselves ineffectual; maybe, they rationalize, another committee or council or citizens group will do the job.

Among the management-related organizations in Syracuse which, because of their alliance with the leadership structure, do have considerable influence is the Manufacturers Association of Syracuse. Originating in 1913 as a luncheon club adjunct of the Chamber of Commerce, it became more formalized, more highly organized as time went on. Finally in the mid-thirties, the era of the New Deal, the need for inter-industry cooperation and exchange of information—particularly concerning labor relations—seemed acute, and a reorganization of the association was undertaken.

This re-organization was in large part the work of Stewart Hancock and Cloud Wampler (whose company, the Carrier Corporation, had just moved to Syracuse). They noted the effectiveness of Rochester's Industrial Management Council and decided that Syracuse could learn from its example. Any problem of community improvement, including the establishment of a strong manufacturers association or a united fund drive, always comes down to getting a group of men to act, Mr. Hancock believes.

"A really representative 'leadership-of-leaders,' which will have the know-how, the organizations, and the means to get things done, doesn't just happen," Mr. Hancock said. "It must be planned." [6]

Syracuse industrial leaders and the staff of the association all agree that the post-reorganization effectiveness of the Syracuse Manufacturers Association is primarily due to its leadership by top management. But to draw outstanding men into community activities, they say, "key individuals" must set both pace and standards. Messrs. Hancock, Wampler and colleagues seem to have set that pace. That the association has thrived—its member companies employ 85 percent of Onondaga County's industrial labor force—is a typical achievement of the top echelon of the city's leadership structure.

The association has two ends: (1) to direct specialized action on specific community problems; and (2) to work continually to strengthen industry's position in the community. The association's board of directors (again, top management men only) is elected by secret ballot with the understanding that the large companies always will be represented. One of these directors heads each of the major standing committees, although committee membership is proportioned representatively among large and small companies and among branch plant and local firms.[7]

The relationship between the association and the Syracuse Chamber of Commerce has been remarkably free of friction. Both organizations include both business and industry in their administrations as well as in general membership. Thus—despite the emphasis on industry in the Manufacturers Association and on commerce in the Chamber—such conflicts as do arise between them have always resulted in compromises. The association also works closely with all other business and professional groups in Syracuse, as with the very active and influential Syracuse Governmental Research Bureau and the Syracuse Citizens Foundation. All these organizations have some interlocking of directorships.

The Syracuse Manufacturers Association, because of its key position in the city's leadership structure, clearly reflects in its membership and in its activities and policies the increase of branch plant managements in the county, and the increasing acceptance of these branch management people as a source of community leadership. Numerically, they equal the representatives of local industry on association committees, and on the board itself, and are, and have been, committee chairmen and officers. There remains the one top spot in the association yet to be filled by a branch plant manager of whatever title.

The Citizens Foundation, begun in 1946, might be described as the educational unit of the community leadership structure. Officers of the foundation wish to make it plain that they are an organization of citizens, and that the foundation's 200 members include professional as well as business management people.

Basically, the purpose of the foundation is to promote community understanding of, and appreciation for, American freedoms. It is purposely a mixture of Syracuse's older, top-level management men and the younger, community-conscious, management-oriented men. The founders saw it as a combination "young spokesmen" organization and training ground for future leaders.[8]

The foundation, which won the Freedom Foundation George Washington Honor Medal in 1953, has indeed accepted its "educational mandate" with great diligence, although perhaps with some inclination to scatter its communication shots.

A third management-oriented and management-supported organization in Syracuse, the Governmental Research Bureau, concerns itself with more tangible aspects of business climate. It aims to assure efficient and economic management of local government. This watchdog of the taxpayer's dollar began in 1948, an outgrowth of a Chamber of Commerce investigation of city and county spending; and like the Manufacturers Association and the Citizens Foundation, it is the creation of local company managements.

The bureau's 38-man board is elected by its supporting membership, mostly companies, although individuals also are permitted to belong. Board members are largely management men of local companies, including the larger retail stores. Insofar as such distinctions are possible in Syracuse, the bureau has more philosophical kinship with the Chamber of Commerce than it has with the Manufacturers Association.

The bureau contends that its research is not an end in itself but is important only to the degree that it promotes beneficial action. Its research publications, printed bulletins and memos, its verbal presentations before other organizations, its consultations with a wide variety of local groups, and its support from both the news and editorial columns of the local press and on radio and TV are among the bureau's means of putting its findings to work.

The Bureau's recourse to the public opinion of property owners is strongly supplemented by its excellent relationships with members of the city's elected Common Council and the county's elected supervisors. The council in fact has used the bureau as a semi-official consulting body. The bureau's studies are respected, if not always admired, even by city and county officers whose budgets are being investigated. Local government is conservative in this Republican community, and the bureau and governmental office-holders have no basic ideological differences.[9]

As will be further evident in the following chapter, the Governmental Research Bureau is the protective and action unit of the business leadership structure. The Citizens Foundation, we have seen, is the educational unit that speaks generally for "the American way" with a highly organized program of communication. The Manufacturers Association and the Chamber of Commerce, themselves, are the organizational umbrellas to cover all locally operating business and industry while taking inter-industry and inter-business stands and cooperative action. All are concerned, although certainly not exclusively, with the development of the community's business climate.[10]

Syracuse industrial leadership is more organized, if less individualistic, than it was in earlier generations. Yet, paradoxically, the leadership structures, both formal and informal, were conceived and instituted by the older local companies for the most part. At this writing, the nature of the city's leadership seems to be in transition. That Syracuse may not long have a "Mister Syracuse," or even several such personalities at the apex of its leadership structure, is not so much a matter of the old leaders dying off as it is a proportional increase in the number of branch managements operating in the city.

Meanwhile, Stewart Hancock and his associates, both of the past generation and present generation, and the functionally specialized organizations they have founded, can regard their community efforts with considerable, if not complete, satisfaction.

2-
Community Leadership and Organization

PART TWO

MANAGEMENT-EMPLOYEE relationships have grown in complexity from the personal, first-name basis of the small owner-operated company of the last century, to the formalized, multi-level supervision that impersonalizes management-employee relations in large corporations today.

A parallel phenomenon has occurred in plant-community relationships.

The town, like the company, has grown complicated in its problems and in its operation. Professional community relations staffs, like professional personnel staffs, become necessary to management's communication. Employers organizations become necessary to coordinate management's relationships with new civic complexities. Charity, even, has become highly organized and depersonalized, and management's community service is now largely a matter of sitting on agency boards and organizing financial support.

The growing depersonalization of management-employee relations in industry historically was accompanied by employee dissatisfactions—and by unionization. This transitional period of misunderstandings likewise had its parallel in plant-community relationships. Managements grew apart from their

25

neighbors as well as from their employees. To some extent, this period is still with us.

The massive administrative units of today's industries, cities and institutions, to quote Professor Williams, "constitute a giant superstructure upon the organic groupings of the old society."

"As chains of interaction and interdependence become longer and more intricate, actions . . . at decision-points have far-flung repercussions . . . (and) each set of decisions elicits massive adjustments"—hence any decision is "freighted with public interest." [11]

Corporate and community leadership—meaning industrial management, to a considerable extent—has never worked within a more difficult context.

Top level community leaders have only two characteristics in common: (1) They are men with influence of one sort or another upon sizable groups of people and/or with influence over sizable sums of money; and (2) They are men willing to give substantial proportions of their time and energy to community affairs. By natural selection, perhaps, the better leaders will become leaders both in their businesses or professions and in their communities; although it is also occasionally evident that community leadership comes with no absolute guarantee of wisdom.

The apex of the city's leadership structure has obvious strengths both in matters of local government relations (police and fire protection, taxes and zoning) and in matters of community service (capital drives for hospitals, local educational facilities, operation of health and welfare organizations, etc.). These all are as much the concern of branch operations as they are of local companies.

This leadership structure, furthermore, has community communications value. Community leaders sit on boards of local organizations; they are leaders of the more important community, business and social groups. They, plus their associates within these groups, are the "thought leaders," the same people who get mailings sent out by the community relations pros on the staffs of some big company plant managements.

It seems obvious that being part of the community's upper echelon "thought leader" structure is better communication than is mailing of printed materials to members of that structure.

Downward communication in a community—from the thought leaders to the rest of the city's citizens—is, of course, by no means the whole answer to community communication. Lateral feeding of information directly into the lower strata of the community structure, e.g. via word-of-mouth communication of employees, via barbers, cab drivers, etc., and via publicity and institutional advertising, is more effective. But the downward aspects of community communication should not be neglected; and these are most accessible to companies with managements that actively participate in the top leadership of their plant cities.

Because every city differs from all others in its pattern, structure, needs and leadership, a community relations-minded management must become an integral part of its plant community in order to understand it and to work with it intelligently. The most intensive study to date of community leadership is Professor Floyd Hunter's *Community Power Structure: A Study of Decision Makers.*[12]

Professor Hunter categorized the leaders of his "Regional City" (a Southern city with a half million population) into first, second, third and fourth rate leaders, as follows:

1st rate: top officers and owners of important industrial and commercial companies.

2nd rate: operations officials of companies, bank vice-presidents, public relations men, owners of smaller businesses; top rank public officials, corporation attorneys, contractors.

3rd rate: civic organization personnel, civic agency board personnel, newspaper columnists, radio commentators, petty public officials, selected organization representatives.

4th rate: professions, i.e., ministers, teachers, social workers, personnel directors, small business managers, higher paid accountants.

Hunter sees these levels of the structure operating something like levels of management in a company, each stimulating the level below into action, each communicating to lower levels.

Here are some ways that the leadership structure of Syracuse differs from the "power structure" of Regional City:

1. Syracuse's structure is more fluid and flexible than Regional City's.

2. Syracuse leaders are strongly community minded, broadly informed about community problems (more than most professionals), and within limits of what they think possible are willing to tackle some—although granted not all—of the harder problems. Hunter found his leaders to be "isolated from many of the problems that affect the average citizen."

3. Unlike Professor Hunter's report of Regional City leaders, Syracuse leaders, so far as I could determine, are not frightened that community improvements will upset the status quo. Although they go in rather strongly for "economic education," I found no evidence, as Hunter did in Regional City, that community leaders in Syracuse are afraid the American way of life is in any real danger from forces within the community.

4. The Syracuse leadership, it seems, is not as powerful as the Regional City leadership. In Syracuse, projects of community improvement have been undertaken by the leadership, and they have failed. Professor Hunter indicates that the "power structure" of Regional City doesn't go in very heavily for community improvement in the first place. In the second place, it utilizes power pressures to get its way—usually to suppress someone or some thing.

These differences may actually be in part regional differences. Syracuse has little fear concerning Negro-White relationships; and the conservative, Republican nature of the citizenry gives the leadership little to worry about. Perhaps Syracuse leaders have more time for constructive activity because they are not so much on the defensive.

Professor Hunter makes no note, either, of local managements' anxiety that branch plant managements shall take on their share of community responsibility. In Syracuse this was a favorite topic of conversation.

Probably more industrial cities throughout the country have leaderships closer to Syracuse's than to Regional City's. Nevertheless, cities dependent upon business and industry have a fairly uniform community structure. Diagrammed, it looks something like the figure on page 30—with the arrows indicating paths of communicative influence.

As the diagram and its explanations indicate, the social structure of a city is important to community relations in two ways:

1. In carrying out a community project: in getting things done through the various community organizations and institutions.

2. In communicating with the townspeople: in reaching them with information about a company, an industry, or the industrial nature of the city in general.

Purpose number two, important as it is, has its definite limitations. Recent research indicates that community opinions in most matters are most influenced by one's peers, rather than by one's socio-economic superiors. Furthermore, people of the lower education-economic levels are not active in social or civic organizations, and have relatively little interest in community affairs. To this extent they are independent of the social structure of the community, and are becoming even

Community policy-makers: relatively few industrialists, businessmen, leading bankers; sometimes an outstanding editor, educator, lawyer or church dignitary.

The "executive level": the captains who associate both socially and in business with the policy-makers, and carry much of the burden of "getting behind" community projects. These, too, are largely industrial and business men but include some at vice-presidential level. Here often are holders of more important political offices, media managers and leading clergymen.

The "thought leaders" or, more aptly, "communicators": most clergymen, school administrators, and some teachers, leading club and PTA women, city and county officers, executives of health and welfare agencies, some reporters and broadcasters, leaders of racial groups and service clubs.

The citizenry: itself divided into education-economic levels. Higher education-economic levels are most commonly members of organizations; those of lower education-economic levels commonly are not.

Lateral lines of communication (communication independent of downward channels that are associated with the many formal organizations represented on various levels of the leadership structure) supplement communication to the citizenry at large. To reach those who are not active in any formal organizations, these lateral communications are the only channels available. Examples: publicity and institutional ads in local media, word-of-mouth communication from industrial employees, etc.

Diagram of typical community leadership structure.

relatively independent of the community's political structure —however dependent they are on community services which they use but do not understand. But these people, by and large, think of neighborhood politicians rather than of industrialists or professional people as being the real leaders of a community. Further, the poorer people are apt to go to local politicians, especially to political party representatives in their own wards, for personal advice. This has been particularly true in larger cities, where party workers have set themselves up as professional champions of the working man. In certain cities and in certain periods of history, the collective grass-root power of wardheelers not only counter-balanced the influence of local industrial leadership, but it decisively outweighed it.

In a study of "Leadership Selection in Urban Locality Areas," Ira DeA. Reid and Emily L. Ehle found people of all but the highest economic levels preferring strength and helpfulness in their leaders to "character" as such. "He (the local politico) gets the things that people want done in the ways that appeal to them as individuals. He is the city's foremost provincial . . . asking no fees for his services, and no special activity for its recipients." [13]

But wardheelers, like the political tradition of "bossism," are not nearly so powerful as they once were. Civil service and merit systems have cut into patronage. Welfare agencies, too, have deprived local politicians of the privilege of dispensing food, clothing and coal to their poorer but enfranchised party constituents.

Despite the great number of organizations in America and their huge memberships, a good many Americans are not joiners at all. A sampling in Philadelphia found that 78 percent belong to no organized group except churches; and that 55 percent of the women belong to no organizations of any kind.[14] Other studies—in New York City, Detroit and New Haven—found a similar lack of affiliation.[15]

Only when income gets above a certain level ($3,000 in 1948), are a majority of people found to be affiliated with organizations.[16] Freedman and Axelrod in 1952 found the following relationship in Detroit between economic level and participation in organizations: [17]

Income	Very Active	Do Not Belong
Under $3,000	8%	58%
$3,000–$4,000	9	34
$4,000–$5,000	14	33
$5,000–$6,000	12	38
$6,000–$7,000	12	35
$7,000–$8,000	19	28
Over $8,000	22	16

These researchers discovered that higher education levels also correlated with activity in organizations. Nine times as many from the highest education group as from the lowest were active enough in organizations to be called "leaders." These richer, better educated, organization-minded people also are the ones who regularly vote, pay property taxes, read books, talk about the community and its problems, and generally busy themselves in community affairs. If they receive and believe management's messages, why bother with the non-joiner who is both inactive and uninterested in community affairs? The only answer is that this non-joiner may well work for your company, perhaps even in a fairly skilled capacity, and hence his opinion of the company and of industry in general is important.[18]

Perhaps too much has been expected also of downward communication via a community's organizations. The people in the first and second layers of leadership belong to such organized bodies as professional societies, private clubs, business and industrial associations, service clubs, country clubs, university clubs, churches, and health and welfare boards. Their wives are members of hospital and agency auxiliaries, two or three of the better known women's clubs, various church committees, and the PTA. Except for churches and the PTA, these organizations cannot readily reach people below the socio-economic levels occupied by management families, for people below these levels do not belong to these same organizations. Only concerning a few projects would churches and the PTA be appropriate or even possible channels of communication.

It is a mistake, too, to think of all hard-to-reach people as inactive and uninterested in the community. Government employees, school teachers, agency professionals, and a good part of the white collar work force are included in the number. They belong to organizations, too, but not to organizations linked to the first and second levels of the leadership structure. In some cities a kind of secondary community structure—usually politically liberal—develops among the professional members of this group. Often citizens committees for this and that, sometimes community councils, are made up in large part of such people.

Despite the high degree of collective intelligence and abilities of most such citizen organizations, their records of achievement are not impressive. They meet regularly to discuss city problems, hear outside experts, appoint subcommittees to make further studies; but ultimately do little except to meet. They may get a street light installed or school bus service extended. But too often they fail in their larger projects because they do not recognize "how things get done in town."

Professor Hunter suspects that in Regional City the power structure, since it fears reforms that would upset the status quo, deliberately diverts the energies of various civic-minded citizen groups to harmless projects like "Paint-Up Week." He thinks the professionals (health and welfare agency staff people) represented in these organizations know what is happening, and resent it. But they are afraid to fight the power structure, which controls their jobs.

Be that as it may, I believe the selection of community

projects and the establishment of priorities among them, in most cities is dependent upon several rather obvious circumstances:

1. Major community projects involve money.

2. The community leaders control corporate giving and most other larger gifts forthcoming in the city.

3. Community projects must await their turn for financing within the limits of available money; and such priorities are set by the leadership which controls the money.

It ought to be added, too, that "financing" is a topic notably absent from the agenda of citizen groups. Some such groups even dislike publicity, and think of it as "propaganda"; hence their projects are unknown to the general public, and certainly unknown to the leadership.

H. Curtis Mial, who as executive director of the New York State Citizen Council, has had as much experience as anyone with community citizen groups of various compositions, reports that the "facts of life" for citizen groups are these: [19]

1. The death rate among community action programs is appallingly high (this is true locally as well as on the state and national level).

2. Most programs are eleventh hour efforts to meet crises. Few develop the continuity that can do a real job of economical prevention.

3. Leadership is all too often of the do-gooder variety that lacks the skills and knowledge to make the program deep-cutting and significant.

4. Programs are often small-gauge where what is needed is 'big ideas.' The frontier lies in achieving the first aspect in our definition of community development—'concern for the whole community.' It takes vision and courage to put the pieces of a fragmented community together.

5. Cooperation from groups with the largest obvious stake in building better communities is often lacking.

6. The resources being thrown into community development are small—very small.

Citizen organizations, despite all that has been said here, nevertheless have had a total democratic impact that is greater than their specific accomplishments; some few have been both astute and courageous; and America owes more to them than has yet been counted. I think the difference between American democracy and the lack of democracy in countries with equally democratic constitutions is due in good measure to the watchdog role of our many voluntary civic associations.[20]

If more business and industry people would participate in these organizations, citizens committees would have better records of accomplishment. And the social workers, teachers, and other socially conscious people in their memberships would learn that businesses, too, are interested in making a better town.

Just as there is no better way of communicating with the leadership structure than belonging to it, so there is no way of communicating with this hard-to-reach secondary leadership structure other than belonging to it, too.

As for those citizen groups whose members might construe this suggestion as advocacy that they allow themselves to be "infiltrated by industrial interests," they should recognize that the classic civic improvement programs in this country are those that have most heavily involved the top managements of locally operating business and industry.[21]

City planning is somewhat like public relations: everyone considers himself to be an expert at it. The truth is that lay groups of whatever composition—from city planning agencies through community councils to government research bureaus —must rely for their technical knowledge upon trained researchers. Independent, impeccable research can bridge the gap between company management and that most neglected of all community "publics"—local government.

Although top management men frequently are active in their political parties, most managements stay away from local governments, to escape accusations of seeking preferred treatment. (The Syracuse management-sponsored program in "Practical Politics," beginning in 1958, is described in Chapter 9.)

Independent organizations like Syracuse's Governmental Research Bureau supply the best possible solution to the delicate problem of a company's community relations with local governments.

If operated strictly on the basis of sound, thorough research, research bodies soon achieve respect in all quarters—including city hall and court house.

Such organizations are established in many cities, and some of them operate with outstanding efficiency; the amount of support they receive from local business varies. A few of the more active ones are: Pennsylvania Economy League (Philadelphia), Citizens League of Greater Minneapolis, Commission on Governmental Efficiency and Economy of Baltimore, the Dade County Research Foundation (Miami), Governmental Research Institute of St. Louis, Cleveland Bureau of Governmental Research, the Metropolitan Study Commission of Allegheny County (Pittsburgh).[22]

Employers' organizations, too, can profit from a degree of objectivity. Manufacturers' associations are most effective for their member companies as their interests and activities are extended beyond strictly business matters. And, conversely, the association that limits its interest to matters that are strictly business-centered will lose some of its credibility and hence some of its effectiveness in the community. This breadth is characteristic of all local employers' organizations

named by the National Association as being among the best
in the country: Manufacturers Association of Syracuse, In-
dustrial Management Council of Rochester, N.Y., Central
Virginia Industries (Lynchburg), Greensboro (N.C.) Industries, Evansville (Ind.) Manufacturers and Employers'
Association, and the Rockford (Ill.) Chamber of Commerce.[23]
To this honor roll should be added the Kenosha (Wisc.)
Manufacturers Association, the Racine (Wisc.) Manufacturers Association, the Worcester (Mass.) Committee on
Business Information, Stamford-Greenwich Manufacturers
Council, the Industrial Information Institute of the Mahon-
ing and Shenango Valleys (Youngstown, Ohio), and I am
sure, others not known to me.

Employers' associations, it is easily observed, have their
periods of effectiveness and relative ineffectiveness, depending
upon the presence or absence of two factors:

1. Active personal support, in terms of both time and
money, of all important top managements in the area.

2. An able, experienced staff well enough paid so that continuity of program is not disrupted by turnover.

An important part of the association's job is advising member companies on almost any subject, but particularly on industrial relations and community relations, and collecting
information and opinions from the community and from all
companies, and passing such information on to individual
companies. Equally important is the association's function as
the medium for communicating management information
and ideas to the community. It can unify member sentiment
when companies should be speaking with one voice, as in
support of a united fund or in opposition to discriminatory
legislation. It can coordinate efforts in community projects,
breaking up big community jobs and distributing pieces to
specific companies.

Cloud Wampler, now chairman of the board at Carrier Corporation, once served the National Association of Manufacturers in its project of self-evaluation. His advice to the National Association has wide applicability: NAM historically has been *against* things, Mr. Wampler said in effect. The Association's future usefulness to its members and to the country requires that it be *for* things, too. No truer observation could be made about employer organizations at the local level.

FOOTNOTES

[1] This and succeeding chapters, excepting the last, will be introduced by illustrative "cases" taken from Syracuse, N.Y. For additional information concerning this industrial city and some of its locally operating companies, see Appendix A.

[2] Mr. Hancock in 1957 was on the boards of both the Chest and Council of Social Agencies, and was President of the Chest in 1942; and from 1943–45 President of the Empire State United War Fund; in 1956–57 on the National Committee of United Community Campaigns of America. He also has been president of Legal Aid Society, County Bar Association, and board member of many foundations and agencies, and currently he is counsel for the Manufacturers Association of Syracuse. Such a listing, however, does not begin to describe his influence in the community over many years.

[3] If the top leadership has a geographical location it is the Century Club, a haven of dark oak paneling and smooth service, located between James Street's eastern elegance and its western busyness. Much modern Syracuse history has been mapped on the Century Club's snowy tablecloths.

[4] The Volunteer Center at the Council of Social Agencies keeps tab of meetings of 200-plus organizations, to help them avoid conflicts in meeting dates. The city's Planning Commission estimated there were 1,200 organized groups in Syracuse in 1949.

[5] Robin M. Williams, Jr., *American Society: A Sociological Interpretation*, Knopf, 1952, p. 472.

[6] From Mr. Hancock's discussion of community organization and leadership at the Cornell Seminar in Community Relations, Summer, 1956.

[7] The full-time staff includes an executive vice president, directors of public relations and industrial relations (the association's two principal areas of activity) plus a librarian and clerical staff.

The Manufacturers Association has its finger in most of Syracuse's industrial relations and public relations pies, although frequently on a cooperative basis with other organizations.

Immediately after World War II the Manufacturers Association of Syracuse took the generally unorthodox (for industry) position of advocating public housing. It worked on the teacher pay problem, with job evaluation men from member companies meeting with the Board of Education and with labor representatives. In the field of labor relations, particularly, the association, because of its collective nature, can frequently fight activities on behalf of individual companies, sometimes taking unpopular stands which the members think are for the popular good.

8 The Syracuse Citizens' Foundation, indeed, is a very active group, with a full-time executive. Some of its more or less regularly conducted activities are:

1. Teachers' Economic Education Workshop conducted, in cooperation with Syracuse University, the Joint Council on Economic Education, and local management groups, for the city's secondary school teachers; the program included workshops, plant tours and question and answer sessions.

2. New Voters' Forum, a get-out-the-vote program addressed particularly to those voting for the first time; bi-partisan meetings are held on the importance of voting and the function of the electoral college. It works also with the Syracuse Good Citizens Voting Council to increase voting; addresses clubs, church groups, Home Bureau units, PTA meetings.

3. An essay contest throughout Central New York on the subject "What America Means to Me." On Bill of Rights Day each member distributed ten copies of the document and encouraged media publicity, sermons by clergymen and public school commemoration.

4. Participation in "The People Act in Syracuse" radio program with the New York State Citizens Council.

5. Presidents' Day, when youth group leaders visit presidents of companies.

6. Membership Forums, held at homes of senior members to discuss tariffs, business ethics, labor relations, public housing, and to meet persons qualified for public office.

7. Future Unlimited, a program à la Junior Achievement.

8. Co-sponsorship of Business-Industry-Education Days conducted for teachers (some 1400 teachers attended the first one in 1952).

9. School Editors Day, with talks and meetings on freedom of the press for student editors.

10. "Guest Teacher" programs in which members teach classes in public and parochial schools.

11. Co-sponsorship of Business-Industry-Clergy Day (100 clergymen visited nine companies at the initial B-I-C Day).

9 One of the bureau's first jobs after its formation in 1948 was to make critical studies, in close cooperation with the local Chamber, of the New York State permissive tax law (pointing out what it called a "threat of three-deep taxation of business"), and of a proposed state gross receipts tax. In one year of investigation of city budgets (1950), the Bureau reported, it found ways to save $850,000 "without impairing essential services." The city administra-

tion protested the study's validity, with the result that the Common Council authorized a Citizens' Non-Partisan Tax Commission to report on budget needs for 1952. Some of the bureau's recommendations were accepted by the citizens group and in turn by the Council, and became part of the city's financial program.

Possibly the bureau's activity was partly the motivation for reactivation of the city government's Municipal Research Bureau in 1952 (established in 1935 but allowed to become inactive) and formation of the Onondaga County Department of Research and Development in 1954. These two government organizations, too, are professionally staffed. Among them, they have made literally dozens of local studies.

[10] The United Fund and Council of Social Agencies are other leadership organizations; and it is through these that philanthropic projects are largely channeled. See Chapter IV.

[11] Williams, *op. cit.*, p. 473 and 477–8.

[12] University of North Carolina Press, Chapel Hill, 1953.

[13] In *Public Opinion Quarterly*, Vol. 14, 1950, pp. 262 ff.

[14] *Ibid.*, p. 265.

[15] See Mirra Komarovsky, "The Voluntary Associations of Urban Dwellers," *American Sociological Review*, Dec. 1948, pp. 686 ff.; Ronald Freedman and Morris Axelrod, "Who Belongs to What in a Great Metropolis," *Adult Leadership*, Nov. 1952, pp. 6 ff.; Floyd Dotson, "Patterns of Voluntary Association Among Urban Workingclass Families," *American Sociological Review*, Oct. 1951, pp. 687 ff.

[16] Komarovsky, *op. cit.*, p. 690.

[17] *Op. cit.* (*see* footnote 15), p. 8.

[18] A most revealing study, with great implication for community relations, is called *Personal Influence: The Part Played by People in the Flow of Mass Communication*, by Elihu Katz and Paul Lazarsfeld of Columbia University (Free Press, Glencoe, Ill., 1955). Where people go for information to guide their money-spending decisions (e.g., women's styles, what movies to attend, etc.) is explored, and the answer turns out to be that mostly they go to their socio-economic peers. But for information to guide their thinking about economics and politics they go to someone slightly above themselves in socio-economic level. In both cases mass communication media are a secondary information source. The study bears out the contention of community relations men that person-to-person communication among neighbors, relatives and friends of employees is the most potent communication medium—for good or bad—operating in a plant town.

[19] Before a National Industrial Conference Board conference, New York City, April 26, 1956.

[20] In their *Parties and Politics in the Local Community*, Marguerite J. Fisher and Edith E. Starratt suggest other ideas on how such groups could be more effective. (Community Study Series No. 2, Bull. 20, National Council for Social Studies, Washington, D.C. 1945–1951, published for Maxwell School, Syracuse University.)

[21] Inclusive organizations at the national, state and area levels furnish knowl-

edgeable guidance to community citizen councils. The National Municipal League (which dates back to 1894) exchanges information among citizen groups. The National Council for Community Improvement, headquartered in St. Louis and organized by Mr. J. C. Penney in 1948, holds an annual Washington, D.C., conference and a cooperative program to help local inter-organizational councils. Among the oldest and best state-level councils is the New York State Citizens Council, headquartered in Syracuse. There are also national organizations to improve specific areas of communities, e.g., American Council to Improve Our Neighborhood (ACTION) to help citizens to up-grade their own neighborhoods; and the National Citizens Council for Better Schools, etc. Almost all major universities have programs to work with community citizen groups.

[22] The national organization in the field is the Governmental Research Association, Inc., New York City, which serves as an exchange for information useful to member bureaus. Comparative statistical studies in the field of taxation may be had from the Tax Foundation, New York City.

[23] Correspondence to the author, March 1956.

3-

The City and Its Problems

Part One: The Syracuse Case

An extreme over-simplification—but a clarifying one—is to say that there are two schools of industrial community relations:

1. The "community-centered" or personal service school, in which company presidents, and hence their administrative staffs, assume great responsibility for the development of the city and its institutions. Members of this school sometimes are described as the "old family" local companies.

2. The "company-centered" school, concentrating exclusively on education of citizens in "basic economics" and on the use of public relations techniques to develop community attitudes favorable to the profitable operation of business and industry. (Locally managed companies are inclined to relegate most branch plant managements and their public relations experts from New York HQ to this school.)

Each school holds vague reservations about the other. A professional, public relations interest in a plant city isn't enough, the first school holds; there must be real devotion of time, energy and money, even personal sacrifice, if the city is to develop to the advantage of all its citizens. Furthermore, high-powered communication of the business point of view might be construed as propaganda.

The second school maintains that cities, too, are in competition. Granted, they say, that the company is obligated to each of its plant cities; but all cities must learn that they in turn have obligations to industry and to the American economy. Community relations programs have responsibility to make this point. What's more, an industry that assumes too much financial and personal responsibility edges dangerously close to "paternalism."

Few company operations, as a matter of fact, are clearly of one school or the other; there is a healthy tendency for the two schools to merge. This chapter will describe just how business-climate-minded local Syracuse company managements are, even if they don't always think of themselves as such.

Cities, like competing companies, prosper or decline with their ability to meet economic needs at competitive prices. This community ability or lack of it rests primarily in locally operating companies and in their individual ability to prosper. But there is more than a little community of fortune among the city's businesses, industries and citizens. A declining city bodes ill for all people who live and work there; its continued prosperity depends in good part on its adaptability to broad economic shifts, on community interest, and on the organizing ability of local leadership.

All the active Syracuse industrialists I interviewed contend that the prosperity of their companies cannot be separated from the prosperity of the Syracuse community, that any project that helps the community, helps business. Thus, in working to maintain a community climate favorable to their own prosperity they find themselves increasingly concerned about slum clean-up, hospital administration, traffic planning, school building programs, welfare economics, and the like. And with such concern come headaches.

Syracuse leaders generally agreed that the most important community problems were: (1) coordination of city and county services and improvements; and financing them equitably; (2) urban renewal, particularly in the mid-town semi-slum area; (3) improvement of local public education; (4) more hospital facilities; and (5) industrial development, of the kind most beneficial to Syracuse. Downtown merchants would like to label parking and traffic facilities as Problem Number One.[1]

This collection of problems is typical of most industrial cities. All of them were discussed in the monumental Syracuse study, The Post-War Report of the Syracuse-Onondaga Post-War Planning Council, published in 1945. This Council, under the general chairmanship of Chancellor William P. Tolley of Syracuse University, and with Sergai N. Grimm, then director of the city's Planning Commission, as executive director, had the backing of the mayor and the chairman of the county board of supervisors. It utilized the services of literally dozens of citizens, as well as experts from the University.[2] Special committees were appointed to undertake research in twenty different areas, from agriculture and credit to traffic and water resources. Three administrative bodies—Research and Planning, Ways and Means, and Public Participation—were given equal billing and powers under the Syracuse Common Council and the county board of supervisors to conduct the project.[3]

Finally, in 1952 the Civic Development Committee, successor to the post-war planning group, published a progress report. It contains a discouraging number of "no progress" notations and recordings of a good many compromises with the original 1945 proposals. Some of the positive achievements of the Syracuse area, one suspects, would have taken place even if no study had been made.

But, whatever its failures of achievement, the post-war study had the positive virtue of concentrating public attention on the important problems of the city and county.

Said *The Post-Standard*, echoing a sentiment encountered by the author in such diverse places as factory plants and the university campus: "We've had surveys by the City Planning Commission, Housing Authority, the parking authority, the urban renewal director, the relocation director, traffic and health committees and just about every public agency you can think of. . . .

"Syracuse probably has more surveys on more subjects by more people than anybody.

"The only thing we haven't had is ACTION on any of them. . . ." [4]

In view of this widespread impatience for action, what are Syracuse companies—individually and collectively through their various organizations—doing to whittle down the community's problems? Because of the intertwined nature of these problems, efforts so far have been directed mainly toward settling on courses of action—particularly concerning government finances.

Syracuse in 1958 had a pay-as-you-go policy, and its great support, as might be expected, came from the business supported Governmental Research Bureau (See Chapter 2). Some few industrial leaders, however, lacked reverence for the policy. Sometimes, they contended, it is good business to borrow money for specific developments, rather than always to wait for accumulated earnings to meet such costs; that same flexibility ought to be permitted the city government.

The Syracuse Governmental Research Bureau and the Chamber of Commerce, at least institutionally, did not agree with this. The Manufacturers Association of Syracuse also formally supported pay-as-you-go. Proponents pointed to the capital improvements made possible by savings on interest and to new industry attracted to Syracuse by its sound financial condition. In one year the city's Capital Improvement Committee allotted a total of $3,625,870 for sewers, fire fighting equipment, parks, libraries, street paving and school buildings.

In a little more than a decade, the city eliminated a $42 million debt and at the same time spent $29,060,000 for capital improvements. The Governmental Research Bureau pointed out that: If the city had bonded for these improvements, the debt cost would have been $870,000 annually, nearly the cost of a small new school building each year.[5] Even with the authorization of a $3 million-plus bond issue in 1955 to finance land purchases for two boulevard projects, the record is enviable. What more, the pay-as-you-go supporters asked, do you want?

Impressive as this argument was, a look around the city in 1957 indicated that such self-discipline had caused capital improvements to lag somewhat. The Syracuse city hall was built in 1890 and looked it; many departments were housed in rented space around town. The police station was sadly decrepit. Many public works vehicles were worn out but still kept in service.

In 1957, the City's Long Range Capital Improvement Committee, a unit of the Planning Commission, foresaw the need for spending $32,532,000 in six years, including $8,265,000 for streets and $9,375,000 for schools. This program would inevitably result in some modification of pay-as-you-go if adopted. Only $9 million in capital improvements would be possible under pay-as-you-go.

Finally, in February 1957, Mayor Donald H. Mead, declaring that at last "we emerge into the sunlight" unfettered by debt, presented to the Common Council his "Blueprint for Progress"—a multimillion dollar public improvement program that included seven proposals for bettering municipal services, administration, and working conditions. First construction project would be a $21 million urban renewal program (costing the city $4½ million) to face-lift more than 100 acres adjacent to the central business district. Also scheduled were a civic center of public buildings and high schools whose total cost would be at least $4 million. Acceptance of the plan virtually assured an end to pay-as-you-go.

Metropolitan Syracuse has grown rapidly in its out-of-city suburbs.[6] As with many cities, population has not merely spread to the fringes, it has jumped out there. Suburban house-building has been five times more rapid than in Syracuse. Suburban village populations have grown so fast that state aid allotments have fallen behind, as, for example, in North Syracuse which grew 2.5 times from 1950 to 1956. Housing developments outside the villages add to the strain on village facilities, particularly the schools. No sooner is a new school built than it becomes overcrowded. Sewer systems become a necessity, as do streets and sidewalks. One of these villages, Cicero, found its assessed evaluation increased 142 percent in a decade—a situation that makes for more county tax revenue, but one that greatly bothers the suburbanite faced with local bonding and taxation.

Meanwhile, the City of Syracuse has been depending on a two percent sales tax for almost $4 million a year, or about 15 percent of its total revenue. The elaborate out-of-Syracuse shopping centers that spring up to serve the new housing developments meanwhile are depriving the city of some of this accustomed income. Hence, it became necessary to raise the city tax rate.[7]

Industry, like residents, prefers to build outside Syracuse. In 1952, 67 percent of the area's manufacturing companies were within the city limits; in 1956, 55 percent were outside. Or, to take a longer view, 40 percent of the area's industrial workers were employed within the city in 1913, and only 18 percent in 1949. This trend, too, adds to the city's financial woe by proportionally decreasing taxable property.[8]

A joint city-county government, or at least more coordination of city-county services, and perhaps a county-wide sales tax, might help both suburbanite and city taxpayers—but in 1957 such coordination seemed unlikely for some time. County voters rejected a two percent county sales tax in 1948, and again in 1951. Although the County Board of Supervisors had the power to impose a sales tax without a referendum, and although the Onondaga County School Boards Association was solidly behind the idea, the supervisors were reluctant to do it.[9]

The county and city welfare departments have been consolidated since 1938 when Syracuse, then in financial trouble, persuaded the county to merge operations. The marriage has not been entirely blissful; county people complain periodically that the arrangement permits the city to keep its taxes down, while the county tax rate continues to rise. (This argument overlooks the possibility of increase in other county expenses at a more rapid rate than city costs.) The Mayor's Blueprint for Progress of February 1957 proposed a study leading to establishment of a metropolitan health department, consolidating city, county and town health agencies.

Meanwhile, even the proposal of consolidating schools leads to bitter intervillage bickering. A referendum for the county manager form of government, supported by the Bureau of Governmental Research, the League of Women Voters, and the press, was defeated by the suspicion of both city people and county people that "other groups" would be favored under a more coordinated arrangement. Among the few signs of cooperation for mutual advantage at this writing have been a joint sewage project, a cooperative civil defense, an inter-town youth bureau, city-county mental health board, public assistance and children's court, and a joint committee to study property evaluations. Perhaps, as one man prominent in the Governmental Research Bureau said, the efficiencies and savings of more coordinated city and county governments can be best achieved bit by bit without arousing the fears of either electorate or the elected that they would be "dominated" by other units of the area.

Another Syracuse problem, important by the area industrialists' own nomination, concerns public housing and clearance of an 87-block semi-slum in the Fifteenth Ward, a few blocks from the city's best stores, hotels and office buildings. Syracuse in 1957 had four public housing projects, one of them, Pioneer Homes, in the Fifteenth Ward itself.[10]

The sub-standard houses vacated by people who moved into these projects were soon occupied by other low-income families. Consequently, the ward, except for the Pioneer Homes project itself, remained as decrepit as it was before the projects were constructed. The ramshackle houses have low assessed valuations; and the area's contribution to the city in taxes is far below its proportional share, particularly considering the central location.

Despite crackdowns on fire law and building code violations, the area has more than its share of fires. Caseloads of all health and welfare agencies are uncommonly high here. Serious crimes are not as frequent as might be expected, but police are called into the area to attend to an inordinate number of fights and misdemeanors. Thus, the cost of city services to this section of town, too, is out of proportion to its geographic and population size.

This blighted area, and several others nearly as objectionable, are apparent even to the most casual visitor to Syracuse. Together, they give the city a dreary, rundown look which must handicap local managements in their efforts to recruit managerial and professional employees; they must hinder the city in its attempts to attract new businesses. And to such "company-centered" aspects of the Fifteenth Ward must be added the humane considerations: the effects of an environment of squalor on the men, women and children who live there.

Local government agencies, "mayor's committees," the League of Women Voters, and others have thoroughly investigated the problems of Ward Fifteen and the related question of additional public housing. Ward Fifteen is a favorite hunting ground for Syracuse University graduate students seeking thesis material. Some of the last generation of the city's industrial leaders were concerned, in a personal way, with the basic problems of Ward Fifteen: Will Hinds of Crouse-Hinds and H. W. Smith of Smith-Corona, for example. Some of the new generation of leaders likewise have been concerned, such as Dr. W. R. G. Baker, former vice president of General Electric, in his capacity as a city planning commission member. But the concern of industry about blighted areas in the city has been spotty, at best.

These intermeshed community problems, plus others to be described in the more detailed case studies introducing later chapters—and still others not mentioned at all—indicate the difficulty of working intelligently in today's industrial community relations. A company open-house, or even a Business-Industry-Education Day, can hardly classify alone as effective community relations, whether one belongs to the community-centered or to the company-centered school of thinking. It is even doubtful that these approaches may be distinguished in their approach to specific community problems.

This complexity means that companies must work within a relatively new social context: the metropolitan region, not just

COLLEGE LIBRARY

the plant community. It means, too, working with inefficiencies growing out of the lack of coordination among governmental units of the region, working within a framework of provincial jealousies and extraordinary tax burdens, working with overgrown towns that threaten to grow right over the factory.[11]

The exploded city and the smouldering slum within it have been "planned about" for years by people who plan as a vocation or as an avocation. Progress to date has not been notable. Industry and industrial organizations, for the most part, have stayed away from those problems in metropolitan Syracuse, as they have in most cities. The problems may be too big for the local industrial leadership to handle successfully. Although it is true that no major community project can succeed without the active cooperation of the industrial leadership, this does not mean that this leadership will be able to achieve whatever it attempts. The Syracuse history provides some bad failures of projects with top leadership. Nevertheless, most cities which have made major and rather fundamental improvements have done so through leadership borrowed from business and industry. Pittsburgh, St. Louis, Miami and Cleveland, among others, are cases in point.

It may well be argued that these social problems are none of business' business. But unquestionably, they are problems important to industrial community relations, whether one belongs to the "community-centered" school or to the "company-centered" school. Whether employees suffer the problems of living in Ward Fifteen or in North Syracuse, or somewhere in-between, management must live with the attitudes and opinions these people bring to work with them.

3-
The City and Its Problems

PART TWO

HIGH and numerous taxes, clogged downtown traffic, duplicated governmental services, spreading city slums, overburdened suburban facilities—all are interacting parts of one comprehensive community relations problem. It is a problem overwhelming in size and complexity, and one becoming more and more troublesome. It is a problem basic to industrial community relations because it concerns the whole environment of a plant's relationships with its area neighbors.

Larger plant cities are fast growing into industrial metropolitan areas, spreading for miles along a transportation route —perhaps along or near a new superhighway, perhaps adjacent to a coastline or strategic river. Some 60 percent of the U.S. population lives in 174 such metropolitan areas. Industry requires large acreages for its modern horizontal, one-story plants and parking lots, which means locating on main transportation routes between cities, or at least well outside of city limits. Families, meanwhile, are moving by the thousands to suburban communities outside city limits, not so much to be closer to their work as to escape to more rural living and (they think) to cheaper living.

Cities lose their middle class families, who sometimes are replaced by lower income immigrants. City property values go down, and so does the city's income from real estate taxes.

The in-city residential property deteriorates, ultimately becoming slums; and builders no longer find it profitable to construct apartment houses unless subsidized by government funds. With less tax money, the city finds it hard to meet rising costs of city services and the new drains on revenue from increased delinquency, old age services, etc. The city's old problem of daytime traffic jams remains to plague the downtown merchant, who at the same time laments his loss of business to suburban shopping centers. As things grow worse in the city, more families who can afford to do so move to the suburbs.[13]

The suburban communities, meanwhile, find themselves swamped with "housing development families," often increasing the community population by thousands. New schools, new sewers, new sidewalks, and indeed the capital services for a whole new city have to be built quickly—and paid for by new residents and old alike. Taxes, these suburbanites discover, are higher even than they formerly had paid in the city. They find themselves supporting a maze of different governments: village, county, various "districts" for special projects, and even indirectly, the city government which may in self-protection have adopted an "earnings" or sales tax.

Will the trend to megapolis, the super-city, industrial region, strip city or whatever one chooses to call this new phenomenon of regional urbanization, scatteration, or suburban sprawl, make industrial community relations impossible, at least in the constellation's central city? America already has one overly developed example of what is prophesied—Metropolitan New York, that tri-state giant with its flinty heart in Manhattan Island.

Any sensible community relations professional will change the subject when the conversation drifts to New York City. None of the community relations principles which apply in other cities seem to work so well in New York. This is generally true despite some demonstrations that New York neighborhoods, such as Greenwich Village, Harlem, Peter Cooper Village and Stuyvesant Town, etc., can be worked with as individual communities.[14]

New York is a city without much of a middle class. New York's upper middle class has bought homes in Westchester, Connecticut and the better sections of New Jersey and Long Island; the rest of the middle class has deserted to the Levittowns of the region.

One in ten residents left New York City between 1940 and 1950, to be replaced by Puerto Ricans and Negroes; so that by 1970 it is estimated that the city's population will contain 14.5 percent Negroes and 13.5 percent Puerto Ricans (a total of 28 percent). Those who remain can afford the cost of New York apartments, or are too poor to leave their overcrowded tenements, or are living in subsidized public housing projects.[15] Meanwhile 20 percent of the city's dwelling units are fifty or more years old, and no builders are interested in replacing them. If they are not now slums, they soon will be.

Industry, too, is moving out of the city's five boroughs, so that the manufacturing employment dropped from 1,080,000 in 1947 to 968,000 in 1955; and except for the ruggedly individualistic garment industry of Manhattan most of the remaining industry is well removed to the outlands of Queens, Brooklyn and The Bronx. Industry, meanwhile, is growing rapidly in Long Island above Queens, in New Jersey, and in Westchester and southern Connecticut.

Nevertheless, New York City, with the help of Robert Moses, is here to stay as the principal headquarters city of American business and industry and as the nation's entertainment and cultural capital. But increasingly, and also with the help of Mr. Moses, its residents will be living in apartments subsidized by governments or labor unions or both.[16] Meanwhile, millions of office workers will continue to pour into the city every week day morning and back to their bedroom communities or mortgaged suburban ranch houses in the evening.

The conglomeration of interesting problems such as one finds in Syracuse—and to an exaggerated degree in New York —seems nearly hopeless of remedy; and most community leaders understandably have limited their efforts to the specifics of taxation, parking, traffic, etc. Perhaps all this is more properly government's business, and not the concern of industry. Nevertheless, in some cities—Pittsburgh, St. Louis, Miami, among others—the community leaderships have taken on the whole complex of interrelated problems in their industrial areas, and what is more they have made some significant progress.

St. Louis's growth, typical of metropolitan regions, is outside the city limits, where industry also is locating. Bridges add to the traffic commuting problem. The St. Louis industrial area involves a multitude of government local units as well as two states. It has its tax problems and its slums, and its suburban headaches.

The citizens' organization that faced the combined problems of St. Louis is called Civic Progress, Inc. Under this organization, the local press, notably the *Post-Dispatch*, and the city government, notably Mayor Joseph M. Dorst, joined forces with top industrial leaders—including the presidents of Anheuser-Busch, General American Life Insurance, Southwestern Bell Telephone, and the board chairmen of Monsanto Chemical and Gaylord Container. Civic Progress dared the controversial—promoting sewer districts, slum clearance and bond issues—and encouraged a study of area governments.

In Pittsburgh, the now famous rehabilitation led by the Allegheny Conference on Community Development, which in turn was led by Richard King Mellon and other industrialists, did not limit itself to building steel and aluminum sky-scrapers on the Golden Triangle, or to angelic projects like supporting the Pittsburgh Symphony and the Carnegie Museum. It included also removing blighted buildings and houses—many acres of them—in various sections of the city. Pittsburgh's slums, like St. Louis', are still extensive. But the leaders of both cities consider slum removal as a necessary part of their programs to preserve their corporate investments.[17]

Wide diversity of committee membership is not enough to insure complete success for large-scale community re-organization plans. The Syracuse Post-War Planning Council (cf. Part One, this chapter) was diverse—and its concepts were certainly imaginative and large-scale. Management men, too, sat on its various committees. Why did it not succeed to the degree that the Allegheny Conference or St. Louis' Civic Progress, Inc. succeeded?

The answer seems to be that such organizations—granted they have diversified memberships that included all important segments of the area—will succeed only to the degree that the community's top leadership persistently drives them to success. The Allegheny Conference had such persistent management drive and discipline. The Syracuse Post-War Planning Council had less persistence or discipline behind it from the men holding most power to make the plans work.

Other post-war planning councils developed in other cities—in Cleveland and Louisville, for example. The Post-War Planning Council of Greater Cleveland and the Louisville Area Development Association were likewise organized for diversification both in their membership and in their projects. Like the Syracuse Council, they achieved considerable good—concentrating public attention on problems of housing, traffic, zoning, race relations, etc. Also like Syracuse, neither proved to be a rival to the Allegheny Conference.[18]

Of all aspects of the community problem complex, none is less likely than slum area rehabilitation to be tackled by individual corporations. Sears, Roebuck & Company, by a somewhat oblique approach, entered this area of slums and housing which is generally avoided by industrial community relations programs. Sears undertook the financing of pilot "housing demonstration" operations in Alabama and Ohio, in the hope that landlords could be persuaded to rehabilitate slum houses and to improve property. To stimulate interest in this possibility, Sears exhibited two houses on a town square in an Alabama town, one renewed, one unrenewed. And in Cleveland the company set up an urban renewal center to which people could come for information about improving their homes.

Sears had considerable help in the projects; unions of electricians and plumbers, and local roofing, building supply and house-moving companies all made their contributions in services or materials. Actually, the nominal sponsor of the project in every city was the local real estate board, acting in coordination with the local urban rehabilitation commission.

It should be emphasized that the Sears' projects were strictly demonstrations to influence landlords that rehabilitating slum houses can result in their increased profit. Sears is *not* redoing houses en masse; it is *not* itself clearing slum areas.

At the demonstrations (e.g. in Columbus), the point was also made to the public that substandard houses furnish but 6 percent of tax revenue, yet 45 percent of the city service dollars are spent on its inhabitants. Taxpayer pressures hopefully might result from this publicity.[19]

As Sears recognized, the profitability of operating slum property—or the belief that slum property is more profitable than other kinds—is key to slum continuance. Building and sanitation codes, as in the case of Syracuse's Fifteenth Ward, are only palliatives. Obviously, slum area rehabilitation and urban renewal are different sorts of projects. Slum area rehabilitation involves attitudes of tenement renters and landlords, and the community's insistence upon vigorous enforcement of local regulations.

The neighborhood conservation campaign, promoted by the National Association of Real Estate Boards, sometimes with the help of such firms as the Henry J. Kaiser Companies, is another attempt to persuade the landlord that there is more profit in property which meets minimum housing standards. The NAREB has outlined for communities a whole program, including ordinances, inspection and condemnation procedures, aimed to inspire owners in slum and near-slum neighborhoods to rescue basically sound structures before deterioration invites wholesale demolition. Some cities, as Milwaukee, New Orleans, Kansas City, Newark, Baltimore and Miami, have reputations for success in such programs; spasmodic "clean-up-paint-up" campaigns interspersed with long periods of public indifference are more characteristic. If the profitability of slum operation is to be removed, ultimately it must be by means of an urban renewal program. Property condemnations, closing down small businesses located in condemned buildings, and displacing tenement occupants are all undemocratic government actions; but from the points of view of both private and public interest, such renewal ultimately must be undertaken when an area ceases to be any longer an economic plus to the community.[20]

Richard L. Steiner, commissioner of the Urban Renewal Administration, pointed out that industry and commerce have these gains to make from urban renewal programs: (1) the opportunity for industries and businesses crowded by slums to obtain additional land for expansion; (2) the reduction of slums and deteriorated areas which are being subsidized at a heavy rate by business taxes. He urged business to purchase land in renewal areas as "demonstration of faith in the future of the city; to sell properties in the path of renewal projects without prolonged legal haggling, and to "demonstrate corporate citizenship" by working with other business and industry people and public officials in the improvement program. Industry and commerce "are asleep if they do not give just as much attention to the trend of the business climate in cities where they have existing capital investments as in selecting new communities in which to locate," Steiner said.[21]

Slum clearance, on the other hand, could possibly take place too rapidly for the health of the city, aggravating housing shortages and forcing the multiplication of public housing. To date, coincidental financial complications have slowed down too hasty programs for demolishing city tenement areas.[22] Max Wehrly of Urban Land Institute points out that the cost of acquiring and clearing slums will often be greater than the new use value.[23] Nonetheless, the long-range expensiveness of slum continuance (meaning both money costs and social costs) is an unfair drain upon a city's resources. A number of cost studies have been made to prove this point, in Cleveland, St. Louis, Newark, etc. A Cleveland slum with 2.5 percent of the city's population, for example, had 20 percent of its murders, 25 percent of its houses of prostitution, eight percent of its families on relief, etc. etc.—all adding up to an annual cost of $1,132,000. Tax income from the area was $225,000, less a substantial amount from tax delinquency. Over a five-year period, the city's loss equalled the value of total property in the area.[24]

Criminals and prostitutes will not reform (and so save tax-payers' money) just because their slum hideaways are torn down. But slum areas not only create such people; they attract them. There is evidence that slums attract more mentally

unbalanced people to them than are driven to mental un-
balance by the living conditions there.

"It is inevitable that individuals who seek the same forms
of excitement . . . should find themselves from time to time
in the same places." So the famous University of Chicago
sociologist of the last generation, Robert E. Park, observed in
the early 1920s. "The result of this," he said, "is that . . . the
population tends to segregate itself . . . in accordance with
its tastes or its temperaments . . . (under which neighborhoods) may assume the character of a 'moral region.' " [25]

Professor Park's observation about neighborhoods to a
degree applies also to cities. The city with fewest slum neighborhoods attracts fewer people of the kind likely to be expensive and anti-social.

Planned, long-term urban redevelopment, with the aid of
the United States Housing Act's "Title I," is being undertaken in a good many cities. In addition to St. Louis, Pittsburgh and New York, these include Baltimore, Cleveland,
Detroit and San Francisco. Some states, as Texas and Louisiana, in 1957 had not authorized city participation.[26] Under
the law, the government absorbs two-thirds of the difference
between cost of buying the land condemned plus clearing
slum buildings therefrom, and the price at which the cleared,
replanned area could be sold for redevelopment. In other
words, the law permits the city to buy land and sell it to a
private builder at a cut price, with two-thirds of the loss taken
by the federal government and one-third by the city. Hence,
the private builder can afford to rent apartments in the new
building at reasonable rents. An example: at Corlears Point in
New York City, a section of property was bought by the city
for $6,500,000, resold to developers for $1,049,240 who built
a $19,650,000 housing project on it for occupancy by families
of the International Ladies Garment Workers Union.

Related to urban redevelopment is, of course, the matter of zoning. "The problem of changing the existing zoning plan and ordinance is much more difficult than the preparation of a new ordinance," says one authority. "The fact that the municipality has designated certain areas for specific uses has not only fixed their future use to a certain extent in the minds of property owners and citizens, but in some cases it has influenced land values." [27] As areas of cities change their character, old zoning restrictions no longer make sense. In Pittsburgh, the zoning ordinance was changed 500 times in thirty-four years, and finally was replaced altogether. With the aid of the University of Pittsburgh Law School, the Allegheny Conference on Community Development devised a uniform zoning plan for the entire region and set up a cooperative regional planning and zoning commission.[28]

Especially in industrial zoning, some changes in codes become logical. "Particularly is there a need for revising industrial classifications to recognize new processes in which nuisances, commonly associated with certain industries in the early days of zoning, no longer exist due to improved techniques." [29] Many city zoning problems lie in what is sometimes referred to as the "blight ring," the area immediately surrounding central business districts, which if unattended will develop into an area of cheap boarding houses, loft-industries, etc., and eventually become slums. Syracuse is solving the problem by encouraging insurance companies and other businesses to erect their office buildings there, and by recruiting quality shops to occupy and maintain the large old residences which in the last century were among the finest in town. In New York City, the answer seems to be public housing and city recreation areas.

Inside the confines of the usual blight ring, office building space grows scarcer and more expensive, and parking lots more and more difficult to find. With little chance of parking down-town, except in an expensive garage, suburbanites are keeping to their villages and shopping centers.

Victor Roterus of the U.S. Chamber of Commerce, Area Development Division, says that parking time limitations, one-way streets and expressways, city parking garages, etc., cannot really meet the problem because of "the potential rider demand that lurks in the hinterland." [30] In New York, for example, the fact that the streets have reached the saturation point is the only reason why more commuters to Manhattan do not drive to work. As the situation is eased by new regulations and facilities, a portion of the immense backlog of traffic potential immediately pours in to make the situation as bad as it was before.[31]

In some newly settled suburban communities there is a rift between "old-timers" (pre-development residents) and the newcomers whose numerous children are raising the tax rates for everybody. The industrial plant that finds itself overnight in the center of a sea of new, cheap houses will appreciate the point of view of the old-timers. Housing projects springing up next to industrial plants historically have been due to management's underestimation of the population growth. As it can, management protects itself by owning land around its plant site, not only to keep taxes down by preventing housing developments from locating there, but also to allow the plant plenty of room for future expansion.

Living close to the factory is no longer considered particularly desirable by America's car-owning workers. In more than half of 137 industries, studied by the National Industrial Zoning Commission, 80 percent of workers rode to work in their own cars. Nowadays, workers choose their homes for the environment they want for themselves and their families; inconvenience and cost of commuting are secondary—to a certain point, a fact which has important implications for new housing plans. Results of this change, Professors Adams and Mackesey of Cornell say, are a greater occupational, industrial and geographic freedom for the worker, a new degree of stability in the labor market because workers can accept jobs further from home; increased effectiveness of wage and fringe benefits in attracting workers; a smoother shift from farm employment to industrial work.

"It is no longer necessary to locate new plants in densely populated areas in order to have an adequate labor supply, but management must estimate the number of workers available within what seems to the workers a reasonable commuting distance." Housing and planning officials, they advise, "must at one point or another make a decision whether the local labor supply, if fully utilized, will be adequate to meet not only current but future requirements . . . long-distance commuters are an important, flexible (part) of the labor supply, and it is these commuters who . . . determine the geographic boundaries of the local labor and housing market." [32]

Plant community relations specialists now consider their operating territory as within twenty-five to seventy-five miles from the plant site. Here is indication that present-day worker mobility justifies this geographical range.[33]

Businesses and industry in the outlying towns of central cities more than pay their share of taxes. A study by Hofstra College's Bureau of Business and Economic Research found that industries in Nassau County, N.Y. contributed in taxes 273 percent of the cost of services they received, and that commerce contributed 277 percent. These findings, the researchers report, are paralleled in other communities; Evanston and Paterson, and in Arlington County, Va.[34]

Industry seldom makes more than a token protest against discriminatory taxes. But the company with a reservoir of local good will can force local government to lower rates under certain conditions. Otis Elevator is one company which successfully protested high municipal taxes. The company sued the city of Yonkers for a reduced assessment, amounting to almost $3 million for each year between 1952 and 1955.

Yonkers recently had lost a major industry, the Alexander Smith Carpet Co. The company threatened to move, and unquestionably would have done so. Cities, it seems, have a natural tendency to want to make up tax losses caused by departed industry by raising the tax on the remaining industry; at the same time such cities realize they can ill afford to lose additional companies and so are psychologically susceptible to demands for tax cuts backed by threats of moving.[35]

Central to the local industrial tax picture is the duplication of taxes within a metropolitan region, to support a variety of local governments which characteristically duplicate services, or at best lack sensible coordination of services. Each governmental unit jealously clings to all portions of its empire, and exploits provincial pride and fear of encroachment by outsiders to oppose any program to unite and coordinate government services. The St. Louis Metropolitan Area at one time contained over 700 agencies of government with taxing power, reports Harland Bartholomew, city planner there; and the Chicago Metropolitan Area had over 1200. "Such taxing agencies," Mr. Bartholomew once observed in an address at Carnegie Tech, "generally are not noted for modesty in the exercise of their powers." [36]

Taxpayers organizations, chambers of commerce, manufacturers associations and such watchdog organizations as Syracuse's Bureau of Governmental Research have not the power to win over the entrenched self-interests of the government units involved. What is needed is area-wide organization, strongly backed by local business and industry and their respective organizations but also including all reputable area organizations of whatever composition, representing as many voters as possible.[37]

Historically, annexation has been the means of drawing independent areas under one city government, but this method is no longer very popular. New York, Philadelphia and New Orleans are cities not included within any county and so avoid some such duplication; San Francisco and Baltimore are amalgamated into a "city and county" unity. Special "authorities" frequently are presented as solutions to lack of coordination—the model organization here being New York's Port Authority which operates the area toll bridges, tunnels, bus depot, airports and airport terminals. The authority's profits, of course, go to improve the authority's facilities; and opponents of authorities (again, state and local governments) argue that this profit ought rather to go to cities for improvement of those city facilities which under city management are losing money. Governments also would like authorities to make payments to them in lieu of taxes; and for reasons of patronage they want some governmental authority to hire and fire the authority's employees.

Proponents of authorities, on the other hand, point to the New York City transit systems, with their lack of coordination and strong tendency to lose money. They suggest that a Transportation Authority, with power to borrow money and build facilities, would not be hampered by the debt limitations that restrict the city's building of transportation facilities, and further that the authority could cut across the geographical boundaries of the tri-state area with a unified transportation system.

The soundest solution to the governmental and tax problems of industrial areas seems to be some form of federated administration with tax-levying power.[38] In this country,

Greater Miami (Dade County) is furnishing a possible model for the many areas faced with similar problems. Florida's Dade County (estimated 1957 population, 650,000) like New York's Onondaga County, is a fast-growing region with growth mostly outside the city limits. It, too, faced the familiar problems of lack of coordination in tax assessments, land use, water supply, sewage districts, intra-area expressways, pollution control, etc. Its already established county-wide school system and public health system indicated to the local leaders the direction they should follow.

The first step was the organization of a "Metropolitan Miami Municipal Board," which, with the aid of the University of Miami, the League of Municipalities, and the Public Administration Service, conducted exhaustive studies of each area problem. Some highlights of the findings were that area police were broadcasting on five different wavelengths, that seventy-one sewers were emptying into local rivers and into Biscayne Bay; that the six area bus lines had little coordinated service; and that a plumber needed twenty-seven different licenses to work in the county.

Public opposition to coordination was considerable, and three variations of federation had to be attempted before one was finally accepted in 1957. The final arrangement, too, contained a number of compromises with local politics. Although there is a joint area tax-levying program, the county government still manages its own finances. Also, the Board of County Commissioners continues to exist, and all twenty-six area municipalities may maintain their governments if they wish. But the metropolitan federation will do the over-all planning concerning intra-area arterials, traffic engineering and parkways, sewage systems, water supply, flood, refuse and drainage controls, police and fire protection, zoning and land use, minimum standard building codes, and health and welfare, recreation and library services. And, most important, the federation is the sole assessor and collector of property taxes.

The operating body of the new setup is a commission, to which five members are elected by the area at large, five elected by specific district elections, and one elected from Miami. The commission in turn appoints a metropolitan manager to serve as the executive officer.[39]

"The truth is," as Meyer Kestenbaum of the Commission on Intergovernmental Relations expressed it, in talking about our metropolitan areas, "that we have developed an economic unit for which we have no political counterpart." [40] Miami's solution might not be the right one for other industrial areas. Certainly the overlay of an additional governmental unit upon existing units is not likely to reduce taxes. Ideally, the subunits would be dissolved or at least decreased. Perhaps St. Louis, which at this writing is studying the possibilities of area-wide government, will succeed in this more completely than Miami has.[41]

Some of the more famous authorities on community problems conclude that cities are rapidly declining into amoral, disintegrated, depersonalized, capitalistic shambles. Lewis Mumford, in *The Culture of Cities*,[42] thinks that tomorrow's leisure, health and comfort will come in spite of business and the profit motive; and he blames our lack of progress toward Utopia on what he considers to be the nation's too big stake in property and profits, and hence in congestion and misery. Queen and Carpenter likewise seem convinced that capitalism is not only partly to blame for our community problems, but also that capitalism may have to go before any real improvement in the situation can be made:

If we were to have really effective physical and social planning of cities, metropolitan areas, and regions, there would have to be a thorough-going modification, if not abandonment, of our tradi-

tional individualism and 'free' competition. . . . Whether the
planning were done by an ambitious dictator, a selfish oligarchy,
or a democratic society, it would mean a complete abandonment
of laissez faire. To devise and carry out comprehensive plans for
urban areas would require fundamental changes in our social
philosophy.

We say this not to frighten any timid soul or to excite those
who are already restless, but to emphasize the vast difference between the unguided scramble amid which our cities have developed in the past, and social planning. We do not like our cities
as they are. Are we ready to pay the price of making them over? [43]

Company managements are not so readily inclined to rule
themselves out in favor of socialism. The far-sighted ones,
indeed, think of tomorrow's civilization and its coming life
of light, color, space, cleanliness and health—exactly as Lewis
Mumford describes it. But unlike Mr. Mumford, they en-
vision this coming Utopia in terms of their own company's
potential profitable contribution to it.

Roy W. Johnson, executive vice president of General
Electric Company, has said: "This urban renewal activity not
only contributes to a basic public interest; it can also expand
the total market opportunity for the General Electric Company and organizations similar to ours in durable and capital
goods." [44] It is this view, in part, that has inspired General
Electric to give strong support to ACTION (American
Council To Improve Our Neighborhoods) and its Advertising
Council promotional campaign.

Some companies, however, may recognize no connections
whatever among (a) tomorrow's higher standard of living,
(b) the company's own product addition to that standard of
living, and (c) the problems of community government,
slums, education, and public welfare in general, as they are at
present and as they will be in the future.

The majority of American companies do not consider the

complex of community problems described in this chapter to be legitimate concerns of their community relations programs. The majority of firms for some time to come will continue to limit their community relations efforts to plant tours, community mailings, publicity, and their support with money and manpower of local organizations and agencies. For one thing, such large community problems inevitably involve local government and politics; and most industry fears the dangers of involvement in such affairs. For another thing, these problems are so overwhelming in their magnitude and complexity that managements prefer to work with the smaller and more specific and manageable segments of the over-all problem.

No one company to any appreciable degree can change a city for the better, but locally operating companies working together as they have in Pittsburgh, and to a degree in other cities described, can, if they will, exert great influence upon the future living of many people and upon the nature of the economy under which we will live.

Good business climate is good social climate, and vice versa. Community attitudes and sentiments which arise out of a city's environment are the source spring of both kinds of climate. The costs to locally operating industry of poor or duplicating local government and city services, or slum areas and inadequate hospitals, schools or public protection, are not only tax costs, needlessly high though they may be. They are also the costs of decreased industrial productivity stemming from badly educated, emotionally depressed, belligerently resentful employees.

FOOTNOTES

[1] The Syracuse Bureau of Municipal Research counted eleven city agencies with responsibility for traffic and parking (see its *Traffic and Parking*, April

1954). Stop-gap devices used in Syracuse are similar to those of other growing cities: downtown parking garages; metering of loading zones for afternoon parking; women checkers to increase turnover in curbside parking; arterials to circumvent the business section, and shuffling—and reshuffling—of the one-way-street system.

2 The city has a real advantage in the availability of Syracuse University research services, particularly from its Maxwell School, Industrial Research Institute, and Business Research Service.

3 The Henry Luce publications supplied consultants and wrote up the project during the time the study was being conducted: "Syracuse Tackles Its Future," Fortune, May 1943, p. 120 ff.

4 The Post-Standard (Syracuse), Dec. 13, 1956. This editorial was in protest of a city allotment of $18,750 for a three-month appraisal of government machinery to see if Syracuse was "geared to expansion." This report, when made the following May, was highly critical of the city's planning, and recommended that the Planning Commission be under control of the mayor, which it subsequently was.

5 In contrast Onondaga County's debt in 1957 stood at $11.8 million.

6 Growth of Metropolitan Syracuse has some geographic symmetry; extensions reach out like the feet of an amoeba. The longest and widest of these is the northern extension, encompassing the villages of Salina, North Syracuse, Liverpool and Clay, the New York State Thruway and Electronics Park. Other extensions reach northwest beyond Solvay, west to Camillus, southwest to Onondaga, east to Manlius and northeast to DeWitt and Cicero.

7 Downtown stores are meeting this competition by joining it—establishing branches at these community centers.

8 An example of industry's importance to village finance is the Solvay Process Division, Allied Chemical and Dye, in Solvay. In 1956, the company asked for a tax reduction. Its operation is assessed at $5,834,000, which it asked to be reduced to $3,100,000. The present assessment is 46% of fair value, whereas other village property is assessed at 25%. The reduction would cost each home-owner an average of $8 a year, according to the village attorney's estimate. Incidentally, the mayor of Solvay Village, an hourly paid supervisor at Solvay Process, led the successful opposition to the company's request.

9 Several New York State counties have a sales tax: Erie, 1%; Monroe 3%; Broome, 2%. Estimates of Onondaga County's income under a 2% sales tax are $6 million to $8 million. In many cases across the country such tax money is earmarked for public education.

10 Locating additional public housing in the city brought vigorous protests from property owners near project sites. They feared that Negroes, who consti-tute about a quarter of Ward Fifteen's population, would devaluate property adjacent to the proposed public housing. These protest groups were successful in several instances, causing the city to resort to a "scattered site" plan.

A Syracuse Housing Authority plan in the Spring of 1957 to raze about twenty-five blocks of substandard dwellings in the Seventeenth Ward and erect a 124-unit public housing project ran into a multitude of snags. Among them, the problem of relocating more than 3,000 families affected by razing operations for the housing and other downtown renewal projects; opposition of the newspapers which argued that private housing is cheaper, more desirable and pays taxes; opposition of residents of existing public housing units in the ward on grounds that units are not well managed and have created congestion in the schools. Finally, while the city's application for condemnation was pending, the owner of the site began construction of a bowling hall.

[11] Carrier Corporation discovered that citizens of the town of DeWitt were petitioning for zoning the company's 400 acres next to its present plant as "residential." This was land owned by the company for company expansion in the relatively near future.

[12] In the vast literature on community problems two works are particularly useful to the non-specialist: *The New York Times* series of eight articles (Jan. 27 to Feb. 3, 1957), available as a reprint; and Stuart A. Queen and David B. Carpenter, *The American City* (New York: McGraw-Hill, 1953).

[13] The suburbs "siphon off not only the wealthier (people) but also (those) who in an earlier period bore the primary burdens of civic responsibility." Where once existed an homogeneous, stable population, we now have an inundation of "restless, migrant, heterogeneous populations who are strangers to one another and to the areas where they find temporary abode, in which they fail to take root, and for which they feel no responsibility because they are neither owners of property nor sharers in the traditions of the community." Louis Wirth, *Community Life and Social Policy: Selected Papers*, edited by Elizabeth Wirth Marvick and Albert J. Reiss, Jr. (University of Chicago, 1956) p. 213.

[14] Banks have had some surprisingly successful community relations activities in New York, e.g., the programs of the Bowery Savings Bank branches on the East Side and in Harlem, working with children, churches and local welfare agencies (handled for the bank by Thomas L. Cotton Associates, New York City).

[15] New York City had more than 84,000 public housing dwelling units for 350,000 people in 1956.

[16] William H. Whyte Jr., analyzing a cooperative survey by *Fortune* and ACTION (The American Council to Improve Our Neighborhoods, a 1956–57 Advertising Council campaign), found some evidence of a back-to-the-city movement among certain groups for whom "homogenized" suburban life is unsatisfactory. Whyte chides architects and city planners for not catering more to these people, e.g., older couples, bohemians, single persons, and Americans working in odd-hour jobs as in radio and newspaper. "Are Cities Un-American?", *Fortune*, Sept. 1957, pp. 123 ff.

[17] The "Pittsburgh Story" has been written many times, for example, cf. *Atlantic Monthly*, May 1951, pp. 66 ff.; *Colliers*, May 30, 1953, pp. 58 ff.; *Time*, Dec. 24, 1956, pp. 55–56.

[18] For descriptions of these Syracuse, Cleveland and Louisville planning groups, see Arthur Hillman, *Community Organization and Planning* (New York: Macmillan, 1950), Chapter IV.

[19] R. H. Hiller Jr. before the Cornell Community Relations Seminar, Summer, 1956. Among questions asked of Mr. Hiller were these:

Q: Why is Sears entering a field which generally is avoided by managements as dangerously controversial?

A: Sears thinks better communities mean better business. The company has found nothing as yet to be frightened of.

Q: What can be done to improve the lot of Negroes in the community, particularly regarding housing?

A: The project described is as relevant to Negro housing as it is to white housing.

Q: How can a company like Sears engage in urban renewal work without being suspected of self-interest?

A: The company has had no such accusations.

[20] For a case description of the chain of circumstances that create slums—as seen in a deteriorating section of Chicago—see Herbert A. Thelen and Bettie Belk Sarchet, *Neighbors In Action—A Manual for Community Leaders* (Human Dynamics Laboratory, University of Chicago, 1954). Church congregation size is a rather sensitive indicator of changing population patterns. It is significant, for example, when Protestant churches in a city's midtown lose members to suburban churches. This process in Syracuse is described by William Ward, *Population Patterning and Social Disorganization in Syracuse, N.Y.* (M.A. thesis, Syracuse University, May 1943). Walter A. Taylor, director, Department of Education and Research, American Institute of Architects and ex-faculty member at Syracuse University, worked with churches in the Syracuse Post-War Planning study; he found that among Christian denominations, those with the best strategy, advance planning and coverage of growing areas were, in order: Catholics, Methodists, Lutherans and Episcopalians. (Letter to author, April 26, 1956.)

[21] Address at the Second Annual Conference on Commerce-Industry Community Relations, New York University, May 15, 1957.

[22] Catherine Bauer, "Redevelopment: A Misfit of the Fifties," in *The Future of Cities and Urban Redevelopment*, Coleman Woodbury, ed. (University of Chicago, 1953).

[23] Address at Chamber of Commerce conference, Portland, Oregon, June 1952.

[24] Queen and Carpenter, *op. cit.* (see footnote 12), p. 178 ff.

[25] Robert E. Park, Ernest W. Burgess and Roderick D. McKenzie, *The City* (University of Chicago, 1925), p. 43.

[26] Nevertheless many more cities have applied for this assistance than available money can accommodate at this writing. A principal difficulty of the Act is that applications granted must be paid out of future budgets, because pay-off time follows acceptance of the project by two or three years, and Congress may not grant enough money in that future year.

[27] Harland Bartholomew and Jack Wood, *Land Use in American Cities* (Cambridge: Harvard University Press, 1955), p. 193.

[28] David W. Craig, *Pennsylvania Building and Zoning Laws, Allegheny County Appraisal* (University of Pittsburgh), 1951.

[29] Bartholomew and Wood, *op. cit.*, p. 140. Their study of zoning regulations shows a definite relationship between population and percentage of land

given to single-family dwellings, commercial, light and heavy industry, railroad property, streets, parks, public property as they are found in (a) central cities, (b) satellite cities, and (c) urban areas. Bartholomew and Wood explain how to figure a zoning plan per kind of city, its population and its available land.

[30] Quoted by H. Clay Tate, *Building a Better Town: A Program of Community Self-Analysis and Self-Help* (New York: Harper & Brothers, 1954), pp. 16–17.

[31] Planners in the more congested cities are now emphasizing pedestrian traffic in shopping areas, and banning all traffic except public carriers. Streets, they say, must be totally used for transportation and not for car storage. See American Society of Planning Officials, *Programs for Central Business District Improvement* (Information Report No. 80, Chicago, Nov. 1955; United States Chamber of Commerce); *Business Action for Better Cities, A Complete Report on the Businessman's Conference on Urban Problems* (Portland, Ore., June 23–24, 1952); numerous articles in *Traffic Quarterly*, published by Eno Foundation for Highway Traffic Control, Inc., Saugatuck, Conn., and technical bulletins of the Urban Land Institute, Washington, D.C.

[32] Leonard P. Adams and Thomas W. Mackesey, *Commuting Patterns of Industrial Workers: A Study of Experience Since 1940 in the Northeast Region*, (Ithaca: Cornell University, 1955), p. 70.

[33] Devices to measure the extent of a metropolitan area are not as easily found as one might suppose. Newspaper circulation, because of the duplication of subscribers, is not as reliable as once thought. Wholesale grocery trade is as good a measuring device as any. See Queen and Carpenter, *op. cit.*, p. 80.

[34] *The New York Times*, Feb. 3, 1956.

[35] Cf. also the case of Esso Standard Oil at Bayonne, N.J., Chapt. 8 Part Two.

[36] Further complicating community affairs, according to John C. Bollens, University of California political scientist, is the proliferation of "phantom" district governments, created largely by state legislatures, which do work legitimately in the province of local governments. Independent of the regular local government, and excessive in number, these agencies conduct activities almost impossible for communities to supervise. See Bollens' *Special District Governments in the United States* (University of California Press, 1957).

[37] In 1952, Chicago businessmen—dismayed by lethargy of the city's twelve official agencies entrusted with slum clearance—studied the problem themselves through their Metropolitan Housing and Planning Council, drew up a tough community conservation law, and lobbied it through local and state legislatures. Under the new program a five-man Urban Community Conservation Board is empowered to purchase, condemn, sell, lease, exchange, remove and demolish property in order to expedite renewal. If its orders to renovate and repair are defied, it may make repairs itself, declaring the cost a lien on the property. Thus Chicago has more power to exact compliance with renewal programs than any other city. *Fortune*, Dec. 1953, pp. 101–102.

[38] Supporters of the federated administration idea include, among other authorities, Luther Gulick, president of the Institute of Public Administration; Commissioner Edward T. Dickinson, New York State Department of Com-

merce; Prof. John C. Bollens, University of California (*see* his *Report to Conference of Governors*, Atlantic City, June 15, 1956); and Prof. Emeritus Paul Studenski of New York University (*see* his thorough, concise analysis "Fiscal Headaches for Metropolitan Areas" in the Governmental Research Association's *Reporter*, v. 7, 1955, No. 1, p. 1).

[39] Toronto preceded Miami with a "Metropolitan Toronto Government" (1954) to provide the area with equalized assessments and coordinated water supply, arterials, schools, transit, sewage disposal, police and fire protection, and over-all planning. It operates under a "Metro Council" (twelve officials of the city and twelve from surrounding communities) and an appointed manager.

[40] Quoted, *The New York Times*, Feb. 3, 1957.

[41] The New York City Metropolitan Regional Conference (made up of mayors of the area) is studing coordination possibilities for recreation, traffic and transportation, air and water pollution control, water supply, and teen-age drinking. No governmental federation is contemplated.

[42] New York: Harcourt, Brace & Co., 1938.

[43] Queen and Carpenter, *op. cit.*, p. 374.

[44] From a letter to General Electric division and department managers and employee and plant community relations managers, July 31, 1957.

4-
Financial Contributions

IN CONTRIBUTIONS-CONSCIOUS cities like Detroit, Cleveland and Syracuse, community chest and united fund campaigns appear to local managements to be central if not downright crucial, to their community relations. It may be that money-raising drives in industrial cities are notably successful only when managements believe that their community reputations as well as their corporate consciences are dependent upon their generous participation in local drives. This belief is widely held by top managements of Syracuse companies, particularly by those with headquarters there; the same is true in other industrial cities with outstandingly successful chest or united fund campaigns. Once local top managements are convinced, it becomes a community relations reality—because the thought-leaders' thinking has made it so. (Sometimes, it must be added, to the embarrassment of branch plant managements dependent upon moderately generous headquarters contributions policies.) This attitude is inclined to spread through all divisions of the local-fund-raising organization and finally throughout the entire community. The result is that ever-larger proportionate goals are set each year.

The wise community leadership works to broaden the base of personal giving—with larger gifts from more people—as well as to raise the level of corporate contributions. The industrial structure of a city is key to success in both aspects of local fund-raising.

Long-range planning wherever found probably began in the minds of the few men at the apex of the community's leadership structure. Such certainly was true in this case history of community fund-raising leadership in Syracuse.

Syracuse, like other industrial cities, historically has had its own mixture of health and welfare hazards, Lords and Ladies Bountiful, and community improvement organizations. It organized a board of health in 1832 to keep the cholera epidemic from coming in on Erie Canal barges. It had a medical association as early as 1858 and a sewer commission in 1868, a Red Cross chapter in 1881 and a free dispensary in 1888. The "Syracuse Moral Survey Committee" of ministers, doctors and educators spent the summer of 1912 studying the local "social evil." [1] Literally scores of organizations—many of them headed by women, all of them supported by personal charity—built hospitals, orphanages, and homes for unwed mothers; campaigned for underground sewers, meat inspection, and school nurses; fought drunkenness, prostitution and horse-racing.

All this was financed largely by private local philanthropy, each project soliciting the city's upper and middle classes in a campaign of its own.[2]

During the Great Depression, that unhappy era of great welfare need and little welfare support, fund-raising still concentrated in good part on "shotgun" appeals to the community at large and on individual gifts from wealthier citizens. The personal activity and generosities of some of these richer men from the "old families," too, were falling off. The city's industrial structure itself remained relatively unexploited.

One year, the Chest's campaign sank to little better than $100,000, with an average gift of two dollars. Under depression circumstances managements felt they should not urge employees to contribute.

To cut administrative expenses, volunteers were brought in to do the chest's office work. Rumors around town were that volunteers were being paid from chest funds (which they were not), and that the chest organization was going completely to pot. One rumor had it that the chest was about to be abandoned altogether.

To a few of the city's leaders, all of them industrialists or professionally allied with industry, the Syracuse Community Chest campaigns of those years seemed amateur efforts guided largely by social workers and an assortment of public spirited citizens. Syracuse is an industrial city and this truth, they decided, must be completely recognized in organization of appeals for financial support. What the Chest needed, they concluded, were techniques to increase employee donations and corporate gifts; and, they further decided, these could be better achieved by expert fund-raisers and top-level management men than they could by welfare workers and miscellany of service-minded citizens. In the remembered words of one of the original planners, Mr. Stewart Hancock: "Let the canny, influential sinners plan and run the fund-raising, and let the trained social workers, with advice of volunteer do-gooders, wisely spend the funds."

It may seem obvious that fund-raising and social work are disparate occupations, and that the talents demanded for success in these fields are altogether different. But recognition of this truth has sometimes come belatedly, and is the explanation for shifts from failure to success in more than one city campaign.

Before techniques could be implemented, the Syracuse planners knew, a pattern of campaign leadership must be established. They devised a "work-up" program of executive development much akin to similar programs in industry. Not all chairmen of the campaign's divisions are presidents of companies, or vice-presidents, or even industrial people, but a good many are. Those who will reach key posts on the campaign inevitably are top management men. By this work-up process, general chairmen of campaigns often have as many as nine years of previous experience in various campaign jobs; all of them know three years in advance of their appointment to the general chairmanship that such is to be their destiny.

If a community's industrial structure is to be exploited, the campaign must have the prestige, the backing, and the power of top management. To be called to serve the Syracuse United Fund drive as a divisional or even sectional chairman now means both social recognition and, perhaps obliquely, career opportunity. Those so nominated are aware of their own bosses' active concern in the fund; they will put all their talents and much of their time into the job; and the fund-raising programs they develop will have the complete backing of their companies.

After several years of participation and, by degrees, taking more and more responsibility, the executive "volunteer" becomes an enthusiastic, evangelistic campaigner; and the fund's goals go up and up.

This kind of organization was not established at Syracuse without some internal friction at the outset. Some devoted people believed that training in social work and concern for the agencies' "clients" must be paramount in any aspect of the chest's work, including fund-raising. The change-over took several years, and used the industrial people active in the old organization to manage the re-organization process from within. As quotas met each year rose by jumps of $50,000 and $100,000, the wisdom of building fund-raising around the city's industrial structure became apparent to all. Old-timers at chest headquarters nevertheless recall some stirring table-pounding scenes.

Another aspect of tying chest campaigns to the city's industrial structure, it was decided, was the involvement of organized labor; but this, too, presented some diplomatic difficulties. During World War II, a union man was hired part-time, and finally one was hired full-time by the chest (then called United War Fund) to educate local union memberships in the value of community agencies' services to the working man.[3] Discussion sessions, "union counselor classes," and visits to agencies soon were involving every local union in the county. The chest board included an AFL representative, the Council of Social Agencies Board included a CIO representative; and, most important, the "Factory Division" of the chest's campaign had union representation. Two places on the chest's budget committee, which allocates the campaign funds among member agencies, were assigned to labor.

All of this, agreed William Bien, the chest's full-time labor staff man, Gerald W. Burke, the chest's executive secretary, and Mr. Hancock, was not enough. They wanted a Labor-Management Committee to be part of the fund's organization.

In 1948 eight union leaders and eight leading industrialists, after much maneuvering, consented to talk it over in the board room of a local bank. The industrialists inside the room on the appointed day became so engrossed in discussing the advantages and disadvantages of the plan that they forgot about the union men waiting outside in the hallway. When finally they opened the door to invite their visitors in they found them gone. "We might have waited a little longer," one of the union men recalled, "if they'd given us chairs to sit on."

When the two parties finally got together (following an

evening of cocktails at Mr. Hancock's home for representatives from each side) it was at the Labor Temple.

The committee created at the meeting in the Labor Temple has helped to raise factory workers' contributions to the fund to an average gift in recent years of almost thirteen dollars and to increase employee participation to around 90 percent.

The Labor-Management Committee was also responsible in large part for United Giving in Syracuse—another project fenced with diplomatic obstacles. Working with the local unions and the Manufacturers' Association of Syracuse, the committee in 1952 instituted the "Industrial Federated Community Services Plan," and soon had eighty of the city's ninety leading companies included. Only ten industrial companies, and 500 workers, were outside the plan. Each company in IFCS agreed to permit only one annual in-plant solicitation, and returns from this single solicitation were allocated among the various campaigns operating in the city throughout the year. In union-organized companies, the decisions of splitting the money among Chest, Red Cross, Polio, etc., were made by a committee of union and company representatives.

The upshot was a series of independent drives requiring many man-hours of administrative time in each plant. It meant that allocations decisions were made by many people, none of whom had the background regarding agency needs that the chest's budget committee had. But it also meant that agencies in Syracuse would be forced into a real united fund before long, which they were beginning in 1954.

Certain health and welfare agencies have opposed the organization of united funds in American cities—largely because they believed they could raise more money with drives of their own, even with the costs of each campaign subtracted from amounts raised. For several years there was much marshalling of figures by these agencies—and by united fund advocates—to prove this true—or false.

Board members of agencies have been conditioned over the years to regard fund-raising drives as opportunities for educating communities about their agency. They feared their agencies (and maybe the board members) would lose some community prestige if they hid their lights under the united fund bushel. In general, these agency board members are important people in the community; and a united fund drive can hardly succeed without their cooperation. In Syracuse these men, nevertheless, were also industrial leaders; and the advantages of UF to their companies proved to be more persuasive than the objections of the agency people.

In Syracuse, too, the strength of IFCS with complete backing of both management and labor, left reluctant agencies little alternative to agreeing to the establishment of a united fund program.

Detroit, as the 1949 pioneer in UF, fought the battle for other cities. One device used there to bring reluctant agencies within the UF fold was to include in the campaign the name of the disease represented by the agency which had refused to participate. For example, when the American Cancer Society refused to join Detroit's UF, and later refused to accept the fund's allotment for cancer, the money went to an especially created organization, the Michigan Cancer Foundation. Next year, the American Cancer Society decided to come into the Fund. Similarly, "polio money" went to a "Metropolitan Detroit Polio Foundation," and two years later the National Foundation for Infantile Paralysis likewise was in the United Fund. Agency revolts threatened again, however, in 1958.

Detroit's United Foundation Torch Drive has become the wonder and the model of UF campaigns everywhere. In 1948, the year before UF was established, 52 separate drives in

Detroit (including the chest, which failed by $300,000)
together raised only $7 million. Under leadership of Henry
Ford II and Ben Young of the National Bank of Detroit,
among others, the United Foundation was established in 1949
with Walter C. Laidlaw as executive vice-president. Since then
it has broken national records for community support of
agencies, and does so with administrative and campaign costs
kept between 4.5 and 5 percent. Mr. Laidlaw's explanation of
the United Foundation's success is the same as Syracuse's: (1)
UF is strictly "a contributors' organization," and its only
connection with agencies is that the money raised goes to
them; (2) among the 60,000 volunteers working for the campaign are the top leaders of every important company in
metropolitan Detroit and all the major unions; (3) the leaders
of the city stand united—as contributors—behind UF and in
opposition to any opponents of the program.

The American Red Cross once issued a booklet that decried
pressures to join the united drive as "un-American." [4] Detroit's
Wayne County Chapter of the Red Cross, nevertheless, in
disobedience of headquarters orders and in the face of threats
of charter suspension, voted to join Detroit's UF. Now Red
Cross, as national policy, accepts chapter participation in
united funds; although it insists that all announcements concerning the campaign link the Red Cross name with the
chest's.

At this writing, only the American Heart Association and
the American Cancer Society continue to fight united fund
participation. Heart disease, "America's Number One Killer,"
beginning in 1956 had the public's sympathy for President
Eisenhower as a peg for support of a drive of its own. If it had
broken away from the fund in strongly-Republican Syracuse it
might, indeed, have done better financially than by staying in
the united fund. Such success, it was feared, might influence

still other agencies to try independent drives. Local industry believed it could not allow this to happen. Syracuse companies and unions to date are standing firmly together in their decision to permit but one in-plant drive a year; they have been successful so far.[5]

National health organizations point out that their most important contribution is medical research; and they complain that chest and united fund boards try to keep as much collected money as they can in their own cities. If these boards would be less provincial, they say, they would be more inclined to participate.

Christmas and Easter Seal campaigns and the March of Dimes, since they do not rely heavily on industrial solicitations, seem immune to united fund pressures; the Syracuse Labor-Management Committee has tried without success to get them in.

The advantages of united funds certainly are worth any unpleasantness in instituting them. By centralizing campaign costs, many millions of dollars are saved across the country. Syracuse United Fund administrative and campaign costs were 5.8 percent in a recent year, and the national average then was only 7.3 percent; whereas formerly independent drives and their administrations had cost as much as 30 percent, and a few even more. Even with the added expense of installing payroll deduction systems, companies find that limiting disruption of work and loans of manpower to one time a year saves them money. One manufacturer estimated his costs of pre-united-fund drives at $40,000 a year, excluding the corporate contributions. From the community's point of view, united fund results in more thoughtful and equitable allocations of total available money; and it gives everyone respite from an interminable series of collections.

The rapid growth of united funds since Detroit's pioneering

in 1949 has been phenomenal. Hundreds of cities are shifting to the plan each year. Companies in cities without united funds are sponsoring their own "united" in-plant drives and permitting no others. Ford Motor does so in all its plant cities that have no united fund. If enough companies adopt the plan, a united fund becomes inevitable, just as it did under the introductory IFCS arrangement in Syracuse.

* * *

Ideas for improving united fund and chest campaigns constantly are being developed in communities everywhere. Here are some, most (but not all) of them practiced in Syracuse:

Organization of the campaign is key to its success, but a useful organizational structure in one community might not work so well in another. Continuity in Syracuse is supplied by an Advisory Council made up of general chairmen of past campaigns and the most experienced people obtainable from the most important publics: labor, manufacturing, government, commerce, etc. Soliciting is by divisions, each having two to a dozen sections.[6]

No less important than the soliciting divisions are the working committees of the campaign: Finance, Allocations, Publicity, Sales Training, Special Events, Speakers' Bureau, Labor Participation, Admissions and National Agencies Relations— all, I think, with self-explanatory titles. Detroit has in addition an Economic Survey Committee to study business conditions and prospects and to determine the amount it will be possible to raise. Detroit, incidentally, is one of the few cities which rather consistently reaches its goal.

Syracuse has no united fund board as such, but its leaders have responsibility to the boards of chest, Council of Social Agencies, and Red Cross. Detroit's 150-man united fund Board is chosen to represent the contributors and not the beneficiaries of the campaign. Whatever the details of structure, this concentration on the fund-raising function must be the underlying principle of campaign organization.

Payroll deduction systems work best when an actual (or seeming) minimum is placed on the weekly contribution. One company accepts contributions of no less than twenty cents a week. Another plan is to sell united fund shares at thirteen dollars each, to be paid for at twenty-five cents a week through payroll deduction; this device tends to establish thirteen dollars as a minimum gift and to raise larger contributions by jumps of thirteen dollars. Receipts are printed to look like shares of stock, and are headed "united preferred . . . a sound investment."

By establishing united fund chapters in each company plant or office, one "joins" by subscribing. This exploitation of the natural desire to belong is used successfully in many industrial cities, and notably in Detroit.

Some plants have found payroll deductions scorned by supervisors who think it more appropriate for them to give lump sums, as executives and salaried people do. For this reason, and because payroll deductions are so painless, even for executives, companies are finding it wise to place all employees under the system.

A major difficulty of the payroll deduction system is that employee layoffs, since the deductions do not accumulate for the worker over such periods, can play hob with agencies which have obligated themselves to the extent of their total united fund allocation for the year. The solution has been to set aside 10 percent reserves in the Fund for these emergencies.

Workers in the building trades in many cities, especially in colder climates, are traditionally small givers. The Syracuse answer is to begin the drive of the Construction Division a month ahead of the united fund's campaign in October and

November, so that building-trades workers can complete their contributions to a modified payroll deduction plan before winter weather interrupts their employment. The slogan of "A buck a week for sixteen weeks" describes this special arrangement. Wisely, the Construction Division has a larger proportion of union people in its administration than other "divisions" of the Fund have.

The "Good Neighbor Day" plan for employee-giving has done well at the Crouse-Hinds Company in Syracuse. Employees there work five hours on a Saturday morning at time-and-a-half, and their total earnings go into a Good Neighbor Fund, administered by elected employees. Voluntary participation is 90 percent. The bulk of the money goes to united fund. Salaried workers are asked to set their contributions at one-and-a-half times what they make per five hours, and so contribute, either in lump sum or by payroll deductions. Because it permits them to contribute generously without actually parting with any money, the plan is popular with Crouse-Hinds hourly-paid workers.[7] The idea is also popular with the united fund because it has a kind of built-in cost-of-living boost tied to current wage levels. The National Cash Register Company also uses this plan in its plant cities.

Fair share formulae for executives' contributions in some cities have raised standards of giving among the better paid. The idea works best if each company establishes its own fair share formula. In one small plant, the plan influenced five management men to increase their gifts from $30 to $150, from $225 to $400, from $120 to $300, from $250 to $365, and from $30 to $120, respectively. The theory behind the idea is that management people want to keep up with their fellows, and that many had been under-contributing out of ignorance.[8]

Advance gift solicitations, which in Syracuse obtain about

50 percent of the united fund goal each year, are handled by about one hundred management people, some of whom head other committees and divisions. Each is given ten to twenty cards of big-gift prospects, according to his relationships. These relationships go by an A, B, C rating as follows:

A—The prospect is obligated or indebted to the solicitor.

B—The prospect and the solicitor are close personal friends.

C—The prospect and the solicitor have close and satisfactory business relationships.

These solicitors are sure to make their own generous personal and/or corporate contributions prior to paying their calls on prospects, because sometimes they are bluntly asked if they themselves have given, and if so, how much. They are also instructed, as a group, to call on the surest and most lucrative prospects first, so that the standards will be set high. They are asked not to leave pledge cards with prospects; but to call back if the prospect wants time to think it over. Contributions are higher if the solicitor is present when the prospect writes out the amount he will give. The sales talk, of course, always is in the community's terms and always is supported with statistical justification of the goal and of the prospect's proportionate responsibility to meet it.

The corporate yardstick plan, as it operates at Buffalo, for example, recognizes that companies in different businesses and industries vary in their ability to contribute to a chest or united fund. The "yardstick" is based on the previous year's average gift per employee in the appropriate trade or industrial classification, multiplied by the number of employees in the company. The "yardstick" plan is a "fair share" formula (see p. 96 ff.), but unlike most such formulas it recognizes differences in wage averages among kinds of industries and businesses. The Cleveland formula likewise includes enough variables to be acceptable to all kinds of firms.

Setting geographic limits to the united fund campaign territory is a worrisome problem in these days of long-distance commuting to work. Syracuse, Onondaga County's only hub, fortunately can limit its drives to the county and its nineteen suburban towns. The 150,000 people covered by the "Towns Division" of the campaign usually give less than the average. The Detroit campaign, covering three counties, before long may extend into six counties—and into areas where some residents are employed in cities outside of the Detroit United Fund jurisdiction.

United fund payroll deductions can seem doubtful investments to long-distance commuters; and in some cases really have little personal application to them. Although it is only a partial answer, Detroit is geographically decentralizing its agencies, constructing or renting branch buildings in suburban areas as quickly as financially possible. Permanent "community service representatives" of the fund are employed to see that residents there are getting their money's worth. The problem of overlapping jurisdictions of rival federated drives remains largely unsolved, however; yet, if payroll deductions are to go beyond 80 to 90 percent participation, some answer has to be found.

Gradual decline in leadership status of individuals heading divisions of united fund or chest campaigns is a natural phenomenon. Sometimes the Syracuse "work-up" system has had to be somewhat telescoped to put higher ranking industrial brass in the campaign's key roles. This was done in the 1955 drive, using pressures possible within the local Manufacturers' Association.

Setting of the divisional goal must in large part be the responsibility of the divisional chairman. He will be more determined to reach it; and, at least, he cannot complain later that it was unrealistic.

A *"task force"* of old hands at campaigning should be free to work with divisions and sections which are doing badly. Such a force, Syracuse finds, is most useful in helping business and industrial firms to analyze causes of failure. (They find it is usually a "personality problem" or an organizational weakness.) The Syracuse "task force" conducted 120 successful missions in one year.

United fund solicitors are trained by members of the Syracuse Sales Executives Club, which includes the sales managers of some important companies. About 90 training sessions are held each year for nearly 10,000 volunteer solicitors. One lesson learned in Syracuse: select solicitors from within an organization who have rank and acceptance there; and let them know precisely what is expected of them. Another lesson: don't force solicitors into a set selling pattern; coach them individually to take the most sales advantage of their own personalities.[9]

Solicitors—and the community at large—can become over-confident or discouraged during the drive if that "red feather thermometer" rises too quickly or too slowly. Announcements of some gifts can be delayed to keep the thermometer from rising too quickly; it is more difficult to keep it from rising too slowly. Syracuse has found it wise to have division heads regularly estimate their remaining potential, a practice that one year resulted in a last minute report to the Manufacturers Association board that the campaign would fail by $22,000. The companies represented among them made up the difference, although they were not solicited to do so. Second solicitations, indeed, are more harmful even than failing to reach the goal; companies thereafter will cautiously dole out a little money at each solicitation, always holding back some for a later "emergency."

Year-around publicity is probably next to leadership and

organization in establishing a united fund campaign's success. Here are some of the better publicity devices used in Syracuse:

A contest sponsored by the local chapter of the American Association of Industrial Editors among company house organs for the most consistent and effective accounts of services and needs of united fund agencies, with the editor of the winning publication receiving a plaque at the campaign's "final report" dinner.

Plaques also are presented to business and industrial companies which achieved or bettered their quotas. The union gets its recognition here, too. Other special awards are given to chairmen of high divisions and sections.

A Red Feather "Thank You Week" of open house tours of each agency is held with considerable publicity in the Spring following the Fall drive. Each agency gets feature treatment on the air and in the press.

Just prior to the campaign, a "Your Dollar At Work" series of articles also features agencies.

The United Fund annual report (in terms both of money and of services rendered) is "released to the people of Onondaga County" with great fanfare at a public meeting, with press and radio coverage.

As money raised is handed over to each of the agencies, a picture and story telling how this money will help citizens of the county is carried in the papers and on the air.

Publicity is calculated to build to a crescendo during the campaign itself, newspegged on a series of "dutch lunch" reporting sessions. At each session, a different division of the campaign is saluted for what it has done and for what it is expected to do before the campaign ends.

In all cities with successful campaigns, the year-around publicity puts more emphasis on agencies' services than on fund-raising as such. Nor is this service type of publicity loaded with "fear" appeal; the lament that "we are not being properly supported" is never included. Investigation has shown that publicity about lack of support leads only to increased reluctance of potential donors. In short, nothing succeeds like success in a united fund and community chest campaign; and, conversely, nothing fails like failure.

Because a campaign was successful this year, it has a better chance of succeeding again next year.[10]

4-
Financial Contributions

Company managements face persistent pressures to give more each year. Fund-raisers the nation over well know there is no place for a contribution policy to go but up. Once a giver, they say, always a giver. Now that corporations are established as contributors to philanthropies (an estimated $500 million in 1956 compared to less than $100 million in 1941) they inevitably will grow as contributors.

This trend is a marked one, despite historic fluctuations due to changes in the national tax picture. Today, much of management recognizes and voluntarily acts upon its corporate responsibility to the nation and to its plant communities.

Following repeal of the excess profits tax, which permitted high-earning companies to contribute to philanthropy at eighteen cents on the dollar, there occurred no *sustained* decline in the upward trend of corporate giving. Just as have individuals, so have corporations given more; all will continue to give more, largely because their communities need more. This does not mean that the public relations motive behind giving is no longer important; honest public relations and honest concern for the community should be corollary. Nor does this mean that all corporations have reached the zenith of community behavior and generosity.

Granted, as Richard Eells, of General Electric Company, says in his thoughtful book, *Corporation Giving in a Free Society:*

The guiding motive for corporate giving is the *enlightened self-interest of the donor company.* Self-interest is necessarily involved; otherwise the gift would exceed the powers of the corporate board. Corporation philanthropy is not almsgiving. Yet it is distinguishable from ordinary business expense in the sense of operating and capital costs. Its purpose is, rather, to serve the long-range interests of the enterprise within broad social dimensions and thus might be described as assurance or conservation costs.

It is often supposed that the chief aim of philanthropy is to promote good will for the donor. Certainly this is a desirable by-product. But corporation giving is not a branch of advertising, nor properly chargeable to advertising costs. Philanthropy is justifiable —and indeed necessary—whether or not the donor-company takes steps to garner the fruits of publicity attending its good works. The aim is to protect and preserve the donor's autonomy by protecting and preserving those conditions within the greater society which ensure the continuity of a system of free, competitive enterprise.[12]

Public relations of corporate giving, Mr. Eells rightly insists, should be as much concerned with gaining public acceptance of company philanthropy as with getting credit for company generosities. This means that the Number One public is company management itself.

"Many corporation directors," Mr. Eells writes, "have yet to grasp the significance of corporation philosophy as a creative opportunity for management." [13] He lists corporate investors, legislators, tax administrators, bench and bar, the press, management consultants, and prospective beneficiaries (organizations) as other groups to be educated in the broader philosophical purposes of corporate giving.

After this education with these publics is achieved, company public relations may move into the "getting credit" phase. Some companies publicize their gifts; many do not at all. Some limit such publicity to the employee publication; others "lead off" fund-raising campaigns, and so get publicity at the initiative of media without themselves trying for it. The fact is, this kind of information always is well circulated in any event, particularly among the more active and important people in the community.

Except for the rare, sardonic stockholder who asks, "Why not give us this money so we can make contributions?" company giving has had surprisingly little opposition from shareholders. This situation may or may not change as corporations give away larger pieces of net earnings. Most companies keep stockholders well informed of their contributions—and only rarely receive letters of protest. Perhaps some quieting effect has resulted from the 1953 New Jersey Supreme Court decision supporting A. P. Smith Manufacturing Company's unrestricted $1,500 gift to Princeton University over the protest of a stockholder.

A question only occasionally asked by the discreet investigator is, "What percentage of corporate profits before taxes does your company give away in your plant communities?" Such a question rarely draws a specific reply. Formulas for giving are not uncommon, however; and considering the companies' primary obligations to shareholders, these policies are, on the average, reasonably generous although the percentage might sound paltry to the man in the street.

In some cities where community fund campaigns utilize industry's help in soliciting both salaried and hourly-rated employees, the corporate contributions percentage actually has been declining (even though corporate contributions are increasing in amount). This is graphically illustrated in Chart A which analyzes the Detroit United Foundation income over a seven year period.

Leland Hazard, vice-president of Pittsburgh Plate Glass

Chart A

UNITED FOUNDATION OF DETROIT
Seven Year Source of Income Analysis

Year	Corporations		Executive & Salaried		Hourly Rated		Residential, Foundations, Retired Wealth		Campaign Total
	Amount	% of Total	Amount	% of Total	Amount	% of Total	Amount	% of Total	
1948	Agencies in separate campaigns raised a total of approximately:								$ 7,200,000
1949	$3,734,206	40.4	$2,427,927	26.3	$1,964,003	21.2	$1,120,909	12.1	9,247,045
1950	3,769,850	36.2	2,804,822	27.0	2,644,247	25.4	1,185,602	11.4	10,404,521
1951	4,338,478	38.5	3,179,482	28.2	2,415,233	21.4	1,341,859	11.9	11,275,052
1952	4,669,450	37.0	3,545,748	28.1	2,991,687	23.7	1,410,094	11.2	12,616,979
1953	4,984,347	37.0	3,913,815	28.6	3,272,614	24.0	1,434,264	10.4	13,605,040
1954	4,804,154	34.3	4,538,890	32.4	3,010,935	21.5	1,654,021	11.8	14,008,000
1955	5,001,027	31.4	5,326,608	33.4	3,856,569	24.2	1,748,796	11.0	15,933,000

Company, thinks—along with Beardsley Ruml and Theodore Geiger—that companies might well give the five percent maximum under the tax law [14]—a total, incidentally, that would rival United States government welfare spending. Mr. Hazard, like Mr. Eells, considers that the choice is between government social spending, with its implied controls, and sharply increased private welfare support.[15]

One company, by board action, budgets one percent of earnings *after* taxes to specified charities and refers additional requests to the board itself. Another gives .5 percent of net profits plus $3 per employee. Very few companies give to the five percent tax deduction limit—most give less than one percent.

Man-hours of executive time given to the study of financial contributions problems, both important and piddling, come to startling totals in many companies. Management cannot be blamed for wanting to reduce it all to quick formulas. Some recipient organizations offer to help companies work out formulas, e.g., the state and regional associations of private liberal arts colleges suggest that companies compute the proportion of their taxes now going to state support of education and give private colleges the same amount.

Sixteen percent of companies use formulas to determine amounts for giving.[16] Here are some of the factors which various companies consider in determining amounts of giving at community levels:

1. Corporate earnings before taxes. (Only three percent of companies use formulas based strictly on gross or net earnings.)
2. Plants earnings relative to corporate earnings.
3. Community sales of company products.
4. Size of work force relative to community size.
5. Plant payroll relative to community's total payroll.

6. Previous contributions by plant employees relative to total community donations.
7. Quota for local industry in each community drive.
8. Averaged contribution of similar local operations multiplied by number of employees.

Statisticians can mix several of these ingredients into mathematical formulas which look scientific and hence inviolable. A solicitor finds his bargaining power more than a little handicapped by such hard and fast equations adopted as a corporate policy; he may be inclined to accept the company's answer as to what x equals.[17]

So-called "fair share" formulas for apportioning corporate gift quotas among locally operating industries may not be fair at all. Certainly no two firms are alike in how they must spend their profits; nor does any one plant's needs remain the same from year to year. A good many firms, e.g. Esso Standard Oil, as a matter of policy, will accept no formulas.[18]

Most company-originated formulas correlate giving with earnings—so that the company's good years are its more generous years. However, a company's period of low earnings and less generous contributions are likely to be the time of the community agencies' greatest need. From the viewpoints both of community need and of company public relations, such lean-year cutbacks are unfortunate. Because resentment would be particularly noticeable following cutbacks on such continuing programs as college scholarships for employees' children, lean-year budgeting is apt to give health and welfare contributions—the more important ones to the community—only second priority. Companies with their own foundations think they have avoided this dilemma.

In Syracuse as in all cities, I suspect, the local industries proportionately out-give the branch plants.[19] Smaller companies with assets under a million dollars contribute nationally an average of 1.13 percent of net income before taxes—notably better than the national average.

Perhaps the discrepancy in giving between locally-owned companies and branch plants creates more local hostility toward branch managements than headquarters staffs realize. It is a hostility that begins with leaders of community thought, some of whom are vocal and vehement in their criticisms of contributions policies set at the distant company headquarters. And, just as "thought-leaders" are cultivated as communicators of favorable information and opinions, so should they be recognized as potential arousers of resentment.

Our community policy, said one headquarters man, is to allow a certain decentralized flexibility in contributions; even for sums over $100 the plant managers are at liberty to petition the contributions committee at headquarters. On the other hand, a local manager confided: "If I succeeded in upping the ante in one case, I'd be before that contributions committee every month or so thereafter. This isn't the issue on which I want to acquire the company reputation as an upsetter of established applecarts. And, as for our community relations, I think the company is big enough to absorb some isolated griping."

Indeed, this local manager may be justified in his point of view, although the griping may not be as isolated as he thinks it is.

What then is the multi-plant company's answer to giving at community levels? One suggestion is that, just as established community wage rates set the pattern for a branch plant's wage rates, so should community standards set the pattern for a branch plant's community giving. An objection to this plan is that a branch operation has a complexity of out-of-town financial and policy obligations that go beyond any one plant town. Adherents to the idea answer, however, that these financial and policy obligations apply equally to wages paid out. They add, further, that wages represent an infinitely bigger piece of money. If there is community relations value in adhering to community wage rates (granted that there are other more important reasons for it), then the community relations value in meeting the industrial community's rates for local philanthropy represents a real bargain.

Show us, then, answer the headquarters men, how to keep peace among our branch managers under such an arrangement. They point out two other facets of the problem: (1) If there is to be planning back of a company's donations there must be centralized decision-making, and (2) local, small but highly-profitable companies, perhaps family-owned and run, can set a pace for giving impossible for other plants. Is this pace to be accepted as a community standard? Maybe, they say, branch managements are entitled to some hostile feelings of their own.

Localized philanthropy, in any case, certainly has community relations importance. Most companies realize this; a few do not. One national company with somewhat misplaced idealism contributes largely to headquarters of selected health and welfare organizations, giving minimum amounts to community chests and united funds in plant cities. The reason: money so given goes directly to an organization and will be used 100 percent by that charity with no "siphoning off" by an intermediary fund-raising chest. National headquarters of the Heart Association and the Cancer Society might regard this as model behavior (if they are among the charities selected), but otherwise the approach seems devoid of public relations virtue. Then again, there is the company which makes all its contributions at plant city levels, with plant managers handing over the money. Turndowns of requests, meanwhile, are always sent out by company headquarters as headquarters decisions to protect local management's relationships in town.

The problem of "how much" is important—and solving it in a multi-plant company has to be, as General Electric Company would put it, in "the balanced best interests" of all its people and all phases of its operations. You can't make a giving formula to fit every company, or perhaps not even a formula to fit any two companies. Utilities, as rate-regulated companies, have additional problems growing out of a variety of state regulations; public service commissions are not inclined to include company contributions as a factor in their rate-setting decisions. According to the American Association of Fund-Raising Counsel, utilities gave .44 percent of pre-tax earnings in 1952, the lowest of any industrial group except transportation.

Percentage giving by industries in 1952 (based on pre-tax earnings): construction, 1.74 percent; wholesale and retail trade, 1.53 percent; the professional firms, 1.46 percent; manufacturing, 1.13 percent; agriculture, .81 percent; finance, banking and insurance, .62 percent; mining, .46 percent; transportation and utilities .44 percent.[20]

But of this I'm sure: a good many national companies might well re-study their local contributions policies in the light of local reactions to their present giving in plant communities.

The "to whom" part of the community giving problem is no less troublesome than "how much."

Westinghouse in one year received 14,186 separate requests at company headquarters, not to mention local requests that went only to branch plants.[21] Basic policy formulations are the only salvation for the contribution committee so confronted. At the 1956 Cornell seminar in Community Relations, participants named seven areas of policy:

1. Policies designed to achieve equitable consideration of requests and equitable distribution of company funds.
2. Policies that can provide a dignified "no."
3. Policies providing for budgetary control.
4. Policies that stimulate good human relations. (Published policies have been found effective in this regard.)
5. Policies that make for prompt and efficient replies.
6. Policies that establish broad categories of recipients and state criteria for giving.
7. Policies that prevent overlapping of gifts.

Probably as necessary as policies is a contribution plan: a stated list of objectives to be met by the contributions program. Such objectives can vary all the way from encouraging research in the company's industry to preserving free enterprise; but whatever they turn out to be, these objectives are the criteria for intelligent, planned selection of both categories and specific recipients of the company's philanthropy.

International Harvester's written contribution policy is recognized nationally as a pioneering document, and is reproduced in full as Appendix C.[22] Like Harvester's, most such company policies state that, since company money is stockholders' money, giving it away must directly or indirectly benefit the company. This is the number one criterion in deciding "to whom" the company shall give. Other frequently included criteria for recipient causes are:

1. That it be in the community's benefit.
2. That it supply benefits not already provided to company employees.
3. That it be supported by the rest of the community.
4. That it be non-controversial.
5. That it be non-sectarian.
6. That it be non-political.

7. That it not be tax-supported.
8. That the recipient organization be included by the United States Treasury Department in its *Cumulative List of Organizations, Contributions to Which are Deductible Under Section 23 (o) and Section 23 (q) of the Internal Revenue Code and the Corresponding Section of Prior Revenue Acts.*[23]

The data worksheet, used by American Airlines, helps to simplify the process of evaluating contribution requests. (See Chart B.)

Fred Jolly, community relations manager of Caterpillar Tractor, warns against too rigid limitations in a contributions policy. Keep it a statement of principles and not of specifics, he says, and you can live with it. Probably no other company gets as much public relations mileage out of its local contributions as does Caterpillar at Peoria. Every solicitor, even of the so-called nuisance variety, gets a red-carpet reception, a full and courteous hearing, and, as soon as possible, a considered answer. Mr. Jolly or one of his community relations staff men will visit a local organization which has requested help and talk over its problems more fully. Caterpillar researches and answers even form letter requests. High school student projects, service club programs for orphans, traffic safety campaigns, etc.—all represent relatively small amounts of money but large amounts of good will. The years since 1944 that Mr. Jolly and his staff have been cheerfully and courteously applying themselves to this time-consuming business have helped establish Caterpillar as a Peoria institution, in the very best sense of the word.

CHART B

REQUEST FOR CONTRIBUTION

(as used by American Airlines)

Organization's name: ....

address: ....

Name of person soliciting................In person........By letter........

Type of organization:...

Purpose of organization:..

Does organization's activity overlap or duplicate that of another agency to which the company contributes?

Yes...........No...........

Is a contribution permitted under company policy?

Will a contribution benefit the company, its employees or stockholders directly or indirectly?

Does the organization meet company standards?

If not, explain.

If organization is not member of Community Chest or United Fund, why not?

Amount of organization's current budget. $.....................

Amount raised during last fiscal year. $.....................

Percent of funds raised during last fiscal year spent on (a) fund raising...............%; (b) administrative costs...............%

Amount of contribution requested $.....................

Amount previously donated $.....................

What amounts do comparable companies give?

Amount of donation recommended $.....................

Reasons for recommending donation:

Request approved .... Date:............. By:.............

Request refused ....Date:.............By:.............

The 1950 Russell Sage Foundation Study [24] of 325 corporations found an average gift dollar division of forty-four cents to welfare agencies (including thirty-six cents to community chests); twenty-six cents to health agencies (hospitals, national foundations, etc.); sixteen plus cents to education (research, scholarships, college funds); four cents to religious agencies; five cents to "free enterprise" proponents; and four plus cents unspecified.

Although in 1955 industry gave more total money, and no category (except "free enterprise" promotion) was cut, a percentage division gave relatively more to education (about 25 percent).[25] Among the larger national corporations, relative percentages going to welfare and to education have been approximately reversed from 1950 to 1956. This does not seem to be true to the same degree among smaller companies.

Industrial concern for the financial plights of endowed colleges and universities, with tuitions at near maximums and operating costs rising sharply, has increased tremendously in recent years. But colleges are not actually competing with chests for the same corporate dollar, as some welfare people contend.

"Obviously, college administrators are outselling us in the market place," complained a chest official from a midwestern city. This seems an exaggeration of his case; contributions to colleges, by and large, represent "new money," not funds that would otherwise have gone into chest coffers. Nor are welfare and education competing against one another in service. Both are needed and both will be supported.

Rising standards of American living and public health continue to make our community health and welfare fund quotas inadequate even as they grow larger—a circumstance compounded by inflation and growing urban-area populations. Increasingly, industry will become more discriminating in its contributions, although no less generous. Increasingly, too, recipient agencies must become more discriminating in spending the money they receive.

More careful budgeting is the answer in both cases. Company contributions budgets are the despair of their makers, what with unanticipated, but legitimate requests eating away as much as half the budgeted amount in six months. Budgeting 40 percent of the total for unanticipated allocation seems to be a common arrangement. Getting complete contributions estimates from plant and division managements is next to impossible, most large companies find, because it is usually at the local levels that unanticipated requests are received.

Thirty-four percent of companies, by one estimate, prefer to play their contributions by ear, and have no budget for donations at all.[26]

A surprising number of foundations were begun in 1953, just before expiration of the Excess Profits Tax.[27] According to Harvard Business School Club of Cleveland, forty such foundations—15 percent of the national total—were in Cleveland alone in 1953.[28] The survey of 200 member companies by the American Society of Corporate Secretaries found that one-fourth of the firms have foundations or trusts.[29] The Sears, Roebuck Foundation, dating back to 1923, but rechartered in 1941, is a national model; although most of its 3,000-plus annual projects have rural emphasis they still are diverse enough to serve as a helpful guide to more recently formed foundations.

A company foundation has the great virtue of stabilizing donations in lean years with extra money fed into it during fat years. Furthermore, it permits commitments to be made more than one year in advance, and it allows contributions to individuals as well as to organizations.

These virtues probably are enough to warrant establishing

a foundation, yet companies should be aware of some disadvantages, too: (1) Money put into the foundation cannot be taken out again for company use, no matter what the emergency. (2) Management of a foundation, as a separate corporation, adds another piece of administrative machinery to companies that may already have more administration than they can cheerfully contend with. (3) The very word *foundation* invites fund-seekers of all kinds to come calling. (4) For multi-plant companies, local gifts of relatively small amounts have to go through the foundation's machinery or else be charged against local operations, unless each plant is to have a separate contributions budget of its own. Because most companies come nowhere near giving away their allowable tax-free limit—either through a foundation or directly to philanthropies—the question of tax advantage is academic in either case.

The alternative to a foundation is a contributions committee of perhaps three to six members, one of them executive to the committee and responsible for preparing budget and screening requests. One company, American Standard, has three levels of committees, at plant, divisional and headquarters levels, each with ceilings on the amount of money it can disburse. Others, like American Can Company, have one headquarters committee to allocate funds both for general office and division office disbursement. Some companies have two separate committees to decide upon charity contributions and "non-charity" contributions (such as organizational memberships). Others draw no such distinction, and a few even consider "good will" advertising in local newspapers to be company "contributions," subject to the committee's decision.

The 1956 industrial contributions study of the American Society of Corporate Secretaries found that contributions committee membership commonly includes vice-presidents and presidents, who make decisions on the basis of information gathered for them by a full-time or part-time staff man. (This staff man sometimes is an assistant secretary to the corporation; more often he is from the public relations department.)

Owens-Illinois Glass Company has a uniquely flexible arrangement that draws in management people at higher or lower echelons according to the size of the contribution requested. Corporate specialists join the committee as advisors, too, as their specializations become involved. Standard Oil Company (New Jersey) has a five-man committee (executive assistant to the president, corporation secretary, head of public relations, head of personnel, and director of budgets) and a full-time executive secretary.[30] This committee undertakes rather extensive continuing investigations of recipient organizations' services and efficiency.

It may be cruel to industrial brass to make the observation here, but one real advantage of a formal organization to handle contributions—be it foundation or committee—is to restrict the big boss from making commitments in an open-handed and off-handed way to people who approach him personally. Let him go in for such unresearched, non-comparative and impulsive generosity with funds from his own checking account, committee and foundation staffmen would say.

Protection against fraudulent and questionable fund-raisers is much publicized, at least in New York State. The so-called "boiler room" promotions of local money drives by fast-moving itinerant operators are not difficult to identify, but tagging the operators with a law violation is almost impossible in some states.

These promoters sell a fund-raising scheme to a legitimate local organization—a Parent-Teachers Association, a youth group or a service club. Perhaps they'll put on a dance for the PTA, sell good will advertising in the program, and, if lucky, the PTA will receive 20 percent of the proceeds. Or the operator may persuade a local service club to sponsor a drive to send underprivileged children to the circus: enough money is raised for 500 admissions, but only 200 youngsters ever receive tickets—the promoter has pocketed the difference as "expenses."

A common practice of these promoters is to hire local women as telephone solicitors, and to remain, themselves, as much as possible in the background.[31] The appearance is that of a reputable local organization using local help to run a legitimate campaign for a worthy cause. The result usually is that the reputable local organization loses community prestige and, hence, some of its usefulness.

The "expenses" proportion of money raised is an indicator of legitimacy, but only an indicator. There are honestly run flops in fund-raising, with total expenses exceeding total profits. Some otherwise legitimate organizations indulge in pitiably wasteful and expensive fund-raising—like mailing out dollar bills to be matched and returned, or fountain pens for signing the gift checks.

Better Business Bureaus [32] have devised questionnaires, now in use in Cleveland and Toledo, so worded as to uncover the promoter-run campaign—and to make sure that both administrative and campaign expenses are set forth in advance. Often a big "keep" has been explained away as "administration cost" in addition to the estimate of expenses submitted before the campaign.

The National Information Bureau, a non-profit organization with headquarters in New York City, is also a clearing house of information about both legitimate and illegitimate fund-raising. New York State Department of Social Welfare publishes a *Directory of Registered Charitable Organizations*,

Professional Fund Raisers, and Professional Solicitors in New York State. Such organizations and people are required by law, passed in 1954, to register complete information before fund-raising plus annual audited fiscal statements, and fund-raisers must post $5,000 bonds. Registered information is indexed and open to public inspection. (Information on fund-raising educational institutions is separately collected by the State Department of Education. Religious organizations and small volunteer groups seeking less than $1,500 a year are exempt from registering.)

Other states, such as Pennsylvania and North Carolina, have licensing boards which, unlike New York, make value judgments in denying or permitting organizations to raise funds. In 1956, twenty-one states had legislation of one kind or another to control fraudulent fund-raising.

City solicitations committees, made up of Chamber of Commerce, labor union, industrial, professional and welfare representatives, have been set up in some cities to survey all appeals for money in the community and to pass public judgment on them. Those at Savannah and at Cleveland are reported to be particularly effective.

Less than half of America's companies utilize the services of available investigative bodies, according to Russell Sage information. Besides checking with the above information agencies, plus police and FBI, companies find that their best protective device is to *require all requests for funds to be in writing,* including complete information about fund-raising techniques, expenses, administrative costs, and money goals.

Discovering and foiling unethical fund-raising is a community as well as a company responsibility. A few sad experiences will make legitimate money-raising difficult for worthy organizations and causes.

FOOTNOTES

[1] Syracuse Moral Survey Committee, *The Social Evil in Syracuse*, Syracuse, 1913.

[2] Although health and welfare agencies earlier had cooperated with one another in an Associated Charities organization, World War I inspired the first unified community fund-raising in Syracuse. The Syracuse War Chest, Inc. was formed in 1917. It became the Syracuse Community Chest in 1921, included twenty agencies and raised $575,000, a creditable sum for its day.

Cleveland's Community Chest, as such, was established in 1919, the first in the nation. Since then the Cleveland Chest has remained one of the best and most imitated. Syracuse's Chest was in part remodeled on Cleveland's, following a 1933 visit there by industrial leaders to study its organization.

[3] Some sixty community funds and councils employed full-time labor representatives in 1956: Arch Mandel, director, Labor Participation Department, United Funds and Councils of America, New York City. (Letter to the author.)

[4] *The Case for Freedom in Fund Raising*, Washington, D.C., no date.

[5] The same sequence of events, at this writing, is under way at Pittsburgh, one of the latest cities to go United Fund. It, too, found itself embroiled in bitter controversy between such "hold-outs" as cancer and heart, and the UF, whose backers—the city's industrialists—are determined to install the one-drive policy. The united fund collected "cause money" for cancer and heart purposes, offered it to national charities; it was refused.

[6] The Syracuse Divisions: Advance Gifts, Construction, Professional, Hotels and Restaurants, Towns, Government, Women's, Financial (including banks and real estate companies), Automotive, Metals, Foods, Schools and Organizations, Retail, Publishing and Business Supplies, Public Service (including transportation companies), Factories. Some cities prefer to work with considerably fewer divisions; sometimes the decision whether an area of the community should be represented by a division or by a section is determined by "political"—or, shall we say, "human relations" considerations.

[7] Probably no company in Syracuse works harder than Crouse-Hinds at acquainting employees with health and welfare agency needs through publicity, talks by agency people, and visits by eight company teams of five people each to agencies in town—all on company time.

[8] Detroit's executive "fair share" formula submitted to companies for their consideration in one year was as follows:

Income Range	Fair Share Gift	% of Income
$ 9,600–$10,799	$130	1.25
10,800– 11,999	155	1.33
12,000– 13,499	180	1.40
13,500– 14,999	215	1.48
15,000– 16,499	250	1.56
16,500– 17,999	285	1.63

18,000– 19,499	325	1.71
19,500– 20,999	365	1.79
21,000– 22,499	400	1.87
22,500– 23,999	450	1.94
24,000– 25,499	500	2.02
25,500– 26,999	550	2.10
27,000– 28,499	600	2.17
28,500– 29,999	650	2.25
30,000– 35,000	700	2.34

For incomes over $35,000, a gift representing 3% of income is suggested.

The plan worked so well with executives in Detroit that now it has been extended to apply to all contributors.

[9] The most spectacular fund-raising innovation since payroll deductions is the "Mothers' March" for the National Foundation for Infantile Paralysis. This technique—which ought to have possibilities for Women's Divisions of united fund and chest drives—depends on thorough organization, so that a mother calls on ten of her neighbors; and every home in town is one of ten assigned to a particular housewife. This large soliciting force, furthermore, does its work in one well-publicized evening, directed by ward captains, district lieutenants and neighborhood chairmen who complete their organizing well in advance. The fouler the weather (the "March" is in January), seemingly the more successful the drive becomes. Everyone is generous to a neighbor he knows who plows through a snowstorm to help crippled children. Recently, some $111,000 was collected in Onondaga County within several hours.

[10] A useful case study of "Three In-Plant Fund-Raising Campaigns" for hospitals in General Electric plant cities is How General Electric Participates in Capital Fund Drives, n.d.

[11] Some of the material in this chapter appeared in the author's article, "Industrial Financial Support of Community Projects," Journal of Educational Sociology, Sept. 1957.

[12] New York: Harper & Brothers, 1956, p. 136.

[13] Ibid., p. 182.

[14] See Federal Code, Section 162, which deals with business expenses, and Section 170, which deals with charitable contributions.

[15] Beardsley Ruml, editor, Manual of Corporate Giving, National Planning Association, 1952, chapters 1, 2 and 4.

[16] A company membership study by American Society of Corporate Secretaries, 1956, quoted by A. A. Paradis at a Cornell seminar in Community Relations, Summer, 1956.

[17] An example of what one can do if one really tries are these formulae found in Corporate Contributions to Hospitals (New York: National Better Business Bureau, 1955), p. 6:

$$\frac{a \times b}{c} \times \frac{d}{2} = \text{company's fair share}$$

$$\frac{a \times b}{c} + \frac{\frac{1}{2}a \times b}{c \times d} = \text{company's fair share}$$

$$\frac{a}{c} \times \frac{d}{2} = \text{company's fair share}$$

Legend: a—Number of company employees in area served.
         b—Average sized family per employee
         c—Population of area served
         d—Amount of campaign goal

[18] Emerson Andrews, in *Philanthropic Giving* (Russell Sage Foundation, New York, 1950) cites on page 65 some criteria for "fair share" formulas based on dollar volume of sales for stores, annual deposits for banks, etc. Other formulas are based on one day's payroll, or *x* dollars per employee, *x* percent of net earnings, etc.

[19] For a statistical documentation of this point in one city see *Corporate Giving in Greater Cleveland* (Harvard Business School Club of Cleveland, 1953), pp. 41–42. As a rather extreme example, Pitney-Bowes Inc. donates about 15 percent of the Stamford, Conn., Community Chest Fund, whereas it employs only 1,600 in a city of 85,000 population.

[20] *Business Week*, Sept. 3, 1955, p. 142.

[21] National Industrial Conference Board, *The Why and How of Corporate Giving*, 1956 p. 49. This conference report contains some excellent case material.

[22] The excellent library of the American Management Association has collected a number of contributions policies available to members. *See also* National Industrial Conference Board, "Company Policies on Donations," *Studies in Business Policy*, No. 49, New York, Dec. 1950.

[23] United States Government Printing Office, $2.50, with supplements.

[24] Emerson Andrews, "New Giant in Giving: Big Business," *The New York Times Magazine*, Dec. 2, 1951, p. 14 ff.

[25] *Corporate Contributions Report*, a company membership study by American Society of Corporate Secretaries, 1956, as quoted by A. A. Paradis at a Cornell Seminar.

[26] A. A. Paradis, American Airlines, before Cornell Community Relations seminar, 1956.

[27] Emerson Andrews' *Philanthropic Giving* contains a sample charter for a foundation (Appendix E). *See also* M. M. Chambers, *Charters of Philanthropies*, Carnegie Foundation for the Advancement of Teaching, New York, 1948.

[28] Harvard Business School Club of Cleveland, *Corporate Giving in Greater Cleveland*, Dec., 1953.

[29] National Conference on Solicitations (*See 1956 Year Book*), 400 Union Commerce Bldg., Cleveland, 1956. This annual conference and the yearbooks present much information valuable both to companies and to agencies.

[30] Claude L. Alexander, Standard Oil Company (New Jersey), is one of the recognized authorities in the field of corporate contributions. *See* his "Problems

and Practices of Corporate Giving," *Public Relations Journal*, Dec. 1950 pp. 5 ff.

[31] Promoters who use their own telephone solicitors and "pickup men" (collectors) are easily identified.

[32] Since Better Business Bureaus are subject to libel and slander suits, keep in mind their need for cautious wording when estimating their reports.

5-
Industry-School Relationships

Part One: The Syracuse Case

As EARLY as the 1930's, Syracuse industrial organizations were grumbling about the poorly trained young people who were applying for jobs: "No math, poor spelling, inadequate vocational training." The executive committee of the local Manufacturers Association in 1947 and again in 1951 asked the Syracuse Board of Education to do something about a centralized, high-level, thoroughly accredited technical and vocational high school, one large enough to meet the needs of the area's business and industry.

This is the case study of the program to obtain this vocational and technical training for the city.

Syracuse has had a vocational high school (at least in name) since 1918. The problem, however, was complicated rather than solved by the presence of Blodgett Vocational High on the city's West Side. A study of Blodgett Vocational graduates in the classes between 1927 and 1937 discovered that few boys trained in the school's industrial arts program were using on the job the skills taught them; that a majority of graduates did not take majors in vocational subjects at all; that the vocational graduates found their first jobs in haphazard ways; that technology had outdated some of the curriculum; and that few graduates ever had taken any additional education.[1]

The New York State Department of Vocational Education, after inspecting the school in 1939, refused to sanction its use of the word "vocational" in its title because it did not meet State standards. Yet here was a school which had had some outstanding teachers on its faculty, and a school with an active alumni association very much interested in Blodgett's future. The Blodgett Alumni Association, as proponents of the project were to learn, was a vigorous, proud, and highly vocal group. If money was to be spent in Onondaga County for improving vocational education, Blodgett alumni wanted it spent to improve the facilities at Blodgett.

Enrollment at Blodgett had declined rather steadily over the years. Such consultation as there was between Blodgett's administration and faculty and local industry appears to have been primarily at the shop and first-line supervisory levels. The School's unfortunate reputation stemmed from the fact that Blodgett had gradually de-emphasized its vocational offerings and increased its academic program. But because it bore the name of vocational, it was judged by the community and by industry as a vocational school.

There were, indeed, people throughout Syracuse who considered vocational education at any location to be totally unrealistic and a waste of taxpayers' money. Vocational schools, they maintained, always attract the less desirable of the generation, the dull or disturbed children; and no employer in his right mind would recruit from a vocational school anyway. Further, the argument went, it is unfair and unwise to force a child to select his career in his early 'teens. Companies, and not taxpayers, should pay for training employees, and such training ought be given on the job and not in public schools.

Whether the fact supports or opposes public vocational education, it was also pointed out that only 10,000 of 80,000 industrial jobs then in the Syracuse area were jobs for which a vocational high school trained its students; and that most industrial employees, such as single machine operators, assemblers, process workers and other semi-skilled and unskilled workers, require only a short period of training, which can be given most effectively on the job.

A strong nucleus of men in industry and in public education were aware of the community value of a good technical education program at the secondary level. With the employment of Dr. Edward H. Lang as Head of the Department of Vocational Education, the program to sell a program in Syracuse was begun, starting with trips to New York, Rochester and Buffalo to inspect the first-rate vocational schools in those cities. From the very beginning, the plan had the full support of organized labor in the county.

Capitalizing on the pressure for educational facilities for GI's after World War II, Syracuse built the H. W. Smith Technical and Industrial High School as a kind of pilot institution in vocational training. Smith Tech was a small school, with enrollment not much larger than 200 boys plus apprentices. Smith very soon demonstrated the possibilities in good vocational programs. It was enthusiastically approved by New York State, and by the Middle States Association of Colleges and Secondary Schools, an established approving body. Job offers were plentiful for the approximately 50 percent of graduates who did not go to college; and soon Smith was having three times as many student applicants as there were available freshman places. The evening program for 400 employed apprentices, plus an additional evening industrial extension program, was no less excellent than the day program.

Smith, in short, brought a scale model of New York's famous Brooklyn Technical and Stuyvesant High Schools to Syracuse and by its example converted much of local industry to evangelical support of vocational education.

As soon as the major policy decision was reached, i.e., that Syracuse should have an expanded vocational education program of high quality, a Vocational Education Consulting Committee was appointed, with invitations to serve coming from the Board of Education. On this committee were executives, mostly of vice president level and below, from Carrier Corporation, Crouse-Hinds, Niagara Mohawk Light & Power, Lipe Rollway Corporation, New Process Gear (Chrysler), General Electric, New York Telephone, C. E. Chappell & Sons (a store), the United Steelworkers (CIO), and the Syracuse Federation of Labor, plus an industrial consultant.

The plan offered by the Board of Education to meet Syracuse's vocational education shortage was the proposed construction of a two-story and basement, brick-faced, concrete block school building adjacent to the city's present Central High School, just a few blocks south of the city's central business and shopping area. When the building was first in prospect, in 1954, its cost was estimated at about $1,250,000. By 1957 its estimate rose to $2,200,000, due partly to inflations in building expenses. The building was to be connected to Central High with a three-story corridor which would close off the street between the buildings, and would be jointly heated from new oil furnaces to be located in Central High, and would share Central High's auditorium, cafeteria and gymnasium, plus Central's academic courses in English, languages, social sciences, mathematics, etc. Central High enrollment had been decreasing over the years as the area became commercial; so the combination was envisioned as a way to utilize fully what had become an under-used facility. It was announced that projected enrollment would be 1,000 in grades ten, eleven and twelve; and that the School would be open to all children, including girls, in the city, as well as to out-of-city students at a fee to be charged the students' hometown educational systems.

Blodgett Vocational High School, on crowded West Side, would be changed completely to a general high school curriculum, offering only the usual industrial arts and shop courses to be found in most modern secondary schools. Smith Tech was to become a "junior industrial school" for students with adjustment problems.

This program, it was rightly suspected, would have some opposition. The backers of the program, notably industrial companies in the Manufacturers Association, labor unions, and the Board of Education, set out to establish the school as a community-wide project. The plan was explained to all parents and PTA groups by speakers from the Board of Education and the city schools. (The strong emphasis to be placed at the school on vocational education for girls turned out to be a major appeal to parents.) Parochial schools, which in Syracuse have almost half the total school enrollment, enthusiastically backed the plan. Syracuse University faculty people, including the Dean of the School of Education, actively campaigned for the school. Some twenty-nine different Syracuse organizations were recruited to participate in public speaking and letter writing programs.

The behind-the-scenes work for this program came largely from the Manufacturers Association staff and from the office of the Superintendent of Schools, and particularly from the Department of Vocational Education. Information circulated by the Manufacturers Association stated that about 50 percent of Onondaga County children did not complete high school; but that in most areas with stronger vocational programs the drop-out percentage was less. It was also stated that in Syracuse 15 percent of male high school graduates had vocational training, but that in Buffalo 50 percent, and in Rochester and

Utica 35 percent, were vocationally trained by the public schools.

The Manufacturers Association maintained that any school system that does not provide the youth of the community with a way of making its living has failed in one of its major obligations. Public school vocational programs, it was pointed out, help small manufacturers and businessmen unable to afford elaborate in-company training programs of their own.

A report of the Board of Education, submitted to the City Planning Commission, and called a *Survey of Vocational Education,* was more detailed in its analysis of community needs. Some of the points made in this report in support of the new school were that:

Opportunities would be open in fields never before available to pupils, and where there were continuing demands for trained employees.

These opportunities would keep in school large numbers of pupils who now drop out because of limited offerings.

These facilities would be available for increased numbers of industrial employees in evening courses.

The downtown location is convenient for pupils from all areas of the city who would attend. . . .

In Syracuse, only 234 boys are included in technical and industrial high school programs, out of more than 5,500 pupils in the total high school population. . . .

More than 50 percent of the jobs available in the Syracuse area are in manufacturing and service industries. . . .

In a separate section entitled "Why Not Blodgett Vocational High School?" it was stated that "By spending about the same amount proposed for the Central High School site, Vocational High School could be redesigned and reconstructed in its shop areas, and adjacent land could be cleared and new shops added, but its pupil capacity would still remain at 1,000 pupils. The Central High School plan will add 500 to the senior high capacity of the city. . . .[2]

Beginning as early as 1953, the Vocational Consulting Committee organized some one hundred people from industry, commerce and labor into fourteen sub-committees to survey different areas of employment in Syracuse and the existing facilities available to meet those needs. These investigations continued over the greater portion of a year.

The central conclusion of the study was that the demand for trained technicians and mechanics in the following fields was far in excess of the maximum possibilities with the then present buildings and equipment:

automobile mechanic	practical nurse
beauty operator	radio and TV serviceman
carpenter	skilled needleworker
electrical technician	sheet metal worker
food worker	office worker
machinist	printer
mechanical draftsman	welder

This conclusion, submitted to the Mayor on February 15, 1954, repeated the proposal that a technical and vocational secondary school be built on the city-owned land adjacent to Central High School in downtown Syracuse.

Involved in this elaborate series of studies were, in addition to city and county officials, the Board of Education, the State Education Department, the Manufacturers Association, Chamber of Commerce, and the central labor bodies: The Syracuse Automobile Dealers Association, the Bakers' Association, National Office Management Association, the Syracuse Builders' Exchange, Syracuse Hairdressers and Cosmetologists Association, the Stewards Club, the Joint Apprentice Committees for the Carpenters Trade and for the Sheetmetal Trade, the American Welding Society, the Syracuse Food

Service Executive Association, the Practical Nursing Advisory Council, and others. These organizations applied pressure on City Hall as needed to achieve the successive steps of the program.

Throughout the program, in fact, community participation was widespread and well organized. In retrospect, and with the assistance again of hindsight, the leaders of the project admit to one omission, i.e., they forgot the various engineers' organizations, which might have helped to forward the technical aspects of the program. Opposition of alumni of Blodgett, it was agreed, would have had to be borne in any event, since no cooperative participation ever would be likely from them.

The individual reports of each of the investigating sub-committees provided overwhelming and detailed documentation of the then (1954) inadequacies of vocational training in Syracuse, and of the employment possibilities in these various industrial specializations. Some sample extractions from these reports:

The Sub-committee on Automobile Mechanics: "Our survey indicated that approximately 1,450 men are employed in the Syracuse area as mechanics in dealerships, garages, service stations, and with fleet operators in the repair of cars, trucks, buses. Using an annual mortality figure of 5 percent, over seventy men are needed each year to fill the places of men leaving the field. The shops recommended above (eleven so listed, mostly dealers) would provide an annual supply (of jobs) to thirty-five to forty graduates. . . ."

The Sub-committee on Beauty Culture: "In the City of Syracuse there are 327 beauty shops, and over 500 operators working in this occupation. Assuming an annual turnover of 10 percent, which is normal in women's trades, fifty operators would be required each year. . . ."

The Sub-committee on Machine Shop Practice: "Statistics from manufacturers in the Syracuse area indicate that over 900 men are employed as machinists, tool and gage-makers, die sinkers and maintenance machinists. These are the skilled positions, usually requiring a number of years of apprenticeship. On the basis of 5 percent annual turnover, at least forty-five new replacements are necessary each year. . . ."

These reports were submitted first to the Board of Education, then to the Mayor and the Planning Commission.

In 1955, the Board of Education conducted a poll of parents to see how they felt on eighteen issues—this being a promotional device of some subtlety. Questionnaires were sent to 20,195 homes and 81.3 percent were returned. One of the eighteen questions was: Should our present technical and industrial high school program be expanded? 10,497 said yes; 958 said no; and 4,013 were undecided.[3]

The Syracuse *Post-Standard*, usually a staunch supporter of industry-backed programs, wrote in an editorial that Syracuse needed a *science-technical school* instead of a technical-vocational school. A trade school cannot be combined with a true technical-science high school of the calibre of Brooklyn Technical High because, said the editor, "the two kinds of schools just don't mix." [4]

Finally, somewhat to the surprise of the project's supporters, the city's independent but largely business-backed Syracuse Governmental Research Bureau opposed the plan in part, and, as might be expected, on the grounds of alleged extravagance. Syracuse already had built one new high school since World War II, Nottingham High on the West Side, costing $4,409,276; total school enrollment in Syracuse was actually less than it had been twenty years ago because of the more rapid growth of surrounding villages.

"The need for schoolhouse construction cannot be justified

by any broad upsurge in enrollments or by so-called emergency conditions." The bureau advocated that additional vocational education be thought of as "an annex" to Central High, and in terms of a 600 to 700 student enrollment rather than 1,000.[5]

This opposition was months in developing, during which time, no doubt, the Bureau's staff and officers wrestled with their loyalties to the industrial community on the one hand and with their instincts to save taxpayers' dollars on the other hand. Certain industrial leaders of the vocational school project privately credit the Bureau's opposition with being the influence that soon thereafter inspired the Planning Commission's long-range capital improvement committee to chop the proposed school from 1,000 student capacity to 600 student capacity.

When this committee cut the size of the school, Carl F. B. Roth, the president of Aircooled Motors and then president of the Manufacturers Association, protested:

"Our studies show that if we keep pace with merely national population projections, we're going to need 50,000 more jobs here," he told the press. "And yet we have one of the state's weakest vocational training programs. . . . The problem is one of vital interest to every parent in Onondaga County, as well as in the City of Syracuse proper. For, under state law, boards of education in our surrounding communities must send to Syracuse—if Syracuse has the facilities and if their towns do not—children desiring vocational training of the approved type. And the approved type robs no one with qualifications from going on to college if he so desires. . . . Once we have given vocational education a fair chance, then 1,000 pupils will be seen as much too small a start. . . ."

The Superintendent of Schools likewise issued a three-page companion protest, reviewing the reports of the fourteen subcommittees on worker needs in various fields, and concluding that, exclusive of commerce, industry alone needed 600 skilled replacements each year, and further, that the community should have a facility to accommodate a stepped-up apprentice and adult education program in trade subjects. A school for 600 students, he pointed out, would cost about $1,716,850, whereas the building to accommodate 1,000 students would cost only $1,898,800 (1955 estimates).

In the winter of 1955–56, after the City Planning Commission had allocated $1,898,000 to the new school, the plan was given a place on the Syracuse five-year program. The plan, however, was for the smaller school: for 600 student capacity instead of 1,000 student capacity. Despite publicity and a letter campaign by people of influence, the 600-capacity figure maintained, although by plan the building is capable of being expanded to the south when and if needed.

Thereafter, the project was approved by the Mayor's Capital Improvements Committee and was submitted to the Common Council in July of 1956. In the Council, the matter of closing the street between the two buildings failed by one vote to get the necessary two-thirds approval. When the matter was brought to vote at a subsequent session of the Council, one member who had voted against the measure and in whose district the school is located, changed his vote to the affirmative, explaining that he wanted the school, of course, but had merely wanted to protest the street closing.

The Council then approved other enabling legislation: the issuing of bonds and the provision of $1,100,000 from the 1957 budget. A similar amount was budgeted in 1958.

One further step was to see that the city did not forget to take up its option on the proposed building site before it expired. The property, which had been cleared by the Syracuse Housing Authority, was being used as a parking lot until the City Planning Commission might make up its mind what to do with the property. Properly deluged with letters, the Mayor gave his approval; and the Common Council on March 5, 1956, unanimously passed a resolution requesting the City and State Housing Authority to transfer title of the land for construction of the proposed new school.

The new school, assured to Syracuse after so many tribulations, was to have two distinct divisions, one technical and the other industrial. Technical graduates would be capable of holding jobs as engineering assistants, draftsmen, and technicians, and of entering schools of engineering, provided that their grades were high enough. About 20 percent of the enrollment would be in the Technical Division.

Male industrial graduates would be qualified for entry jobs as mechanics, machinists, electricians, radio and TV repairmen, welders, printers, painters, sheet and metal workers, carpenters, and photographers; female industrial graduates would be qualified for entry jobs in fashion design, nursing, beauty culture, and food service, plus home-making. (Commercial subjects are taught at other Syracuse high schools.)

Each subject has its own committee of high-level people from industry and labor to see that the instruction shall be geared to work situations at local plants.

Instructors in the technical program must be graduate engineers with training also in teaching methods. A New York State-approved high school industrial program, as the new school would offer, includes three full hours per day in a specified shop, under an instructor with the required five years' occupational experience plus teacher training. The remainder of the school day is given to mathematics and science related to the student's major subject and to blueprint reading, English, citizenship education, and health and physical education. The school day for industrial and technical programs is six hours a day (eight periods of forty-five minutes each) as compared with four and one-half hours in general high schools.

The new building was also to be used extensively for apprentice and extension training of industrial personnel, and these programs likewise were to be closely tied to the work realities of Syracuse business and industry.

The School was to open its doors a year or so after this book is published. It will, hopefully, be a model of modern technical and industrial education. But no matter what its future, it already has proved to be a model of how to get things done in a community.

5-
Industry-School Relationships

Part Two

Industry has a stake in the quality of vocational education being given to its future employees. How heavy a stake the community itself can have in vocational education is dramatized by the recent history of Utica, a city fifty miles east of Syracuse in upstate New York.

Utica used to be a textile town with 30 percent of its workforce in the mills. The movement of textiles to the south left the city near depression as welfare cases increased with each closed mill. The last large mill left in 1952, adding another 3,000 persons to the city's unemployed. The Chamber of Commerce's Industrial Development Division knew that replacement companies, if any, would not be other textile firms. Textile workers who had spent their whole working lives in the mills were not at all sure that, as they put it, you could teach an old dog new tricks—or teach him new skills for new trades.

Under the inspiration of a few leading businessmen, local industry, government, labor and education put together a remarkable vocational training program. The project was organized under a Community Action Committee of twenty-four members, all of whom had sub-committee assignments. This was their program:

1. To give the former textile workers a battery of aptitude

tests to discover their labor conversion possibilities. This was administered by the local staff of the New York State Employment Service, who, together with the unions, also handled the promotional program to bring in the men to take the tests.

2. To survey the area for building space, teachers, and equipment that could be used in the re-training program. Much equipment was borrowed, in part as a club project by Rotary. Public schools, Mohawk Valley Technical Institute, and Utica College (a branch of Syracuse University) supplied most of the classroom and shop space.

3. After consultation with a number of expanding companies, to get their assistance in predicting the skills that most likely would be required by in-coming companies. The emphasis turned out to be on machine job operations.

4. To organize a training program in light of the above and to begin retraining some 1,500 men, who had been screened as likely to be successfully retrained. All courses were tuition-free, and administered by the school housing the course.

Loom fixers, for example, became machine setters—and soon were working for a company new to the town, Chicago Pneumatic Tool, perhaps, or General Electric. At this writing, Utica is far from replacing its 15,000 lost textile jobs, and indeed is suffering badly from unemployment, but the community achievement nonetheless is commendable.[6]

A by-product of the project was the establishment of community appreciation of vocational education in Utica, so that the city has one of the better vocational training programs in New York State.

In too many cities, it seems clear that the public schools are not training children to fit into the industrial structure of their own communities. Among the notable exceptions are the four counties in Ohio and Pennsylvania within the Mahoning and Shenango valleys centering in Youngstown; and the industrial area around Evansville, Indiana.

The organizing body of management men in the first mentioned area is the Industrial Information Institute, Youngstown, which includes 125-plus companies. A committee of industrial engineers and personnel men from Institute companies spent three years studying the area's job opportunities and the specific qualifications of each, after which they reported their survey in a popularly-written manual they entitled *Achieving Your Career*. This booklet, distributed in 3,260 copies in twenty-one area school systems, described the qualifications and training needed in ten vocational areas or job "families," and showed the student how to go about determining which of the job families would offer him the most opportunity. A guide manual was prepared for teachers and counselors to help them use *Achieving Your Career* most effectively. A committee of twenty-one guidance administrators from area school systems then expanded on the manual by making and collecting visual aids and other dramatic means of presenting local job opportunities to high school students. A motion picture, *The Right Road*, was made for presentation to students and their parents.

Related to the survey of local job opportunities and their qualifications is the program of the group's Schools Advisory Committee in evaluating area vocational and industrial arts courses, and of organizing and sponsoring a particular "model curriculum" from time to time. This committee also runs periodic surveys of member companies' attitudes toward, and criticisms of, local vocational and industrial arts training. In short, the Institute wants to keep the schools informed of industry's needs and preferences, and keep industry informed of the various programs in effect at the schools.

More than incidentally, the Institute has financed the writing of social studies texts by a local teacher, the preparation of several series of radio scripts, and even comic books, all to describe the area's history, geography, economics, and its opportunities and future possibilities.

Another notable community-centered education program began when the Evansville (Ind.) Manufacturers and Employers Association, and the Evansville public schools themselves, became disturbed at a survey in 1949 which indicated that very few local high school students could name any of the products manufactured by locally operating companies. They were further disturbed when one-third of the students said they planned to look for jobs outside of Evansville, "because the town lacked variety of opportunity."

In response, the Association began a long-term guidance program, one purpose of which was to integrate local job opportunities with the training and counseling programs at the city's seven high schools. It was supplemented with publication of four six-page supplements to the social studies program on the community's economic history and with a $1,500 student essay contest on a number of themes, all of them having to do with local career opportunities. Companies stepped up their open house, plant tour and school visitation programs.

The major project was a three-year survey of area jobs, by four job analysts on loan from the Indiana Employment Security division and five staff people from the Association. More than 130 plants participated, filling out a thirty-two-page questionnaire. In addition, the job analysts selected thirty key plants as pilots, where they interviewed and checked job information in great detail. This tremendous study came up with 300 "types of work" which the analysts called "key jobs." None of these were entry jobs, but rather represented career

stations or career terminals, although attention was placed on
how to reach these jobs in each case.

The collected information, useful as it would be to school
guidance programs and curriculum committees in vocational
education had to be written to appeal to the youngsters, who
needed to be convinced that Evansville could provide them
with careers. The result was a 190-page, two-color, thoroughly
illustrated book called *Your Career Opportunities in Evansville Industry*, in itself one of the recognized classics in industrial community relations literature. Seven thousand copies
went to students; and a number of copies are in local manufacturers association offices across the country, waiting to be
used as a model when and if money should ever be available
to them for such a survey. The costs at Evansville, incidentally,
were paid by fifty-nine of the larger companies.

Theme of the book, other than its stress upon job opportunities obtainable in Evansville, is this plea for the best in
vocational education:

"There is no future for the unskilled, and very little for the
semi-skilled. . . . In 1900, America required the services of
11 million common laborers. Now, although the population
has more than tripled, this nation needs only about 6 million
unskilled workers. There will be even fewer required ten years
from now. . . ." [7]

Despite all that has been said so far in this chapter, vocational education has little respect in most American cities,
even from the companies which ought to be benefiting from
it. The small manufacturer and small businessman, those who
could profit most from local vocational education programs,
inevitably are the men who pay least attention to them. A
study of companies around Ithaca, N.Y., by Harold J. Steffens,
found that only 2 percent of the area employers he interviewed
preferred vocationally-trained new workers, and that 95 per-

cent of employers wanted new workers to have academic educations. Most employers, Dr. Steffens found, did not know what the area schools were offering as vocational or technical education, and thought of vocational education still as the old-time manual training course.[8]

Vocational schools all too easily degenerate into corrective or "problem boy" schools. If academic standards are not maintained, the unintelligent and the more difficult children will fill the rolls. As the school loses reputation over the years the quality of entering students drops further. The end result is that the graduating classes finally are almost entirely unemployable.

All of this, admittedly, begs the question of what is to be done with children who drop out of school because they do not like (or can't take) the discipline and standard of the academic units of the secondary system. Employers no longer are interested in child labor; most will not hire workers under eighteen years old, and prefer new hires to be in their twenties. Yet, if the less intellectually gifted boys are not to be kept in school, and if no jobs are open to them, they may get into trouble.

In all studies of student drop-outs there is an *a priori* assumption that students ought to be kept in high school—or in some kind of school—at all costs and for as long as possible. Only a fifth or less of drop-outs leave school because they must go to work for financial reasons; most just do not like school. Their teachers were "unfair"; the students lacked interest in subjects being taught them. Many drop-outs come from broken homes; and in most cases parents did not talk with anyone at school prior to the student's leaving.

These so-called drop-outs make very poor employees, which in part explains industry's reluctance to hire workers under eighteen years of age. A follow-up study of teen-aged drop-outs in New York found that they carried their old personalities with them into jobs: they were restless, inattentive, low-production workers.[9]

Other reasons why companies are reluctant to hire minor workers have to do with the insurance rates, draft service, social security taxes, and the minimum wage law. Among 19,000 job holders in manufacturing in New Jersey companies, only 3 percent were under twenty-two years of age. The principal explanation seems to be "poor job attitudes" of the 'teen-ager.[10]

Every generation has its group of difficult young people to contend with, distinguishable by their eccentric fads of dress and hair styling. If industry won't hire them, and it will not, should they be put into vocational schools and trade classes? Such classes, more than incidentally, are substantially more expensive to the taxpayer than are other classes. This "solution" is obviously unsound from the point of view of the students, the companies, and the taxpayers. Yet it is in effect in most American school systems.

In this writer's opinion, all of this indicates the sensibleness of raised secondary school standards, and particularly, raised vocational program standards. The maladjusted and emotionally disturbed should have psychiatric help, but such help ought not to be considered a part of the city's vocational training program.

Those few public vocational and technical schools which have maintained high standards now enjoy academic reputations equal to the finest private preparatory schools. Engineering schools prefer their graduates to those from any other sort of secondary institution. And there is no need here to belabor the national demand for technicians, scientists and engineers.

To be sure, vocational courses should not be as rigorous as upper division mathematics and physics college-preparatory courses; for the nation's average I.Q. is, after all, at a theoretical 100; and engineers presumably have to be smarter than machinists. But the fact is, too, that fewer and fewer students will take such "hard" subjects as mathematics and science unless some pressure is put on them. In Syracuse, in 1940, 52 percent of students took math and 29.5 percent took sciences; in 1955, 33 percent were taking math and 20.6 were taking sciences. Such figures stack up oddly with the rather characteristic statistic from one company (Du Pont) that in 1947 one employee in ten was a college graduate but in 1956 one employee in seven was a college graduate. At the other extreme, furthermore, the number of unskilled jobs in industry is decreasing.

A Columbia University professor in the field of conservation of human resources reports that his research indicates most students can do more difficult work at their respective educational levels than they are given, and that a majority of students are working at levels as much as four grades below their capacities.[11]

All schools which had post-war experience in educating GI's admit that never before nor since have there been so many outstanding students on American campuses, nor students who got so much from their educations. Just as industry discovered that a little aging makes a man a better employee, so did educators find that a little aging helps a man to become a better student. It seems that some people in their 'teens are just not ready to take being educated, or being employed, either; but that given a few years of military experience, or of just plain living, they get over it. A rather dramatic illustration that one ought not to feel too superior toward high school drop-outs is supplied by James Nolan, community relations and training man for Oxford Paper at Rumford, Maine. Mr. Nolan wondered how many people in his one-industry town would be interested in getting a high school education through the state's "high school equivalency program." He asked the question on the bulletin board and around town, and discovered that seventy-three people in his small town wanted such education, and that he had started a whole back-to-school movement in Rumford. Mr. Nolan found himself, also, working as the in-mill representative of the program almost as hard as he did at his regular duties.

Professor Miner's research convinces him that only those in highly skilled employment, for the most part, have reached their saturation points in levels of education. He found that more than half of skilled (63%), semi-skilled (60%), and un-skilled (52%) workers were capable of going to higher educational levels than they attained.[12]

California has succeeded better than other states in raising the educational level of its citizens through its numerous junior colleges, some attached to city systems, some to county systems, some to districts. These schools (no longer called "junior colleges" but just "colleges," perhaps because "junior" has unhappy connotations to a true Californian) are accepted units of local public school systems to the extent that the popular education level of their communities now includes the fourteenth grade. A great many of these 625 junior or community colleges in California and elsewhere have extensive technical and vocational programs.[13]

The age and grade level of industrial education programs is rising [writes Professor Emeritus Lynn Emerson, formerly of Cornell, the man who has contributed perhaps more than any other to the advancement of this field]. Twenty-five years ago many vocational schools admitted pupils at the end of the sixth grade, gave them two years of intensive instruction, and placed them in industry. With the rise in entrance age into industry, and with social pressure on youth to remain in school longer, the school level at which vocational work is offered has risen steadily. Today few high schools offer specific vocational work below the ninth grade, and much of it is offered in the tenth and eleventh years. There is a marked tendency toward placing the specific industrial training on the adult and post-high school level. This change was intensified by the subsidy for veterans' training but was under way long before the veterans' programs were developed.[14]

Professor Emerson found, in an investigation of industrial education throughout the country, that in California two-thirds of the unit trade classes are in adult schools and junior colleges. He found post-high school trade school programs operated by cities, as at LaCrosse and Spokane; by areas, as at the North Georgia Vocational School; and by universities as the one at the University of Houston. Some were distinct, state-operated collegiate units, as the California State Polytechnic College at San Luis Obispo and the Fashion Institute at New York City. New York State has a rather wide-spread collection of community colleges and technical institutes which derive one-third of their income from the State; one-third from tuitions and one-third from city, county or district taxes.[15]

Unless vocational training is kept at post-high school levels, school systems find themselves expecting children to determine their careers while some are still dreaming of a life as cowboy, policeman or space cadet. Probably because it seems so ridiculous, vocational guidance is not much stressed at the seventh and eighth grades; and business and industry are all too rarely called in to help in guidance at this junior high school level. Yet actually these children soon will be deciding whether to enter a "regular" high school, a commercial high school, or a vocational high school. Most children of that age know nothing about the kinds of jobs to be had in industry, and neither the schools nor local companies have done much of anything to help them find out.

It is asking much—perhaps too much—of children of twelve, thirteen and fourteen to settle on a particular trade. Even high school students seem unrealistic and immature in their job preferences; and certain occupations become, first, fashionable, then unfashionable.[16] For example, how realistic are the following stated career preferences of Syracuse high school pupils, in order of frequency of mention? Radio and TV-related professions (695); beautician (557); airplane pilot, stewardess or other jobs in air transportation (533).[17]

Some probing into the personal histories of workers, however, seems to add some elements of reasonableness to early counseling. Taken from interviews with some 900 randomly selected wage earners at Oakland, the following findings make it plain, to use the researchers' words, that "lack of advice falls most heavily on those whose very lack of education presumably accentuates their need for advice. . . . [Also] those who do receive advice in school are mostly ill-advised . . . those few [teachers] who did give such advice made no attempt to brief their students for the real labor market" . . . and suggested to at least 60 percent of the young people that they choose professional careers. Some pertinent percentages of this Oakland study:

55% of the sample reported they had no specific job plans while in school. (The proportion of those with no job plans drops as education is continued.)

78% of those going no farther than 8th grade stated they had no job plans.

47% of those graduating from high school said they had no job plans.

13% of college graduates said they had no job plans.

67% of those going no further than 8th grade said they had received no vocational advice from anybody (parents, teachers, etc.).

45% of high school graduates said they had gotten no such advice.

31% of college students said they had gotten no such advice.

87% of those going no further than 8th grade said they'd gotten no vocational advice from teachers.

63% of college students said they had gotten no such advice from teachers.

53% of graduate students said they had gotten no such advice from teachers.[18]

Assistance in vocational guidance certainly should be one of the major contributions of local industry to community schools. In Syracuse, in addition to Career Day, local businessmen participate in two other organizations of a student guidance nature—all, however, at secondary levels. One is a Business Education Advisory Council to work with the city school's Supervisor of Business Education both in counseling students and in assisting teachers with materials and class problems from locally operating companies. The other is called the Annual Central New York Science Congress, put on by the local unit of the Science Teachers Association to display student projects and exhibits and to hear students report their research. Local business and industry help with the finances of the latter, in prize contests, tours of technical installations, etc., all in cooperation with the area science teachers, whose show it is.

Lederle Laboratories, Division of American Cyanamid, regularly holds a "Science Evening" at Pearl River, N.Y., when both students and science teachers see Lederle exhibits and demonstrations and hear talks on aspects of biochemistry and career opportunities in pharmacy and chemistry by Lederle's thirty scientists. This affair is Lederle's contribution to Chemical Progress Week, nationally sponsored by the Manufacturing Chemists Association with essay contests, lectures and publicity encouraged by member companies in all plant cities.

Vocational guidance on an industry-wide basis is supplied by the Automotive Manufacturers Association in the form of a book of standards for automotive instruction, distributed to the 1,250-plus vocational schools in the country. This manual outlines courses of instruction, provides shop layouts, and supplies information on teaching materials and where they may be obtained. General Motors uses a somewhat less formal kit of its own, designed particularly for Career Days to interest boys in becoming mechanics. GM also has some thirty training centers of its own throughout the country, to train thousands of mechanics every year. Ford and Chrysler go in more for traveling schools of instruction in automotive mechanics.

Another organization active in this particular area of vocational education is National Standard Parts Association, which also helps school systems to set up automotive courses and supplies them with teaching aids and materials.

Similar assistance in their respective industries, plus teaching aids at various grade levels, are supplied by the Manufacturing Chemists Association, the American Iron and Steel Institute, American Petroleum Institute, American Gas Association, Association of American Railroads, and the Institute of Life Insurance, among others.

Perhaps the best kind of counseling program is one that provides the student with a chance to work within a company. Not many large corporations do this at the high school level. The relatively few companies with integrated summer work programs for high school students, it seems, are those employing many technicians, and those located amid somewhat superior socio-economic populations.

The Retail Association of Syracuse and the city's Board of Education have a Cooperative Retailing Program for three schools (Central, Eastwood and North Highs). Students get retailing credit while selling or performing office duties under instruction in the local stores. The retailers find that the program helps them to spot employees they would like to hire upon graduation. To make the venture more attractive to teen-agers, a club called Future Retailers Club has been formed.

Similarly, Lederle Laboratories, again, provided on-the-job training to high school commercial students for a full semester. The company made it clear that the experience was not a guarantee of hiring; and the students were not paid.

The Sunray Mid-Continental Oil Company's "Science for Youth" Club in Tulsa allows seventh to twelfth graders to develop their own research projects in the company laboratories, while supervised by both teachers and company scientists.

Most work-study programs at the secondary level were largely war-time devices to provide industry with man-hours it needed for stepped-up production, and the bulk of the literature in the field has to do with war-time experience. Some of the present reasons why employers dislike to hire teen-agers were also applicable then, and mitigate against the success of attempted work-study programs today. Current limited experience indicates that work-study programs do better in higher socio-economic level communities and in relations with companies which have a fairly large proportion of professional employees.[20] The most useful treatment of the subject is a staff-written bulletin by New York State's Division of Vocational Education. It recommends two moves as first steps in setting up work-study programs:

1. Determine community occupational training needs, on the basis of potential training facilities in local establishments, and determine occupational trends of pupils and graduates.

2. Utilize the services of a Vocational Advisory Board. (The New York State education law provided that a board of education operating any type of vocational school shall appoint a five-member advisory board representing local trades and industries.) This advisory board can be used in cities where they exist already for the vocational school, but should be created for schools setting up work-study programs.

"In selecting members," the bulletin suggests, "careful consideration should be given to representation of business, industry and labor, keeping in mind that any major organizations interested in education may also be included." The coordinator of the program, too, should take active part in organizing the committee. "An alert coordinator will recognize the valuable support such a committee can offer in organizing and operating a cooperative training program; in helping to locate employment opportunities; in recommending course content; and in preserving desirable relationships with employers, with labor organizations, and with the general public." [21]

Another variation of work-study programs, although seldom thought of as such, is the frequently encountered company program of sending employees to area schools or colleges. General Electric has such arrangements at most plant locations. In Syracuse, GE has a "College Level Apprentice Training Program" which pays all tuition and book costs for employees in pre-engineering courses (English, mathematics, physics, chemistry) at Syracuse University; at the end of a work-study apprentice period, the apprentices are accepted as full-time juniors in the School of Engineering. A number of other companies, in fact, have similar arrangements with various schools of engineering.

In Syracuse the Manufacturers Association found that eighteen larger member companies, employing about half the area's industrial workers, have such programs. Two-thirds of the employees eligible for tuition-paid education are restricted to colleges or universities.[22]

A National Industrial Conference Board survey of 166 companies, published in 1956, found that the median-per-capita expenditure was $48 per employee-participant; that 24 percent restrict courses to subjects pertinent to the employee's work but 46 percent permit "cultural subjects"; that two-thirds allow correspondence courses, with certain restrictions; that four-fifths of the programs are administered by the personnel department; that 80 percent require a passing grade in the course before reimbursing the student; and that 47 percent pay full costs and 39 percent pay half-costs or more.[23]

Industry has been more active in working with high school teachers than it has with students. For reasons of recruiting employees, as well as for promoting community understanding of the company via one category of so-called "thought leaders," many companies encourage plant visits by teachers. As in all plant-tour and open-house operations, these affairs will be more interesting and useful if planned for as homogeneous a group as possible, e.g., for all science teachers, or for all parochial school teachers, or better still, for all parochial science teachers. (GE in Syracuse entertained forty such on a day's visit to Electronics Park.)

B-I-E (business-industry-education) Days are sponsored by chambers of commerce all over the country to bring teachers to local company operations for a day or for a half-day, to learn about student employment potentials, production and business processes, and business problems and concepts. The procedure sometimes alternates with an E-I-B Day, when the management people visit the local schools. Unless tightly disciplined by a local employers' organization, the latter can become a devastating failure, as it did in a particular Florida city when the teachers readied themselves for a day of visits from local businessmen and industrialists—and no one came. The teachers there reached some bitter conclusions about business.

In Syracuse, the Chamber of Commerce and Manufacturers Association, with the help of the mayor and local newspapers, sponsor a dinner for all new public school teachers each fall. Another program at Syracuse is the occasional Workshop on Economic Education, run by Syracuse University and local industry and labor for visiting students and teachers from area high schools as a Joint Council on Economic Education project. On at least one occasion, a local company was selected as a case study in economics, with union, management and academic people presenting their respective versions of economic problems, plus their attempted solutions in the "case" company and elsewhere.

Industry is concerned, too, with the shortage of teachers, and particularly with the shortage of science teachers and the improvement of the quality of science teaching.

President Lee A. DuBridge of Caltech said bluntly that the reason high school students avoid math and science courses is because the classes are badly taught and the texts are poor: ". . . an endless procession of dull useless problems . . . an avalanche of useless details." Dr. Benjamin Fine of *The New York Times* reported that "between 1950 and 1954 the number of college graduates qualified to teach mathematics dropped 51 percent; the number qualified to teach sciences dropped 56 percent." Dr. Howard L. Bevis of the National Committee to Develop Scientists and Engineers said that some of this talk was alarmist and untrue, but adds that there "is evidence that teaching is not always good." [24]

The New York City schools have appointed a lay committee chaired by the Dean of Engineering at Columbia University to interest able young people in becoming science teachers. This committee sponsors summer institutes for science teachers at New York City campuses and works also to get summer jobs for present high school teachers in science. The Esso Foundation has contributed heavily to the New York City program. The companies which have cooperated most readily with summer jobs for teachers are the oil companies, the chemical companies, and the electrical manufacturers, plus General Foods, Procter and Gamble, Timken Bearing, and a few others.

Most companies involved announced before hiring the teachers that under no circumstances would the teachers be considered for permanent employment after the summer experience. As with every scholarship or fellowship program, accepted practice is to turn over to educators the responsibility for selection of winners from among applicants. The delicate matter of what salary to pay the teachers has been met with various policies: some pay the teachers' own regular monthly salaries; some pay them at salary levels of others in the company doing similar work; some pay on a general evaluation of what the man is worth to the company.[25]

The National Science Foundation has financed a three-month training program for high school science teachers at Oak Ridge, administered by the Oak Ridge Institute of Nuclear Studies and the Atomic Energy Commission. After their training at Oak Ridge, these teachers are supplied with station wagons (courtesy of Ford Motor; gasoline and oil, courtesy of Gulf Oil) and with demonstration materials; they are then assigned to nine months of traveling across the county, spending one week at each high school in the itinerary to teach sophomore and junior students about atomic energy and its applications to physics and chemistry. The National Science Foundation also has endowed fellowships at a number of universities for high school science teachers.

In Southern California, an Industry-Education Council has been formed, endowed by Hughes Aircraft, as an outgrowth of a 1957 conference jointly sponsored by the National Academy of Science and Hughes Aircraft. Its purpose is to encourage talented young people to become science teachers and to keep science teachers from leaving the teaching profession. To these ends, the Council sponsors lectures by working scientists from industry to high school classes, finds summer jobs for science teachers, and locates talented prospects for careers in science and encourages them with summer jobs and other assistance.

One industry-education cooperative venture in the area of high school science teaching has had much publicity but little action—the suggestion by General David Sarnoff of RCA that industry loan capable professional men to act as teachers in public schools. General Sarnoff's plan would establish a National Education Reserve of scientists from industry to meet the emergency dearth of science teachers, and do so with salary costs met by the sponsoring company.

Present science teachers have not been enthusiastic, saying that teaching isn't a job that just any old scientist could perform, especially if the assignment involved classes in different subjects and perhaps even supervising a study hall. Nor are there many major corporations willing to free capable professionals even for visiting professorships at universities, much less for teaching at the high school level.

In at least two instances companies were willing, however, to take on the teaching of a class in a local college as a group assignment. The Adding Machine Division of National Cash Register, in Ithaca, N.Y., teaches a senior course in business administration at Ithaca College. The executive in each management capacity is responsible for from one to several weeks of instruction in his own specialization: finance, sales, production, personnel, etc., using also the assistance of managers of sub-departments like sales promotion, purchasing, safety, etc. The plant manager opens and closes the course, which throughout attempts to bring together in the focus of one "case" all the important business principles learned since the students entered college.

Sixteen executives of Ralston Purina have performed very much the same service for a senior course in business at Washington University in St. Louis, with the organization of the class placed in the hands of the vice presidents of Research and Product Control, Personnel, Public Relations, and Advertising.

Many executives, of course, will accept spot speaking or demonstration assignments before classes in nearby schools. NAM circulates a roster of people from member companies who are willing to address students, and on what topics. Racine, Wis., businesses very intelligently asked the teachers what topics they'd like their students to hear discussed by local executives. Here, for the guidance of management everywhere, are some of their answers:

History and Growth of a Representative Industry or Business in Racine.

How Is Production Planned?

Planning for Vocational Opportunities. Emphasize opportunities in Racine and particular skills marketable here. Training and apprenticeship programs.

What Does Industry Expect of High School Graduates? Personality, basic skills, specialized demands of particular jobs.

To What Extent Does Racine Depend on Foreign Trade? Confine to one or two industries.

Techniques of Advertising. Different Appeals. Determining what techniques to use.

Labor-Management Relations. How are conflicts resolved?

Making a Job Application. Writing an application, handling the interview, placement, and promotional procedures.[26]

In the matter of company or industry-prepared teaching aids, too, the best examples, the most widely used, and no doubt the most rewarding to industry, are those that were created primarily to meet the schools' teaching needs rather than to carry management messages. This means that teaching aids should be designed and written for a specific grade level (the same piece will not do for both junior high and senior high distribution). This means, really, that a teacher or a committee of teachers ought to act as consultants for every such project. Every one whose job involves working with schools ought to read the pamphlet, *Choosing Free Materials for Use in the Schools*, by the American Association of School Administrators, Washington, 1955. Its theme, obvious as it seems, bears repeating: "The only defensible basis on which to select materials, either free or purchased, is the degree to which they will make a positive contribution to the basic educational purposes for which the school exists. . . . The schools have a definitely assigned task of helping children learn certain things. All that is introduced to the process must aid in the discharge of this responsibility or it should not be used. . . ." [27]

A few outstanding examples of teaching aids are: the entire program on nutrition education and on the economics of foods, prepared by General Mills; GE's counseling aid called "Why Study English?"; the entire service for business teachers, by the Institute of Life Insurance; the Chemistry teaching aid, "Experiments with Gas," by the American Gas Association; American Petroleum Institute's helps in Boy Scout merit badge programs in geology; Sears, Roebuck's numerous materials for farm children; and the oil industry materials, centering around models of an oil field and an oil refinery, by Standard Oil Company of California.

The National Science Teachers Association and its affiliated state associations are doing much to develop life-like and challenging teaching materials, NSTA, an affiliate of National Education Association, has a "Business Industry Section" with 150 companies enrolled. Two outstanding and widely accepted contributions in mathematics teaching are *Math Problems from Industry* (Chrysler Corp., Detroit), and *Math at General Electric* (General Electric, Schenectady). Equally valuable in teaching high school chemistry are the lab experiments worked out by the Manufacturing Chemists' Association.

A sort of summarizing roundup of business-education techniques is furnished by Dr. F. Kenneth Brasted, former education director for National Association of Manufacturers. As his Ph.D. thesis at New York University, he queried 1,262 Connecticut companies as to their use of various education-industry cooperative activities (the list itself had been obtained and graded by another group of 300 respondents from education and industry). These activities in order of frequency of listing by the companies were:

1. Summer employment of college students
2. Opportunities for plant visits
3. Participation in B-I-E Days
4. Participation on Advisory Committees
5. Participation in E-I-B Days
6. Service on Boards of Education
7. Provision of speakers for public schools
8. Provision of speakers for colleges
9. Provision of teaching aids directly to schools and colleges

(Low on the list were endowment of professorships; graduate fellowships; equipment of laboratories; employment of professors of business subjects.)[28]

He sent the list also to sixty-three school systems and to seventeen colleges and universities in the state, and compiled the following listing, in order of frequency of mention:

1. Opportunity for plant visits
2. Provision of teaching aids directly to schools and colleges
3. Participation on advisory committees; provision of speakers for public schools (equal rating)
4. Provision of teaching aids through trade associations
5. Education-Industry conferences
6. Service on Boards of Education; cooperation in evaluating instruction (equal rating)
7. Employment of public school teachers
8. Provision of leadership through trade associations re curriculum
9. Participation in B-I-E Days
10. Vocational counseling—school

(Low ranking was given to professorships; graduate fellowships; cooperation in establishing college refresher courses.) [29]

This would indicate that industry's activities, and education's needs coincide to a degree, but that industry is missing some opportunities—in employment of school teachers and vocational counseling, for example.

In his summary, Dr. Brasted said: "Even among the relatively few industrialists who complained about . . . some phase of school . . . operations, and likewise among the relatively few educators who made comments critical of industry . . . there was definitely the feeling that these were problems which, if the two groups could get closer together more frequently, would largely be solved to the satisfaction of both." [30]

Thomas R. Reid, Director of Civic Affairs for Ford Motor, with refreshing candor once described relations between businessmen and educators as "slightly phony." "This tendency to subdue our opinions and enthusiasms in the interest of a sort of sweetness and light," Mr. Reid said, "is the greatest single barrier to communications between the two groups."

Mr. Reid went on to say that the businessman had three admittedly self-interest reasons for wanting good relations with educators: (1) the desire of the modern corporation to be accepted as a constructive force in our society; (2) the desire to "receive a steady flow of new blood" (young people "well grounded in the fundamentals," particularly mathematics); and (3) the desire that "our young people . . . understand that this free, individualistic, unsentimental, business system of ours, driven by the goad of the profit motive, has more that is good to offer by far than those statist systems which chain men to the pursuit of the theoretically perfect society." [31]

To continue in Mr. Reid's vein of candor, the resentments of the educators are (1) the businessman's implication that teachers are treating industry with unfavorable and unfair bias in their teaching, and (2) that they collectively are proponents of statist systems of government. Educators, it may even be, react more feverishly to criticism than most people.[32]

Perhaps the best philosophical summary of this subject is supplied by the group conclusions reached by the community relations specialists attending a Cornell management seminar a few years ago.

1. In a democratic society it is vital that all citizens should be as completely and intelligently informed as possible on all subjects

important to them, including the basic principles of economics.

2. American business is based upon the free enterprise system. It has the right and even the duty to broadcast the values of this system.

3. Education is the prerogative of the school systems. If business leaders become educators, too, they ought to seek that elusive goal so dear to educators: objectivity. For business will not attain the stature worthy of educators if it tries to present unsupported opinion as fact.

4. If either business or education should attempt to indoctrinate without educating, it will deserve the vast public resistance which it will surely meet.

Footnotes

[1] William J. Hageny, *A Follow-up Study of the Occupations of the Graduates of Commercial and Vocational Courses of Blodgett Vocational High School of Syracuse, N.Y., of the June Classes of 1927 to 1937 inclusive.* Unpublished MS thesis, Syracuse University, July 1953.

[2] Processed, undated.

[3] This Syracuse questionnaire and its very favorable responses may be of interest to other school systems doing good jobs while harassed by a vocal minority. The questions and their totals, hence, are included in Appendix F.

[4] *Post-Standard* (Syracuse), December 2, 1955.

[5] Syracuse Governmental Research Bureau, *School Building Needs in the City of Syracuse; A Review of the Proposal Submitted by the Board of Education,* processed, 1955.

[6] Local people in education, industry and labor all agree that cooperation by many groups is what made the program a success. Utica is about 90 percent unionized, but has an outstanding strike-free record. The Utica Federation of Labor belongs to the Utica Chamber of Commerce, to my knowledge an arrangement unique in industrial communities. The International Association of Machinists has seen the city's changeover from a textile town to a diversified industrial town as its opportunity to become the most important local union. I.A.of M. contributed both leadership and work to make the re-training program a success; needless to say, it since has greatly increased its membership locally.

[7] *Your Career Opportunities in Evansville Industry,* Evansville Manufacturers and Employers Association, Public Relations Division, Evansville, Ind., 1953, p. 166.

The 300 jobs described are arranged under various chapter-heading categories: wood products, metal products, textile products, chemical products, food products, printing, utilities, maintenance, clerical jobs, professional and technical jobs, management jobs. The first chapter, "Choosing Your Career," counsels the student on analyzing abilities and interests . . . "measuring your choice" . . . "fixing your goal" . . . "what kinds of education?" . . . "the facts (economics) of industry." In the appendix is a "dictionary and index of job opportunities in Evansville industry," plus a general index.

H. F. Williams, Jr., who as then Director of Public Relations for the Evansville Association, acted as editor-in-chief of the book and as the executive officer for much of the project. Mr. Williams presented "the Evansville cases" to the Cornell Community Relations seminar in the summer of 1956, and much of the above information is taken from his presentation.

For the company or community seeking additional experience in local employment surveys correlated with guidance programs, cf. also the work of Racine (Wisc.) Manufacturers Association, and the occupational Inventory of Cuyah County, Ohio, for the Welfare Federation of Cleveland.

8 Harold Jean Steffen, *A Study of Common Elements in Entry Jobs*, unpublished Ph.D. thesis, Cornell University, June 1955.

9 See Harold J. Dillon, *Early School Leavers: A Major Educational Problem*, National Child Labor Committee, New York, 1949. An unpublished M.S. thesis at Syracuse University (Alfred J. Lewis, *Study of Problems which during the Past Fifteen Years have Caused Boys and Girls to Leave Syracuse Central High School before Graduation*, 1951) showed that personal dissatisfactions of one kind or another were responsible for most drop-outs. Some programs in various cities to reduce drop-outs are described in *Improving School Holding Power*, a report of a Chicago conference on "Life Adjustment Education" attended by representatives from cities larger than 200,000 population; (Federal Security Agency, Office of Education Circular No. 291, Washington, 1951). Cf. also *Summary of Findings and Recommendations of Work Group on Working Conditions and Experiences as Related to Personality Development of Youth*, Bureau of Labor Standards, U.S. Department of Labor, Washington, April 1951 (mimeographed).

10 Herbert G. Zollitsch, "Barriers to Employment of Young Workers in Manufacturing Plants," *Industrial and Labor Relations Research* (New York State School of Industrial & Labor Relations, Cornell University), November 1956, pp. 13 ff.

11 John B. Miner, *Intelligence in the United States* (New York: Springer Publishing Co., 1957), p. 11.

12 *Ibid.*, p. 125.

13 See Edmund J. Gleazer Jr., "Two Year Colleges Growing Rapidly," *Pride* (American College Public Relations Society) March 1957, pp. 9 ff.

14 Lynn A. Emerson, *Industrial Education in a Changing Democratic Society*, Bulletin No. 33, New York State School of Industrial and Labor Relations at Cornell University, October 1955, p. 71.

15 Onondaga County of New York State has been planning for such an institution for some years, in part to save the money that has been exported to pay a third of costs of educating local boys and girls at state community colleges at Auburn and elsewhere in the state.

San Diego's community project to obtain a state scientific college, which would place particular emphasis on airplane and missile manufacturing, was led by the managements of the airplane industry there, and particularly by Convair Division of General Dynamics which contributed $1 million to the building fund.

[16] Cf. *Social Prestige of Occupations: A Study of the Relative Prestige of Occupations Among Greater Cleveland High School Seniors* (with contrasts noted between 1954 and 1950); The Occupational Planning Committee of the Welfare Federation of Cleveland, 1955.

[17] These preferences were expressed in anticipation of "Career Day" which every spring is sponsored by the Syracuse Council of Service Clubs and which attracts about 350 people from business, industry and the professions to address and counsel local high school students on career possibilities and on relevant post-high school education. A how-to-do-it manual in the putting on of Career Days by the National Association of Manufacturers, is called *Career Conference, a Program for Vocational Guidance at the High School Level*, New York, n.d., mimeographed.

[18] Seymour Martin Lipset, Reinhard Bendix and F. Theodore Malm, "Job Plans and Entry into the Labor Market," *Social Forces*, March 1955, pp. 224 ff.

[19] Summer work programs for college students are, however, quite common, e.g., at Union Carbide, RCA, General Electric, Bloomingdale's and other large department stores, among others.

[20] Two examples of such war experience literature still with some pertinence to present problems are *Cooperative Education and Other Work-Study Plans*, National Association of Manufacturers, New York, 1946 (although the concern is largely with programs at the college level); and Caroline E. Legg, Carl A. Jessen and Maris M. Proffitt, *School-and-Work Programs, A Study of Experience in 136 School Systems*, Federal Security Agency, Office of Education and U.S. Department of Labor, Division of Labor Standards, Bulletin No. 9, Washington, 1947.

[21] *Industrial Cooperative Training Programs—A Work-Study Plan*, State Education Department, University of the State of New York, Division of Industrial Education, Albany, 1950, p. 3.

[22] Manufacturers Association of Syracuse, *Educational Subsidies for Employees*, Information Bulletin IB 56–28, Nov. 7, 1956.

[23] Doris M. Thompson, *Tuition-Aid Plans for Employees*, National Industrial Conference Board, Studies in Personnel Policy No. 151, New York, 1956.

[24] *The New York Times*, December 2, 1956.

[25] This program to hire teachers for summer work in business and industry has had the cooperation of a number of trade associations and professional societies, including the National Association of Manufacturers, American Chemical Society, and Scientific Manpower Commission. The Future Scientists of America Foundation, affiliated with the National Science Teachers Association, distributes a flier, *Let's Help America's Science Teachers Find Science-Related Summer Jobs*, obtainable from the Association's office in Washington, D.C.

[26] William D. Stansil and Ernest G. Lake, "A New Window for the Classroom," *The American School Board Journal*, March 1956.

[27] A comprehensive but slightly dated study is Thomas J. Sinclair, *A Report about Business-Sponsored Teaching Aids*, F. A. Owen Publishing Co., Dansville, N.Y., 1949. This is a popular version of Mr. Sinclair's Ph.D. thesis at Northwestern University.

There are a number of booklets giving general information on working with schools: NAM's *Activities and Services for Education-Industry Cooperation* (n.d.), Manufacturing Chemists Association's *How Industry and Education Can Work Together* (1957), and various publications by Hill and Knowlton Inc., some by American Iron and Steel Institute as *Education and Industry Cooperate; Teacher for a Day;* and *Partners in Community Enterprise.*

[28] F. Kenneth Brasted, Ph.D., *Education-Industry Relationships, A Connecticut Study with National Implications*, National Association of Manufacturers, New York, 1953. Table IV, p. 13.

[29] *Ibid.*, Table V, p. 13.

[30] *Ibid.*, p. 22.

[31] From an address at the first annual conference of the Industry-Education Cooperation Group, sponsored by the Michigan Manufacturers Association of School Administrators, Michigan State College, East Lansing, Feb. 17, 1955.

[32] As a result of popular articles criticizing the public school system, the National Education Association and the American Association of School Administrators asked the Advisory Public Relations Committee, U.S. Chamber of Commerce, to make some recommendations. This committee appointed a sub-committee to prepare a report. The sub-committee members were Ralph C. Champlin, Vice President for Public Relations, Pennsylvania Railroad; Denny Griswold, publisher and editor of *Public Relations News;* Stewart Schackne, Manager, Public Relations Department, Standard Oil (N.J.).

The Report made this point: "To us who are not in the field of education, but who follow the press and other public expressions of opinion more carefully than the average person and who are familiar with the practices and predilections of journalists, it seems that, too often, the reaction of educators to criticism is a refusal to examine its possible validity. Instead there appears to be an attempt to assert for education an immunity to inspection which is granted to no other segment of our society, including the clergy." *See* Ralph C. Champlin, "Applying Public Relations to Attacks on Education," *Public Relations Journal*, June 1955, pp. 12 ff.

6-
Air and Water Pollution

PART ONE: THE SYRACUSE CASE

SYRACUSE butts into Onondaga Lake, and Greater Syracuse industrial and residential areas stretch themselves around the lake's eastern and western shores. This lake (three-fourths to one and three-eighths miles wide and four and a half miles long, 364 feet above sea level, fifty to seventy feet deep) once was half-circled with salt springs that gave Syracuse its industrial start in life. It is connected with the New York State Barge Canal system, still operative although the Erie Canal, as such, is only a romantic memory. Its outlet is the Seneca River, also part of the Barge Canal system.

Onondaga's brackish water never was good drinking, even in Hiawatha's day. Nor is Onondaga Lake naturally attractive. Its shorelines are low, and in early days were swampy, bleak and unhealthy. Filling swamp land, and controlling the courses and overflows of low-banked creeks which empty into Onondaga Lake, have been perennial public works activities over the years.

Any beauty the lake acquires must be man-planned and man-made. To date, a county-operated park along the northeastern shore is its only such beautification.

Garbage and sewage disposal units and some industrial installations line the city-side shore. Along the southwestern shore in the town of Geddes are two large operations—the Solvay Process Division of Allied Chemical and Dye, and the Sanderson-Halcomb works of Crucible Steel, plus several smaller plants.

Prior to 1924, the city of Syracuse piped all raw sewage into the lake; and the lake seemingly was able to absorb it without greatly offending the sensibilities of residents.

In 1925, a primary settling-tank type of sewage treatment plant was completed. Liquid effluent, after screening and settling, was pumped from the tops of the settling tanks into the lake to be naturally digested and oxydized there. The lake's capacity to absorb the necessary oxygen from the atmosphere (about 1600 pounds needed for each million gallons of sewage effluent) was estimated as sufficient to care for the city at its expected rate of growth until 1945. The city and its sewage grew faster than expected, to the detriment of the lake, which slipped to a septic condition about five years ahead of schedule. The hope at this writing is that someday the lake's western end may be brought up to a "B" (swimming) classification, and the eastern end to "C" classification.[1]

Sewage solids which settled on the bottoms of the settling tanks (called "sludge" in the parlance of sewage engineers) were pumped to the waste product beds of the Solvay Process Company, there to be sterilized by the company's waste chemical slurry in the company's waste product lagoons.

The Syracuse Intercepting Sewer Board's report on its then new installation, presented to the citizens in 1925, contains this paragraph:

The unique opportunity afforded by the close proximity of the Solvay Process Works and the Syracuse Sewage Treatment Works was recognized by the Intercepting Sewer Board engineers. Through the courteous cooperation of the Solvay Company, [this] has served to save the city many thousands of dollars in construction expense, that would otherwise have been necessitated by the construction of sludge digestion and drying works. Through this method of mixing the Syracuse sludge with the Solvay waste, the sludge is buried inconspicuously, inexpensively and inoffensively and the discharges of the supernatant liquids as finally enter Onondaga Lake from the waste lagoons are completely sterilized.[2]

Solvay Process, since 1920 a unit of Allied Chemical and Dye Corporation, utilizes Onondaga County's only two mineral resources, salt and limestone, to manufacture soda ash by a process perfected by the Solvay Brothers of Belgium. This process was established commercially in Syracuse in 1881 by F. R. Hazard, "father of the American alkali industry," and his engineering associate, William B. Cogswell. The Solvay plant's location in the Town of Geddes in the Village of Solvay on the west bank of Onondaga Lake is ideal: limestone may be had from quarries near Jamesville, and salt from the underground salt fields near Tully, both in Onondaga County; an unlimited water supply needed for cooling purposes is available from the lake at the plant's front door. The process uses many millions of gallons of water a day—more than the whole city of Syracuse. Because of algae living on sewage in the lake, the water must be chlorinated before it is used in the plant; so, except for some addition of salts, it is returned to the lake considerably purer than it was when drawn into the company's two large intake pipes.

The bulky waste product of the Solvay soda-ash process is the inanimate and sterile hero-villain of this peculiar case study. Since soda ash production at Syracuse first began in 1884, this waste has been accumulating on company land near the lake. When you drive your car onto the 400-acre parking lot at the New York State Fair grounds, deeded to the state by the company, you are riding on a flattened mountain of

Solvay waste product. This area at one time was swamp land. And it was this same waste product, when mixed with Syracuse sewage sludge, that saved taxpayers millions of dollars over more than a quarter of a century.[3]

Yet to the citizens of Onondaga County this waste product is more villainous than heroic. They think of Solvay waste beds only as unsightly blots upon the landscape. Waste beds, as a matter of fact, do lack natural beauty; acres of them on nearby company land cause neighbors and local governments to worry about property devaluation.

Much research time and money have gone into seeking possible uses of this gray, crumbly mixture. Among other failures, it has failed as a building material and as a road surfacing agent. There's too much of it to bury or to transport any great distance either by truck or by pipe. Nothing will grow on it, and for some years—or until it is well settled— nothing will grow in top soil spread over it.

Back in the nineteenth century, when Syracuse was a town instead of a city, dumping the waste along the banks of the lake offended no one, and in fact helped get rid of some of the swamps. Today, as always, the waste, as a semiliquid slurry, is piped to a company lagoon which, when filled and dried out, in time will become another company waste bed.

Events to follow can be appreciated better after a little background on Allied Chemical and Dye Corporation and its Solvay Process Division plant at Syracuse. Prior to the 1950s, Allied was non-communicative as a matter of principle and as a matter of top-management policy. Not until 1953 did Allied ever run an advertisement in any publication. Always a blue chip company that never missed a dividend, even during the depression, it nevertheless experienced in 1933 a stockholders' revolt (an unsuccessful one) against management's secrecy. Management even banned Who's Who listings of Allied executives as contrary to its anti-publicity policy. With such a tradition, the Syracuse officers of the company were hardly practiced hands at making public speeches or issuing communiqués to the local press.

The philosophy back of this secrecy went something like this: If you run an honest, efficient, profit-making company and do your best to be fair in your dealings with people, there will be no need to worry about this new-fangled clap-trap called public relations and personnel relations. This philosophy no longer dominates Allied, mostly because of the new leadership provided by Fred Emmerich (president in 1946, chairman of the board in 1957) and Glen B. Miller (president in 1957) who do not agree with their predecessors that isolationism is the best industrial policy. Perhaps the change, which inspired *Fortune* to write an article for its October, 1954, issue entitled "You'd Hardly Know Allied Chemical," was also partly a result of events at Syracuse during the period of the late 1940s and early 1950s.

The cooperative spirit and sense of social obligation evident in the Solvay Process arrangement to care for Syracuse sewage sludge were genuine; but the company saw no reason to talk publicly about its good deeds.

In 1943 a break occurred in the supporting entrenchment around the waste bed then being used, a bed on the lake shore in the town of Geddes where the plant is located. The slurry-sludge mixture poured across a road, damaging a number of houses, automobiles and shrubs in its path. On another occasion Solvay was shut down by a strike, and for a while produced no slurry to sterilize the city's sewage sludge. These incidents disturbed people, and strengthened their opinions that the company lacked concern for the community and that it was a polluter, not only of air and water, but of scenery as well.[4] Available records of the period, verified by memories of citizens, express worry that Solvay waste beds by the lake shore were somehow dangerous polluters of the lake itself. The feeling, furthermore, was that the company was antisocial for so endangering the lake.

Foreseeing the need for future waste beds, Solvay in the 1920s had purchased some land in the adjoining township of Camillus. After World War II the company also acquired an abandoned airport there. Perhaps it was the purchase of the airport land that triggered the organized opposition to waste beds in Camillus. But, whatever the immediate inspiration for it, the Camillus Planning Board drew up a zoning ordinance in 1949 that would prohibit Solvay from using its property for waste deposits. The board behaved democratically: it held a series of public meetings, invited correspondence from interested parties and interviewed almost everyone in the township. The residents, the board reported, feared devaluation of their property; they didn't know where this thing would end; and maybe Solvay intended eventually to make one big wastebed of their town. With the whole town deteriorated, they feared, undesirable establishments would move in to hasten further deterioration.

Public sympathies, judging by letters to Syracuse newspapers, usually favored "the little people" in their fight against "the giant corporation." And the newspapers themselves gave little or no opposition to the Camillus Planning Board's position—largely because they could obtain no counter statement whatever from the company, which obviously (and suspiciously) did not want to talk to the press.

As the situation grew more tense, the company finally did make an announcement. It told the Camillus Planning Board that, without available waste beds, continued operation of the Solvay plant would be impossible. It said that unless the

prohibiting ordinance was killed the company would regret-
fully have to move out of the Syracuse area.

At this point, Syracuse's well-organized and experienced
industrial bodies, the Manufacturers Association and the
Chamber of Commerce, went into the battle "to save Solvay
for Syracuse." Accepting the Camillus Board's invitation to
correspond, the Chamber of Commerce sent a two-page statement, with copies to the press and civic and social groups all
over the county. The Solvay notice of intent to move, the
statement said, was no idle threat. For some 3,000 men to
lose their jobs—which for generations had been the steadiest
in the area—would affect not only their own families but also
many other families in the county who depended, however
indirectly, on Solvay's $10 million annual payroll. The many
older workers at Solvay probably would be unable to find
other jobs and would go on relief. The area would lose a big
local taxpayer (a half million dollars a year), and any future
attempt to persuade Crucible and other companies to make
up the difference might influence them to leave the county,
too.

Meanwhile, various planning agencies of the county, with
the active cooperation of the company, searched the area for
alternative sites for waste beds. They found none; and this,
too, was publicized.

In less than a month, the Planning Federation of Onondaga
County Municipalities had worked out a compromise plan
designed to remove the fears of Camillus people and to give
them a substitute for Solvay's scalp. The plan—which in large
part originated with company management and the company's
then newly engaged public relations counsel, G. Edward
Pendray—called for horticultural buffer strips around future
waste beds, to be maintained by the company. Old beds, it
was also proposed, should likewise be screened by plantings

of trees and shrubs. A key feature of the plan would be the building, at county expense, of a community park in Camillus, complete with swimming pool, athletic fields and picnic grounds "to protect the area against any direct or indirect effect of proposed expansion of Solvay waste beds." In addition, the county would throw in a cross-county road through Camillus.

The plan had the very active backing of the Chamber of Commerce and the Manufacturers Association (although strangely the various village chambers of commerce across the lake placed themselves on record as being definitely opposed).

Coup de grâce to the Camillus ordinance was a meeting at the County Court House, sponsored by the Civic Development Committee and attended by top officers of such bodies as planning commissions (county and municipal), Manufacturers Association, Chamber of Commerce, Veterans Council of Onondaga County, Community Council of Camillus, Camillus Board of Supervisors, village government of Solvay, New York State senate, the Catholic Church, American Federation of Labor, Greater Syracuse Industrial Council, Federation of Women's Clubs, League of Women Voters, and—last on the program—the Camillus Planning Board.

The session consisted of a series of testimonials by these people to the economic importance of Solvay to the area. When his turn came, the man from the Camillus Planning Board kept his remarks brief and noncommittal. The meeting closed with a unanimous vote of approval of the compromise plan outlined above.

Solvay Process had been rescued—of all things—by public relations.

Then, only two years later, the citizens of Geddes grew resentful of big neighbor Syracuse using their township as a dumping ground for its sewage sludge. Some of the resentment was transferred to the Solvay company for its complicity in an operation which was considered offensive to township dignity, and occasionally offensive in other ways, too. In recognition of this sentiment, the company moved its waste depositing operation inshore to Solvay property in the town of Geddes, near the tiny village called Lakeland. The city of Syracuse built a pipeline costing $85,000 to Solvay's new bed. It was expected that the old money-saving arrangement of mixing the sewage sludge with Solvay slurry would be continued.

But this time Geddes residents, through their organizations and government, informed the company that they would no longer tolerate this indignity.

The company was forced to decide which community it would accommodate, Syracuse or Geddes. Management decided to accommodate Geddes, and refused to allow Syracuse to install the necessary sludge pumps on its property.

Unhappy as it may have made city taxpayers, the decision had the virtue of forcing Syracuse and Onondaga County into facing up at last to their long outgrown sewage disposal systems. Committees were appointed, studies were made, reports presented and duly recorded in the local press. This tedious process, enlivened occasionally by city vs. county conflicts, went on for four years. The problem of what to do with the sewage sludge meanwhile was solved by burying part of it in trenches on city land on the south shore and dumping the remainder into the lake, so that, as worried State officials expressed it, the lake became "visibly polluted." [5]

A poll of people in Syracuse probably would record, even at this writing, a lack of understanding of the company's position, and would almost certainly nominate Solvay Process as the greatest single polluter of Onondaga Lake. Yet, looking back over these years of waste bed trouble, it seems that the company has been remarkably community-minded and conscious of its social obligations. Management made the decisions that seemed right to them; I am sure that in the long run these decisions will prove themselves to be right for communities as well as for the company.

For the happy ending, you have the recent new outlook at Solvay and at Allied Chemical and Dye. Allied is going heavily into product research, enlightened industrial and personnel relations practices and public relations. Syracuse papers and area weeklies now carry occasional institutional ads for Solvay. Solvay has one of the best plant newspapers in the Syracuse area, a program of in-plant seminars to develop its management people, a series of easily read pamphlets about the company, and a staff of able public relations professionals.

Solvay has found that the only way to keep from being misunderstood is to tell people what they should know about the company. With this new approach, the company's community relations have climbed out of the basement, and still are going up.

When you visit the plant now, your tour is likely to include a ride in a company car around the landscaped shrubbery which screens the waste beds from view.

6-
Air and Water Pollution

PART TWO

G. EDWARD PENDRAY of Pendray & Cook, public relations counsel to chemical companies, among others, has found that management's community relations thinking about its plant pollution problems often follows this sequence: [6]

1. Initial denial of excessive pollution.

2. Announcement (when pressed) that the plant was located at its present site before the community built up around it, and that the builders and buyers of homes in the area knew what they were getting into. (The plant's economic importance to the community may also be mentioned.)

3. Official silence, sometimes maintained on legal ground. (This silence may continue despite installation of expensive control equipment.)

4. Dismay as community pressures increase and "unfair" anti-pollution regulations are passed by town and county governments.

5. Finally, with the plant's black eye shining for all to see, the company resolution to begin a program of community information and education.

Public criticism of industry's pollution is inevitable. Opinion Research Corporation's, Erie, Pennsylvania survey in 1949 indicated that dirt, smoke and stink are what people hated most about factories and mills in town. Polluted water kills fish, prevents swimming, damages boat bottoms, and may look and smell terrible. Polluted air gives people red eyes and sore throats, dirty houses, streets and clothing, plus a decidedly unfavorable opinion of smoke stacks and the companies operating them.

Anti-pollution regulations aimed at local industry may have political motivation, but basically such legislation stems from public opinion rather than politics. Regulatory laws have been passed by all states and many counties and cities, and more go into effect each year. Basic to every public relations program to meet a pollution problem is this helpful little rule: stop polluting. Or come as close as reasonably possible to stopping. And tell people about your efforts.

Spending huge sums on pollution control at first blush seems unsound economics, even from the point of view of the public who eventually must pay the bill. But the truth is that people want pollution controlled; and the company job is not to dissuade them, but rather to convince them that management is doing all it can as fast as it can, and that the effort is costing a pile of money which the company is happy to spend to get results.

A community shouldn't expect its heavily used industrial river to support swimming and fishing also. Pollution standards for the Mahoning River as it flows past Youngstown's steel mills must be based on that particular river's immediate uses to humanity; there seems little sense in expensive pollution treatment of a river clean enough to meet legitimate community needs and health standards. The Manufacturing Chemists Association does not consider that air pollution exists "unless . . . concentrations [are] definitely offensive to human senses, or impair the normal functions of the human body, or detract from the value, usefulness or enjoyment of property." [7]

These are sensible opinions, but without very much public appeal. DuPont's well-publicized policy (which is also operative at other important companies) is positive rather than defensive: Expenditures for pollution abatement shall require no justification in terms of dollar return on investment; all new installations must include modern facilities for pollution control; and all pollution problems must be solved in advance of construction.[8]

Industry may with justification feel a scapegoat for other kinds of offenders. But industry is easy to pick on, compared with thousands of owners of smoking incinerators and ancient autos. Comparative statistics on pollution sources seem to leave the community public relatively unmoved.

Some fear is combined with the public's dislike of industrial dirt. Twenty persons died in a five-day smog at Donora, Pa., in 1948. The 400 percent increase in lung cancer in twenty years cannot be proven to be a result of air pollution, although cigarette manufacturers might be happy if it could. In 1937, *Fortune* reported that in twelve typical smoky cities the death rate was 31 percent greater than in less smoky cities, and that smoke cuts out important ultra-violet light from the sun by 40 to 60 percent.[9] Dirty looking water, particularly if it has chemical scum or odor, frightens people.[10]

The compounded result of all this is that industry has no sympathizers with its pollution problems, but plenty of critics. Sometimes regulations resulting from public demand are unreasonable; but those at city, county and area levels by and large are cognizant of industrial problems. When Erie County, N.Y., attempted to get municipal approval of a stringent anti-smoke law, the Town of Lackawanna vetoed it. "I am never going to vote for a law that would drive Bethlehem Steel out of Lackawanna," the town supervisor said, "especially when I know they pay 72 per cent of our taxes."

Nevertheless, regulations come to cities which have the worst pollution. Back in 1931 and 1933, a Public Health Service investigation showed that St. Louis, Pittsburgh, Chicago, Boston and Baltimore had the heaviest air pollution—all of them with an index of 137. (Normal or average cities have an index of 100.) [11] In 1956, St. Louis and Pittsburgh, with the cooperation of locally operating industry, had highly effective regulations and a much improved situation. Chicago, Boston and Baltimore also have regulations and improvement. The 1954 investigations by the U.S. Environmental Health Center found the worst air pollution in Charleston (W.Va.), Detroit, Los Angeles, Anchorage (Alaska), and New York City, in that order—a completely different list. [12]

Local regulations, when designed to meet the pollution problems peculiar to specific communities, are better than state regulations from industry's point of view. Usually local industry has cooperated in their formation. [13]

St. Louis' 1940 smoke control code, which prohibited the sale of highly volatile bituminous coal within the city, was among the first to apply and vigorously enforce the rule: "Use smokeless fuel and burn fuel smokelessly." [14]

In 1949, the Allegheny County Smoke Control Ordinance was passed to take Pittsburgh out of the running as America's smokiest city. The Mellon-sponsored Allegheny Conference on Community Development is primarily responsible for this ordinance which gave industry a deadline for converting from high-volatile bituminous. The ordinance also established a research program to discover practical methods of reducing stack emissions from blast furnaces, open hearth furnaces and bessemer converters. In addition, several steel companies in the Pittsburgh area set up cooperative programs of research and "self-policing." Each company has a "smoke abatement coordinator" to record plant infractions of the Smoke Control

Ordinance, their causes and the corrective measures undertaken or planned. Advantages of this "self-policing" are listed by G. A. Howell, assistant to the chief engineer of steel manufacturing, U.S. Steel Corporation at Pittsburgh:

First, all operators of combustion facilities are made more cognizant of their responsibilities to perform their duties correctly and efficiently. Secondly, it brings to the attention of the plant officials those operators who are dilatory in their approach to smoke abatement, and disciplinary action is applied if previous instructions and warnings have been disregarded. Finally, an overall picture is presented to company officials as to what is being accomplished. They in turn can discuss the different aspects of the smoke control problem with the coordinators and plant officials.[15]

The clean-up program at Pittsburgh is one of the nation's remarkable civic achievements made possible by cooperative industry. Here in this heavy industry area with 1.5 million people and with soft coal cheap because near at hand, the problem was to give Pittsburghers clean air for the first time in a century—and to do so without putting local industry at a competitive disadvantage. In this the city succeeded—largely because it had an engineering approach. Careful studies were made of the technical problems of each industry so that standards set would not be unreasonable. Plants which could comply with the ordinance were required to do so to the extent of their technological advancement. Those with unsolved technical problems were required to "embark in good faith" upon joint research with industries in the same boat. Steel companies using bessemer converters, for example, were exempt from certain smoke abatement standards provided they joined together in a five-year research project.[16]

Laws may not be the total answer to pollution, but, as

Henry B. duPont has said, industry must help to implement them "as a matter of good business." [17]

The cooperative and engineering approach has proved remarkably successful, too, in Indianapolis, where 75 percent of the work of the Bureau of Air Pollution Control is in lending assistance to companies in research and in the training of industrial personnel in refiring methods. Significantly, air pollution control publicity in local media stresses, not violations, but the achievements of local plants in reducing air contaminants.[18]

How does this sort of approach come about? It develops largely from the good relationships existing between agency administrators and staff and industrial management and its staff. In communities where management is accustomed to cooperative organization and unified action in other fields, pollution problems, too, are attacked cooperatively. In one New Jersey area, newcomer companies are politely but firmly instructed on what's expected of them, not by agency people, but by industrial neighbors. If industry helped form the local control agency, with research and cooperation in mind, the publicity will be positive and progress faster.

A Pendray & Cook survey found that in one year sixty-seven cities were planning crackdowns on violators of air pollution ordinances out of impatience with delays.[19] Much of the ill will and bad publicity of such hassles could be avoided with a cooperative and engineering approach like that of Pittsburgh and Indianapolis.

A population of at least 100,000 is estimated by the Air Pollution Abatement Committee of the Manufacturing Chemists Association as necessary to support a local air pollution control unit because of the costs of investigation and analysis.[20] To retain control of pollution as much as possible at local levels, this MCA committee recommends formation of community air pollution control commissions which would utilize the investigative and analytical facilities of a state bureau. Membership for such a local commission might be: a municipal official, a county official and a public health official (representing the public); a representative of local agricultural interests; a public utilities representative, and two representatives of industry (an executive and a technical man, such as a professional engineer).

Unlike air pollution, water pollution has been regulated primarily by states and not by communities, although a number of area and bi-state and tri-state central boards have been established. All states now have laws regulating discharge of wastes into water courses. In addition to older federal laws to protect boats and marine structures,[21] there is also the Federal Water Pollution Control Act of 1948, Public Law No. 845, which was revised, amended and passed in 1956 as Law S-890. It authorizes the Surgeon General to suggest remedial measures to a water polluter and to the official water pollution control agency in the state of origin. If the pollution continues, the Secretary of the Department of Health, Education and Welfare, through its component, the U. S. Public Health Service, is authorized to appoint a board to conduct public hearings and to make recommendations to the Secretary. The Secretary may then bring suit on behalf of the United States against the polluter.

At this writing there is no federal law regulating air pollution.

Research is the basis of both pollution control and public relations to meet or forestall pollution criticism. The classic negative demonstration of this point is to be found in the smog story of Los Angeles. When newspapers seized upon an experimental thesis and called it a scientific fact, they had Southern Californians convinced that smog was caused by

sulfur dioxide. Public pressure forced industry, especially refineries, to spend millions to control emissions of sulfur
dioxide. Then the thesis was disproved. At another period,
synthetic rubber manufacture took its turn as suspect.

Actually, air pollutants from the city are walled in by
mountains inland, kept from drifting over the ocean by inshore sea breezes, and pushed down close to the ground by an
"inverted" layer of cold air. Add a strong mixture of ozone,
plus sunshine to warm and semi-liquefy the pollutants, and
you have smog—as Los Angeles does with disturbing frequency
the year around.[22]

Manchester Boddy, when he was publisher of the now
defunct Los Angeles *Daily News*, pointed out that pollution
research is a job for scientists and not for newspapermen.
Certainly communication about research must be carefully
handled, as all public relations men for universities, medical
centers and research institutes at some time in their lives have
found out the hard way. It is better to have a three-inch accurate story below the fold on an inside page than a mislead-
ing speculative story with a banner head on Page One.
Sometimes it is necessary to work hard to keep from getting
the unwarranted banner head.

One clipping service collected 55,000 column inches of
news space devoted to Los Angeles smog between 1949 and
1951, plus 6,500 column inches of editorial space.

Los Angeles is huge and sprawling: a conglomerate of
suburbs. This diffusion, plus the city's history of bickering
and jealousies among organizations, both political and civic,
has made difficult the sort of cooperative approach which
achieved such wonders for Pittsburgh.[23] Los Angeles City
(forty-five square miles) sometimes acts unilaterally without
consultation with the Los Angeles Air Pollution Control District, which tries to integrate activities of the entire Los

Angeles Basin (7,000 sq. mi.), with its forty-four cities running into one another.[24] Demands for "crack-downs" on industry are commonplace, and have been since smog began to be a nuisance during World War II. Politicians and would-be politicians try to capitalize on public anger by accusing the Control District of being soft toward industry. All this is routine for Angelenos.

Actually, the major guilty party in Los Angeles is the public —with 2.5 million automobiles (two cars to a family: one old, one new) traveling great distances across the spread-out city. Until 1957, when a county ordinance outlawed them, backyard incinerators added to the pollution. In part due to appeals from Los Angeles, leading automobile manufacturers began their efforts to engineer hydrocarbon pollution out of cars with fuel injection systems, after-burners, catalytic mufflers, etc. James C. Zeder, vice president of Chrysler Corporation, estimated that automobile companies were spending $450,000 in one year in this research.[25] Carburetor attachments to reduce discharge of unburned fuel were promised by General Motors.[26]

Smog research is well centered in two privately supported organizations, The Air Pollution Foundation and the Stanford Research Institute.[27] The Foundation was started in 1953 and the Research Institute began its work in 1947 with financial support of the Western Oil and Gas Association, whose membership, incidentally, has been subject to more than its share of "crack-down" hysteria. With all its lack of geographic and social cohesion, Los Angeles County is given to daring plans and imaginative thinking. Some day it will solve its problem, no matter what the cost may be. And the solution, when it comes, will be developed from research. Smog will not be blown away by giant fans, as has been suggested; instead, the answer will lie in chemists' discoveries, e.g., of inexpensive ways to reconvert nitrogen oxides back to nitrogen and oxygen immediately after it is formed by the combustion process.

The federal government has gotten into air pollution research, too, with a $25 million program administered by the Department of Health, Education and Welfare through grants to foundations, abatement agencies, universities, etc. National regulations are not contemplated; and the Interdepartmental Committee on Community Air Pollution which recommended the project to Congress in June, 1955, specifically stated its belief that regulatory control is the province of state and local governments, "except with regard to radioactive air pollution resulting from operations directly controlled by the federal government or interstate and international air pollution." The Committee also made it clear that its interest was in the broad picture of community pollution and not merely in pollution from industrial operations.[28]

But by far the greatest effort and money expenditure to control pollution comes from industry. Pulp and paper companies are reported to have spent $40,000,000 to $50,000,000 in ten years to reduce their pollution of waterways.[29] A sizable proportion of the chemical industry's $300,000,000 annual research budget is devoted to pollution research; an estimated $40,000,000 a year is spent on control apparatus for present plants; and 2.5 to 4 percent of all chemical industry construction costs goes for anti-pollution equipment.

Investments by individual companies make impressive statistics: DuPont, $5,500,000 in one year: Union Carbide, $2,700,000 at one plant (its largest, at South Charleston, W.Va.); National Petro-Chemicals, $1,650,000 on water pollution at a single plant; Kaiser Aluminum, three years of research and $6 million to reduce air pollution at its Chalmette, La., reduction plant; Ford Motor, $1,500,000 to control stream pollution at its River Rouge plant. The listing could go on indefinitely.

A 1954 *Fortune* survey of industries given to polluting water asked this question and got these answers: [30]

"Roughly how much has your firm spent since the end of World War II on water pollution abatement?"

	Minimum	Maximum	Average
Steel (two replies)	$3,000,000	$50,000,000	
Chemicals	460,000	10,000,000	$4,500,000
Petroleum	2,500,000	9,000,000	4,700,000
Pulp and paper	400,000	3,000,000	1,500,000

Research included in these expenditures is clear demonstration to the public of industry's concern and activity in pollution reduction, or would be if the research were more widely publicized.[31] An editor's normal preference is for stories of public attacks upon polluters, instead of stories about research to reduce pollution. Once a story is carried on a company's expensive piece of control equipment, the newspaper is not inclined to repeat it unless some newsworthy "new angle" is developed to interest readers.

Nevertheless, newspapers persistently kept informed of pollution research and control efforts will be inclined to fairer treatment of industry even though they may never use the information as news stories.

One incidental virtue of research has been to demonstrate that industry is not the nation's major polluter of air and water. Soil erosion pours tons of mud into rivers to destroy aquatic life. The District of Columbia Sanitary Engineer believes that lack of soil conservation along the Potomac River costs Washington, D.C. two-thirds of its water treatment budget.[32] Among 11,800 municipalities with sewers, *Fortune* found that 5,200 (serving a population of 35 million) had no treatment of sewage before dumping it into the waterways, and 3,100 municipalities serving 25 million had only partial treatment. Of 10,400 industrial plants, 3,700 had no treatment of their waste discharge—a proportion, granted, that looks favorable only in comparison with city records.[33] Los Angeles research definitely tagged the automobile and the backyard incinerator as infinitely greater polluters than industry. All of this, as pointed out earlier, is more comforting to management than it is pacifying to the public. For industry to point its finger at farmers, car owners, apartment house superintendents, city departments of sanitation, etc., while protesting its own relative innocence is (a) dubious public relations practice, and (b) futile.

The most enlightening case study to make this point is the story of Consolidated Edison's pollution problem in New York City, as described by George Minasian, Con Ed's community relations manager, before the 1954 annual Cornell management seminar on Community Relations.

The problem concerns fly-ash from the coal burned in the company's boilers; and because Con Ed uses half the coal burned in the city the problem remains a real one despite the most modern fly-ash catching equipment which corrals upwards of 95 percent. The company had spent $27 million on pollution control up to 1954. Whenever new generating units have been added, a considerable part of their cost has gone for modern control equipment. All of this received some recognition, especially in the measured and careful columns of The New York Times and The Herald-Tribune.

Then in 1951, two men made air pollution in New York their special province. One was a new deputy commissioner for smoke control and the other was a feature writer for the New York World Telegram and Sun. Their joint publicity efforts, as Mr. Minasian moderately states, "tended to give casual readers the impression that the utility company was the major pollution offender, and that it was reluctant to take certain obvious steps which might result in quick improvement." The World-Telegram reporter dressed a mannequin named "Cinder-ella" in a fluffy white dress, carried her to various sections of the city, and attributed the dirt collected on her dress largely to Con Ed's belching stacks.

The company renewed its attempts to tell its story through the press and at public meeting after public meeting. Ultimately, more notice was given to Con Ed's efforts to keep its stacks clean, as well as to some other pollution sources in the city, particularly pollution from the City Transit Company plants. Complaints became fewer, and, as always, these were answered. Sometimes complainants still mistake other stacks in the city for Con Ed's; sometimes the company's stacks are smoking due to emergency or cleaning operations. Actually, complaints provide a communication channel that should be capitalized on, Mr. Minasian believes.[34]

In passing out a 1952 summons to Consolidated Edison (resulting in its third fine), the director of the city's Bureau of Smoke Control told a New York Times reporter that such court action would "prompt (the company) to push installation of smoke-prevention devices." [35] A few days earlier The Times had run a story of the city's own pollution, together with five columns of pictures showing smoke belching from the Board of Transportation's West Side power plant, and fly-ash—inches thick—on the roofs of neighboring buildings. The chairman of the Transportation Board admitted to the reporter that "equipment was not up to present engineering standards" and that "the City always moves slowly, but its present dour financial status has forced it to purchase less costly smoke-control equipment than the best engineering practice dictated." [36]

Perhaps this situation could develop only in New York City. It would be unlikely to happen in Syracuse with its powerful and cooperative industrial organizations. Certainly, too, it is a far cry from the success stories of Pittsburgh and Indianapolis.

Throughout its period of trouble, Con Ed displayed remarkable self-control and adherence to its educational approach. Politicians and feature writers find utilities easy targets for popular attacks; yet to become angry with these people would be disastrous. Eventually the community can be sufficiently educated so that attacks on the company no longer pay dividends in community popularity, and at that point the attacks will cease.

The lesson to be learned from Consolidated Edison's experience—and from Solvay's experience—is that no company with a pollution problem can expect good deeds to speak for themselves. Both companies admit in retrospect that they took their own good efforts too much for granted, and that management's strong tendency to "let the sleeping dogs of pollution lie" can only lead to disaster. Earlier education programs, they believe, would have forestalled some, if not all, of the community attacks upon them.

The problem of early and continuous communication in matters of pollution abatement must rely for its solution on educational methods rather than publicity methods. We have seen how sparse the publicity for actual pollution reduction can be, and how uncontrollable such publicity can become, to the detriment of both industry and the community.

In handling pollution problems, the chemical plant or the paper mill, the gas and electric company or the steel mill must operate much like universities, with programs of:

1. Research—continuing investigations to find more and better physical means to reduce pollution.

2. Education—a planned, organized, long-term program to inform the community through its groups and organizations of research under way and of research findings being utilized to reduce pollution—and to counteract misinformation and distortion of fact.

The one group closest to the company is, of course, the employees who very much want to be proud of their company instead of ashamed of it when they talk with their friends and neighbors. Furthermore, if they know about all the work and money going into pollution control, and if they are made to feel a part of this effort, they will be more careful that the boilers they tend will belch no more smoke than necessary. Educating employees in pollution control and its importance is primarily the job of supervisors; but all management contacts and internal communication media should be utilized to this end.

City, county and state officials concerned with passing or enforcing pollution ordinances are another important group to be kept informed. Part of their job is keeping abreast of developments in their field, and they will appreciate information (if not condescendingly offered), not only of the company's plans and activities, but also of research findings the company may have from its industrial associations and other sources.

Local high school and college classes in science and social sciences can be interested in problems of pollution control, if the approach to the instructor concerned is made in terms of his curriculum requirements.

It would be hard to find a group in the community without interest in the air they breathe and in the neighboring bodies of water they use. Plant visits by special groups are more effective than talking about them in their own meeting rooms. They are more readily impressed, for example, to see for themselves how effectively fly-ash is being caught. Parent-Teacher Associations, service clubs, women's organizations and civic bodies really want to know what is being done about pollution. It's obviously better to tell them *before* the company is forced to do so in a defensive manner.

Auxiliary to this preventive or educational approach to the pollution problem is the assignment of specific staff to guarantee immediate and responsible action, both to locate needless pollution at the plant and to investigate complaints from residents of the community as quickly and thoroughly as possible. Esso's Bayway (N.J.) refinery, for example, has had a corps of "air men" since 1927 on an around-the-clock schedule to investigate all calls from neighbors, and to see that corrections are made at the refinery if any such are indicated. It is important, Esso believes, that every person known to have complained about the company's pollution be interviewed by a company representative.

Reducing air or water pollution is not easy, cheap or quick; and one aspect of the education program is to communicate the difficulty of the job. People must not be led to expect their solutions right away.

Too much neglected in community education programs are the historical aspects: what industry already has accomplished, and the long series of successes and failures that led to those accomplishments. A play-by-play account of efforts to solve a pollution problem can be made interesting when told informally and in laymen's language. This may be in the form of dramatized and rehearsed talks to be given before community groups, or a reprint of a published article to be distributed throughout the community.[37]

The "five-year study" approach—with installation of testing stations, numerous and wondrous instruments and devices, etc.—provides some opportunity to keep anti-pollution efforts current in the minds, both of citizens in general and of news-papermen in particular. By way of experimentation—and of making a point—one company has planted a garden of flowers and vegetables adjacent to the plant; and sees to it that this garden is one of the finest in the state. Similarly, another plant installed a small farm, featuring prize milch cows, almost beneath the company stacks.

But whatever devices are to be used, one educational point is paramount: that industry is concerned with the *complete* burning of its fuel, not only because this is the smokeless way but also because this is the most economical way. Specifically, townspeople should be told the dollars and cents cost to the company of inefficient combustion. It is important that the community understand that the company has a double motive for trying to reduce pollution. And there is another obvious but neglected point to be made: that modern civilization itself is built upon the burning of fuel. Burning of fuel—and in large quantities—is necessary to modern living. "And," goes the chorus, "we are trying to find out just as fast as we can how to burn the fuels of our industry without polluting the air."

The educational approach, I am sure, is the wisest one for any emotion-laden or potentially emotion-laden situation: the installation of an atomic energy plant nearby, the introduction of jet-propelled airplanes, or air and water pollution. Obviously emotion cannot be reduced by meeting it with emotion, nor by expressions of the company's own self-interest.

The Manufacturing Chemists Association, like other industrial associations, advocates a cooperative, inter-company community relations program in areas that support a number of chemical plants. This approach works well, once the more progressive managements become convinced that the institutionalizing of the problem has plusses which outweigh the minuses inherent in dragging along the indifferent and backward managements in the area.

To maintain educational objectivity may involve the enlisting of out-of-company people to study a community problem —such as a pollution problem—encouraging them to report their findings with complete impartiality. At Pearl River, the Lederle Laboratories Division of American Cyanamid was accused of polluting a stream that flowed nearby, crossed the state line into New Jersey and passed through several towns en route. Even though the stream was some distance from the Lederle plant, community grapevines in the towns downstream named Lederle as the culprit. Newspapers in these communities carried emotional letters to the editors, and finally editorials of their own. To meet the criticism, a committee, headed by the mayor of one of the larger towns concerned, was appointed to investigate, first, Lederle's excellent and expensive system of waste treatment, and, second, the pollution content of the stream and the source of the pollution. The committee finding was that the pollution was not Lederle's doing, but came from a housing development downstream from the plant. The mayor announced this finding to area newspapers over his own name, and not as a publicity release from Lederle.

Yet even when charges have been so intelligently disproved, a remainder of suspicion and antagonism aroused in a case of this sort persists.

The community relations problem in the field of pollution, as I see it, is not to formulate ways to meet such situations as Lederle, Consolidated Edison and Solvay experienced. Infinitely more important is finding the means to prevent them from happening in the first place. Perhaps the clue is in the Manufacturing Chemists' recommendation for formation of citizen's pollution abatement committees *before trouble breaks.*

Could permanent committees of citizens, with industrial as well as public and government members, have forestalled the attacks upon Lederle in Pearl River, or upon Solvay in Syracuse, or perhaps even have mitigated the attack on Consolidated Edison in New York?

Management quite naturally shies away from citizens' committees in areas so important to the company and over which the company would have little control. This, they might say, is like tailoring your own hair shirt which must be worn once it is made. Old management hands in the chemical industry, whose tradition is to manage their plants with productive efficiency and meanwhile to say nothing to anybody, would consider such a plan to be outrageous poppycock.

Granted, certain circumstances and certain community personalities may make unwise this educational technique of bringing in the "students" to participate actively in solving the problem. Nevertheless, plant management must be aware of the following facts, and consider them as a sequence of possible misfortunes that could happen to them:

1. Community attacks on pollution by chemical, paper, steel or power companies are, if not inevitable, quite possible.

2. In the heat of such attacks, and in order to push rezoning restrictions, anti-pollution legislation, etc., citizens committees may be formed among the attackers.

3. Emotionally expressed misinformation about the company, growing out of the attacks, will adversely affect worker recruitment, employee morale, and perhaps eventually, productivity.

Let the company honestly concerned with reducing overall community pollution get credit for this concern in a sound and educational way; and to this end let management use to the fullest every applicable educational principle and technique.

An educated community will not be likely to join in unfair attacks of any kind, from whatever source, made upon the company.

Footnotes

[1] Consistently the Manufacturers Association of Syracuse has publicly supported the New York State Water Pollution Control Board's suggested classification for the lake.

[2] General Description of the Sewage Treatment Works and Other Improvements Constructed by the Syracuse Intercepting Sewer Board, Syracuse, 1925, p. 8.

[3] The waste product is largely sand and particles of limestone which do not react in the process, plus salt. As it passes from the plant, this slurry is hot; its powers of neutralizing sewage sludge come from heat more than from chemical reaction.

[4] Solvay's electrostatic precipitators catch most of the plant's fly-ash. Generally prevailing easterly breezes blow most of the smoke from Solvay Process and Crucible Steel stacks over Onondaga Lake. Crucible uses natural gas except in its boilers, and these, too, are equipped with fly-ash catchers. When Crucible purges its furnaces by injecting oxygen into them, a fast-rising colored smoke results. Even so, this heavy industry on the lake is not a real air pollution problem to Syracuse and the rest of the county. Except for one small flurry by the League of Women Voters, air pollution in Syracuse to date has escaped public censure. And in comparison with most industrial cities of similar size the air is reasonably clean.

[5] In 1956, work began at last on a completely modern Greater Syracuse sewage plan, including secondary treatment plants with sludge digesters that will inject no sewage at all into the lake; even the effluent will be pumped to the Seneca River, which is the lake's outlet.

[6] G. Edward Pendray, "Public Relations Aspects of the Industrial Waste Problem," Public Relations Journal, April 1950, p. 9.

[7] Manufacturing Chemists Association's Air Pollution Abatement Manual, Washington, 1952, p. 4.

[8] Henry B. duPont, "Management Looks at Air Pollution," Proceedings, Second National Air Pollution Symposium, Pasadena, May, 1952, pp. 58–61.

[9] The Fortune Survey, Fortune, June, 1937, pp. 100 ff.

[10] For discussion of biological aspects of air pollution see William G. Frederick, Proceedings, Second National Air Pollution Symposium, pp. 106 ff.

[11] The Fortune Survey, Fortune, June, 1937.

[12] The New York Times, Feb. 29, 1954.

[13] The New York State Air Pollution Control Act of 1957 received industrial support in some industrial cities, including Syracuse; but the local employers' organizations made it plain that they did not want the state to usurp operations of local ordinances. American Society of Mechanical Engineers has written a model ordinance which has become the basis of many enactments. Others are based in principle on the model written by the National Institute of Municipal Law Officers. Arthur Stern of the New York State Division of Hygiene and Safety thinks there can be no such thing as a model ordinance because of local differences in (1) kind and quality of fuel used, (2) nature of industries present, and (3) topographical features and meteorology. ("Problems in Drafting and Administration of Air Pollution," *Air Pollution: U.S. Technical Conference on Air Pollution* (New York: McGraw-Hill, 1952), pp. 685–94.

[14] *Ibid.*, Raymond R. Tucker, "The St. Louis Code and Its Operation," pp. 726–31.

[15] G. A. Howell, "Air Pollution Control in Steel Industry," reprint by U. S. Steel from *Iron and Steel Engineer*, Oct. 1953.

[16] Ralph H. German, "Problems of Compliance with Air Pollution Ordinances in Alleghency County, Pa.," *Air Pollution: U.S. Technical Conference on Air Pollution*, McGraw-Hill, New York, 1952, pp. 695–701.

[17] Henry B. duPont, *op. cit.*, p. 59.

[18] Robert H. Herrmann, "Indianapolis Clears the Air," *Foundry*, May 1953, pp. 212 ff.

[19] *The New York Times*, March 26, 1955.

[20] Manufacturing Chemists Association, *A Rational Approach to Air Pollution Legislation*, Washington, 1952, p. 13.

[21] Sec. 13, *Rivers and Harbors Act* of 1899, and the *Oil Pollution Act*, 1924.

[22] Ozone itself is a pollutant, formed by oxygen plus hydrocarbon vapors plus nitrogen oxides, under action of sunshine. Clear desert air has no ozone at sea level; Los Angeles on smoggy days has .6 to .8 of a part per million.

Unlike Los Angeles' smog, London's is a winter phenomenon due principally to domestic coal burning. Very little coal is burned in Los Angeles. A Kettering Laboratory analysis of gaseous pollutant samples collected by mobile unit in a number of industrial communities found the following, in order of abundance: carbon dioxide, carbon monoxide, oxides of nitrogen, aldehydes, sulfur dioxide, chlorides, ammonia and ammonia salts, fluorides and particulate matter. (Jacob Cholak, "The Nature of Atmospheric Pollution in a Number of Industrial Communities," *Proceedings, Second National Air Pollution Symposium*, pp. 6 ff.).

[23] California's 1947 air pollution law created an air pollution control district in every county with jurisdiction within cities as well as in unincorporated sections. The district is not activated until after a hearing and finding of polluted conditions. The county board of supervisors is the ex officio pollution board. (Harold W. Kennedy, "The Legal Aspects of the California Air Pollution Control Act," *Air Pollution: U.S. Technical Conference on Air Pollution*, pp. 702–11.)

[24] The California state legislature has given the Los Angeles Air Pollution Control District power to declare "alerts" when instruments show dangerous amounts of pollution in the atmosphere: Stage One alert, all outdoor burning stopped; Stage Two, health menace emergency with curtailment of car, bus and truck traffic and shut-down of refineries; Stage Three, all industry and virtually all traffic stopped and martial law imposed, if necessary. Thus far, only Stage One alerts have been needed. (*American City*, Jan. 1956, p. 142.)

[25] Hydrocarbons, found to be the principal source of smog damage to green plants, is emitted ten-fold from car exhausts while the car idles, and 35-fold when the car slows down in gear. (James C. Zeder, "Million Dollar Search: What the Automotive Industry is Doing to Help Los Angeles Fight Its Smog Problem," *Proceedings, Third National Air Pollution Symposium*, Pasadena, April 1955, pp. 97–101.)

[26] *Ibid.*, Dr. F. W. Went of Caltech describes recent research of smog effects on vegetation in his "Global Aspects of Air Pollution as Checked by Damage to Vegetation," pp. 8–11.

[27] The Stanford Research Institute will loan free of charge its 28-minute color film, *The City That Disappears*, an excellent description of the smog phenomenon. The Institute maintains laboratories at both Stanford University and at South Pasadena.

[28] *The New York Times*, July 11, 1955.

[29] *Ibid.*, Sept. 17, 1954, report of Cincinnati meeting of the National Council for Stream Improvement.

[30] The Fortune Survey, *Fortune*, March 1954, p. 148.

[31] William C. Foster, as president of the Manufacturing Chemists Association, has proposed a National Advisory Committee on Air Pollution Abatement to coordinate activity, represent various interests, prod and encourage the government, guide research, advise on regulations and ordinances, and collect and distribute information. ("An Approach to the Air Pollution Dilemma," *Proceedings, Third National Air Pollution Symposium*, pp. 207 ff.)

[32] *Business Week*, May 7, 1949, p. 34.

[33] *Fortune*, March 1954, p. 124.

[34] How the Memphis works of International Harvester enlisted its unfriendly neighbors in wholehearted support of the plant's smoke abatement program is described by the works' public relations manager, James Robert Massey, in *Public Relations Journal*, Sept. 1954, p. 13.

[35] *The New York Times*, April 11, 1952.

[36] *Ibid.*, April 3, 1952.

[37] As an example of the real interest inherent in such a story see Michael V. Consentine (an Olin Mathieson engineer) and his description of a four-year fight to beat an odor problem. *Public Health News*, N.J. State Department of Health, Aug. 1955, pp. 287 ff.

7-
Strikes and Community Relations

PART ONE: THE SYRACUSE CASE

UNION relations is not synonymous with public relations, but in some instances of labor-management strife it is hard to tell where one begins and the other leaves off. An outright blending of the two—as in the eight-weeks strike at the General Electric plants at Syracuse in 1953—can be significant in the conduct, and even in the results of the dispute. Really to understand the case of the General Electric Syracuse strike, one must be aware of the company's philosophy of union-management relations.

Here, in extracts from an Employee Relations News Letter reviewing the year 1954, is a statement of the GE philosophy. Pointing out that the local plant managers negotiate separate local contracts with local representatives of some ninety bargaining units, the News Letter remarks:

An occasional top union official will [be] upset about us because we don't . . . conduct ourselves for his benefit [rather than for] what we honestly believe is . . . [to the] balanced benefit of our employees, neighbors and all others concerned. . . .
. . . Meanwhile, we don't think there should be any silence on our part that might be taken to admit . . . false charges. We think we should speak up with what we claim is the truth—and then let all concerned decide whom and what to believe.

Another thing that upsets one particular union official is that he feels we don't 'bargain' . . . to fit in with his particular skills and personal desires . . .

He wants us to make an offer and then, almost immediately, raise it for no good reason except to prove we are 'bargaining.'

He wants us to . . . conduct ourselves . . . so that any final settlement appears to be one to which we are not . . . agreeable, but one into which we have been driven unwillingly by brute force. We think all this is out of keeping with the change from bargaining as a 'class struggle' to bargaining as a joint search for what is . . . in the fair and balanced best interests of all concerned.

To be sure, some may [still] associate bargaining with horse trading . . . downright deceit, or . . . pointless haggling.

But the objective of competent and honorable 'collective bargaining' is for employees to get for their individual contribution no less and no more than is fairly coming to them. . . .

Thus, our bargaining [aims at] the most mature approach possible by management and union representatives: to arrive at the facts and then take action . . . in the balanced best interest of all. We don't want any more or any less than what's right for anybody. We are seeking facts and sound conclusions. We don't care where the facts come from, or when. We are not concerned with credit or face-saving. We just want to do right. . . .

. . . we are always freshly amazed when a top union official . . . claim[s] . . . this is a 'take it or leave it' program and that our efforts at 'doing right voluntarily' represent [a] challenge to the whole usefulness and survival of unions. For nothing could be farther from the facts. . . .

. . . Every one of our offers has stated we would be glad to change on learning of any valid reason why we should. . . .

. . . we have wanted to tell the full truth in the beginning as to what our studies indicated was right. We have refused to try to fool our employees into thinking we were trying to get away with less than we thought was fairly coming to them . . . where old or new facts show [that] we ought to improve a previous offer, we are always happy to do so at once, and in no sense [do we] have to be beaten into doing so. . . .

We do our level best to see that no employee ever has a valid reason to strike—and we mean 'valid reason' from *his* standpoint on the basis of all the facts. . . .

But . . . if the strike instrument is available to the one [party] for what he feels is a just cause, the other [party] should also be permitted to stand the strike in order [not to be] forced to do what he believes [is] wrong for the balanced best interest of all those for whom he is responsible.

The real complaint is that the strikes called here by the official in question have been unrewarding. . . .

The "official in question" might well be James B. Carey, international president of the International Union of Electrical Workers, CIO. And the policy here outlined is the company's philosophy, according to which its own role in that drama was played.

Such a policy ignores, as not being part of management's responsibility, the union bargainers' reputations with their constituents. Union negotiators, so confronted, feel that they have two alternatives: to strike—or seem to capitulate to management's first offer.

Since the company has become so decentralized, unions find that simultaneously striking any sizeable number of GE plants is difficult. And, because each of GE's many plants is usually an independent producer of a saleable product, a strike at any one of its 130-odd plants does not disable the company's operations. Long local strikes without gains for the members can make union leaders look "irresponsible" or at best ill-advised.

All of this constitutes an industrial phenomenon with some curious community relations aspects. Strikes, research by Opinion Research Corporation and other organizations has discovered, tend to damage temporarily the community reputations of both company and union. It may be, however, that certain advantages to the winner may compensate somewhat for the temporary loss of good will.

These advantages—whether anticipated or not—are a possible increase in the winner's bargaining power at future labor-management negotiations, and a discouragement of strikes in future years. Some companies may consider these to be meager and chancy recompenses for losses of large sums of money, of good in-plant relationships, and of good community relationships. It becomes a matter to them, perhaps, of making the most of a bad circumstance.

Such a bad circumstance developed about three o'clock in the afternoon of Good Friday, April 3, 1953, when a group of skilled employees walked out of GE's campus-like Electronics Park plant at Syracuse. That same afternoon a picket line carrying signs of the International Union of Electrical Workers, CIO, Local 320, was patrolling the gates. Although a good many second shift people crossed the picket line, most walked out by 8 P.M.; and few of the late shift went to work at all that night.

The business agent of Local 320 explained that the walkout was in protest against management's "moving work to other plants." Both the walkout and the picketing, he said, were "purely spontaneous" and "based on local issues."

Meanwhile, for the month past, national IUE-GE discussions under a contract re-opening clause had been going on, but getting nowhere. IUE's international president, James B. Carey, as early as January that year had announced his bargaining program to the industry—in order to give employers time to study and prepare for negotiations, he said. His program called for:

1. Bringing wages up to the cost of living.

2. Automatic wage increase of at least 2½ to 3 percent per year, based on minimum estimates of the increase in national productivity of the worker (an amount later stated as 16 cents).

3. Revision of an incentive system to assure take-home increase proportionate to production increase.

4. Guaranteed equal pay for equal work for women, with corporation-wide minimum wages of at least $1.25 an hour.

5. Employment security fund to supplement state unemployment compensation—a step in the direction of GAW. This would serve to ease the plight of workers idled temporarily by changeovers from defense production to civilian production.[1]

As part of union forehandedness, a strike vote by Local 320 was taken on February 6.

When national negotiations under the re-opener actually got under way in March, GE offered a percentage increase based on the cost-of-living index which the company said would amount to about three cents an hour. Mr. Carey said he thought the offer "insulting," and that by his computation it meant only a one-fourth-cent increase. GE and IUE negotiators had met again a few days before the Syracuse walkout, but without making progress.

Although IUE persistently referred to the Syracuse GE strike as "local," there was evidence that national pressure on the company was at least contemplated. On the day of the walkout, IUE's secretary-treasurer told a union group in Cincinnati that "I guess the workers in Syracuse are getting an early start," and that "the rest of them [presumably other GE plants] can be struck at any minute." [2]

In that April a number of IUE locals at GE plants were to decide whether or not to strike. Local 320's time for decision came early. Certainly, the union had considered 320's potential both of strength and of example to other locals. It seems, however, that the strike came earlier than Mr. Carey expected, and indeed that he had counseled delay.

The business agent's claim that the company was "moving

work to other plants" referred to the movement of certain defense projects to the Utica plant as part of a long-term plan. Determining the location of production projects, the company answered, certainly classified as a management prerogative; it was said, too, that the movement would not result in decrease of over-all employment at Electronics Park.

The statement by the business agent that the walkout was "based on local issues" derived from the fact that plant management had indeed been negotiating with the union on "local supplements" to the national contract.

Still emphasizing to members that the walkout was strictly local, the union called a mass meeting for Monday, April 6, in the city's largest theater. Newspapers on the day of the meeting carried what was to be the first of a long series of full-page GE ads.

LAST CHANCE TO STOP A STRIKE

The Strike that began at Electronics Park on Good Friday could become a long, tough and costly strike—but it can be stopped.

It can be stopped at the local union meeting tonight.

It can be stopped if enough union members say they do not want a senseless strike. It can be stopped if enough union members say they do not want to lose pay at the rate of nearly half a million dollars a week.

Tonight may be the members' last chance to ask their leaders: "What do I gain or what will I lose by this strike?"

And here are some more questions to ask the union leaders tonight:

If the Good Friday picket lines were caused by the false rumor that we are sending work to other plants, why is the union claiming in other cities that Syracuse employees voted to strike on national issues?

Why are 7000 Syracuse workers threatened with loss of pay today by picket lines set up in *advance* of the union voting tonight?

Are the Syracuse workers again, as they were in 1950,[3] being asked to make a senseless sacrifice—on the orders of the IUE national leaders?

Are these union leaders again making "whipping boys" out of Syracuse workers on pretense of local issues while other IUE members in other GE plants are working and getting paid?

If all local IUE-CIO members turned out tonight or if they were allowed an orderly secret vote in the plant, would there be a strike?

General Electric workers in Syracuse know we can't do more than is right even under the pressure of a strike.

Tonight, if enough union members turn out for the membership meeting—and have *their* say—they have an unusual opportunity: a last chance to call off a senseless strike.

(GE signature and trademark)

To this statement, Clyde Harrison, manager of employee and community relations at Electronics Park, added the following, quoted in the news columns:

We expect our Syracuse operations to be open on Monday and we will have work and pay available for all. The union has said there will be peaceful picketing and we believe this should not be a payless Monday for employees, but if pickets should attempt to deny free entry to the plant, we do not want anyone to take chances with his personal safety, despite the illegality of any such action by pickets. To repeat, we do not want any employee to take a chance with his or her personal safety, if pickets should illegally attempt to deny entry to the plant.

At the union meeting, some 1,700 of the 7,000 membership "roared their approval," as one reporter phrased it, to the suggestion that Friday, April 3, be considered the first day of a strike. Officers of Local 320 again emphasized to members that this was strictly a local strike, and talked about unrecognized grievances, wages below levels paid elsewhere, speedups in some departments, and the "move out" of some tools, fixtures, and dies to other plants.

Following the meeting, Dr. W. R. G. Baker, then vice-president and general manager, announced the company's decision to close the plant because of what he termed illegal mass picketing. IUE estimated the number of its pickets at various gates to be about 1,500.

The second GE ad appeared the following morning:

SOLD DOWN THE RIVER—AGAIN

Last night the leaders of Local 320 IUE-CIO sold 7,000 Syracuse workers down the river again.

Last night members of the local union again were denied a fair and secret vote—and a chance to call off the senseless strike of the Syracuse GE plants.

Last night a small group of union members pushed through an endorsement of the Good Friday Strike that is costing Syracuse workers nearly a half million dollars a week.

Saturday one of the national officers of the IUE said that a nationwide strike could come at any minute, and indicated the Syracuse union "was getting an early start."

In spite of what Syracuse union members have been told by their leaders, this seems to make it clear that "local issues" regarding which the union leaders raised so much dust were only a smoke-screen to hide the real purpose of the strike. It seems clear now that the whole plan was directed from the headquarters of IUE President Carey as it was in the 1950 strike. Again, as in 1950, Syracuse workers are paying the price by losing pay while other IUE workers in other GE plants are working and getting paid.

In all this smoke and dust several things are clear:

GE wages have risen more than 22 percent since Korea while cost of living has risen less than 12 percent.

GE recently offered another wage increase while only yesterday 1,300,000 railroad workers took an actual 3 cent-an-hour cut under cost of living wage agreements.

As for "local issues," we have sincerely tried to reach agreement over many weeks. But it has become increasingly clear that the local union leaders wanted no agreement—they wanted excuses to promote a strike.

We say again, we cannot be forced into any action that is not right—under pressure of a strike no matter how long that strike might last.

We suggest again, as we have many times in the past, if their leaders really feel that local union members favor this strike that they agree to a fair and secret vote in the plant. Let's find out if this strike was planned by Mr. Carey to support his own ends, or truly represents the interests of the workers.

(GE signature and trademark)

These GE ads always are recalled by Syracusans as the most memorable feature of the strike. Some, including management people, consider that such hard hitting tactics were questionable, either philosophically or strategically. Others think they were completely justified, both morally and practically. Union leaders and adherents remember them with extreme bitterness.

Among the ads published during the first two weeks of the strike was one bearing a photograph of a shirtsleeved man rolling dice. The copy read:

WHO'S GAMBLING WITH YOUR PAY CHECK?

The paychecks of 7,000 Syracuse workers
the rent and the grocery money
the vacation and the Christmas funds
the money for clothes and for church
this is the money that is being gambled
Ask yourself
and the other workers who are kept out by picket lines
who's gambling with your pay check?
Do the union leaders, the men like Carey and Callahan and Clancy, who say it will all be over soon
do they know what they are talking about?
Do you know who's gambling with your pay check? And why?

Another featured a facsimile of a newspaper clipping headlined "Government Reports Big Drop in Cost of Living." The ad's message was:

General Electric pay is up—the cost of living is down.
Doesn't this make the Syracuse strike seem senseless?
35,000 IUE members in the automotive industry yesterday took
a one-cent-an-hour pay cut, but not IUE members with GE.
Doesn't this make the Syracuse strike seem senseless?
Lower prices and higher GE pay, including the new wage offer,
boost buying power of GE workers about 8%—11 to 16 cents an
hour higher than last July.
Doesn't this make the Syracuse strike seem senseless?
Local union leaders took Syracuse workers out on strike on
excuse of "local issues" when statements of national IUE bosses
strongly indicate this strike was planned at IUE national headquarters.
Doesn't this make the Syracuse strike seem senseless?
Syracuse workers are losing pay while other IUE members in
other GE plants are working and getting paid.
Doesn't this make the Syracuse strike seem senseless?
*We say "YES!" Again inept leadership on the part of union
bosses Carey, Callahan and Clancy is costing 7,000 Syracuse
workers needless and senseless pay losses.*

Still another ad, with its headline in a type style reminiscent
of early American documents, appeared thus:

"NO PERSON SHALL BE . . . DEPRIVED OF LIFE, LIBERTY, OR PROPERTY, WITHOUT DUE PROCESS OF LAW . . ."

The history of America is the story of a continuing battle to
protect the rights of individuals . . .
. . . a secret ballot is the only real safeguard against those who
would ignore the best interests of the individual.
Our government has insisted on a secret ballot when workers
select a union to represent them. Once a union has been chosen,
its most powerful weapon is a strike.
Few of the remaining problems of labor today justify the all out
industrial warfare of a strike. Union members realize this, and
strike votes seldom represent the wishes of the majority. For this

reason strike votes are held by a minority of the members at late hours in cramped, obscure voting places . . .

The leaders of the union representing Syracuse General Electric workers persistently have denied their membership this fundamental democratic right (of a secret ballot). There is no law which requires these leaders to grant that right. We think there should be such a law to protect the rights of individual workers.

Congress is now considering laws affecting unions. We urge you to write.

> R. Walter Riehlman
> (House of Representatives)
> Irving M. Ives
> (United States Senate)
> Herbert W. Lehman
> (United States Senate)

The information and opinions in these ads were broadcast in five daily radio programs. In addition, letters over the signature of Dr. Baker were occasionally sent to employees' homes. Here is the first such sent a few days after the strike began:

Fellow Employees:

I cannot agree that . . . 'we won't be on strike long.' Instead the union has made it clear that it's time to tighten your belt for what looks like a long and costly strike. Your next paycheck may be the last one for some time, and that could mean long, lean weeks ahead.

You are out on strike on the excuse of 'local issues.' But no matter how much these are blown up, it seems clear that this strike is part of Mr. Carey's national strategy.

Now Mr. Carey will sit tight hoping for the pressure to build up from Syracuse in advance of the next national meeting April 16. This means you can count on being out at least two weeks by April 16, and perhaps for long after that. General Electric has offered all that is justified in a wage increase under present conditions, an increase at a time when other workers in other industries are taking cuts. We can't be forced into doing more than is right, even under pressure of a strike.

The union actions show there is no reason for anyone to hope this strike is just a short spring vacation. That is why we must in fairness inform you that while other IUE members in other GE plant cities are working and getting paid, there may be many pay-less Fridays ahead for Syracuse workers. This could be stopped if you and enough other workers tell the union you are not in favor of this senseless strike.

Publicity was constant, of course, throughout the strike; and both Syracuse daily papers included statements of both sides on all aspects of the strike. The afternoon paper, *The Herald-Journal*, consistently and frequently took the editorial middle position that union and management compromise was neces-sary to settlement. *The Post-Standard*, the morning paper, editorially supported GE throughout. At every opportunity IUE accused *The Post-Standard* of "biased" and "unfair" treatment; letters making this accusation were regularly printed in *The Post-Standard*.

The union's messages were carried largely in the local's paper and in handbills, as well as via personal contacts with strikers. IUE had considerable help from other unions, par-ticularly United Auto Workers and United Steelworkers of America.

The company held one press conference at the Hotel Syra-cuse (where plant management moved its headquarters during the strike) rather early for the purposes of backgrounding reporters who would be covering the strike. The union scheduled a press conference, too, but cancelled it.

To the indignation of the union, GE foremen began to talk with employees, usually by telephone, about the strike. This, IUE said, was a direct violation of the Taft-Hartley Act: the company must bargain with the union and not with individuals.

"No one," the company replied, "is making any adjustment or settlement with individuals. If we had anything more to offer as a basis for settlement, we most certainly would offer it through the appropriate union representative."

Meanwhile, IUE locals at other GE plants one by one voted against striking: Lynn, Bridgeport, Pittsfield, Ft. Wayne, Tell City. GE played the theme in an ad headed "Who's Out of Step?" Then, on April 22, a long-anticipated company-union get-together in New York City failed. The union said the company had refused to bargain. General Electric said it saw no reason to budge, and wouldn't. The company said it saw no reason, either, why employees should not return to work. Mr. Carey took the occasion to insist that local grievances of long standing were the sole issues at Syracuse.

The negative strike votes by other locals had indeed removed any national wage significance from the Syracuse strike. From this point on the strike was in truth—and completely so —a local issue. From this point on, too, GE ads for a time grew sharper in their criticism of union leadership.

The Post-Standard editorialized that strike meetings were attended by only a small fraction of the union members and that "the vote itself reflects an even smaller percentage. . . ."

This newspaper proposes that a strike vote be held, either in the General Electric plant or in some centrally located and convenient place such as the War Memorial, and that the balloting be in secret and supervised either by the Commissioner of Elections of Onondaga County, or under the direction of a Justice of the Supreme Court.

Only by secret balloting of the full union membership can the union justify its own position and can the company know the true feelings of its employees.

No man should ever be denied the right to work until the majority of those affected have spoken.

A few days later The Post-Standard ran a second demand for secret balloting. GE's ads daily took up the cry:

We believe it is long past the time for General Electric employees in Syracuse to face the facts squarely. It is time for them to realize that a strike is easier to start than it is to stop.

It is time for them to realize that a union leadership which denies (members) a secret ballot at a convenient voting place permits a few union leaders to ignore the wishes of the majority . . .

It is time for a change.

You can decide if you are tired of being dominated by a small group of irresponsible union leaders who stage slow-downs and wildcat walkouts that cause unnecessary layoffs and lost pay, who use emotional charges and spread false rumors to maneuver a strike.

. . . write . . . wire . . . phone . . . union leaders to demand a secret vote . . .

Local union leaders denied GE workers a truly secret vote in 1950. The 1950 strike cost GE workers $1,250,000 in pay losses.

Union leaders denied GE workers a truly secret vote on the question of accepting various pay increases offered by the company since 1950. Rejection of these pay offers cost GE workers $210,000.

Local union leaders denied GE workers a truly secret vote on the strike now going into its third week. This strike to date has cost GE workers $945,792.28.

This is a voting machine. [A picture of one was included]

It is more than a machine. It is a symbol of freedom. It is a weapon for defense of human rights.

. . . Voting machines are feared by dictators because voting machines permit everyone to have a truly secret ballot. Some union leaders oppose truly secret ballots.

Later, ballots were mailed to employees with a note from Dr. Baker, asking them to express their preference between continuing the strike and returning to work. The company reported that 6,600 ballots were mailed, that 2,387 were returned, and that only one in ten favored the strike.

Although it scoffed at the validity of the company balloting, the union finally capitulated to this kind of pressure, and announced that it had hired the War Memorial Hall for a secret balloting of the membership on April 30. The union invited Dr. Baker and Mr. Harrison to address the gathering, but they replied that "employees already have enough information to enable them to make a decision." They did, however, make two points before the election:

1. The company had not withheld, before the strike, "any possible concessions in order to have them available as a means of ending a strike."

2. Arrangements had been made by the company to maintain various insurance programs for employees in their absence, and these would be continued.

The meeting turned out to be lively, with much booing of union proponents of both sides. Empty chairs on the platform were labeled reserved for Dr. Baker and Mr. Harrison. Union officers spoke in favor of the strike. After two hours of speeches and voting, ballots were counted by union officers at union headquarters, observed by a committee of five selected from the audience.

The announced result: 1,860 opposed to ending the strike; 1,137 in favor of accepting management's offer. Whatever the announcement, however, management has said that it believed a majority of the 7,000 strikers wanted to return to work, but lacked leadership to unite opposition against the strike.[4]

For the first time in the strike, the union ran an ad in the local press:

WHAT'S WRONG WITH G.E.?

For more than four weeks GE employees in Syracuse have been out on strike.

For more than four weeks GE employees and their families have been bombarded with full-page newspaper ads, with propaganda letters to their homes, with radio programs, with visits by GE foremen to their residences.

GE has spent nearly $125,000 in its attempt to break this strike.

Rather than sit down and negotiate in good faith, GE has squandered $125,000 to defeat unionism.

Finally, GE conducted a "return-to-work" vote, sending ballots with stamped return envelopes to every one of the Syracuse GE workers.

On April 27th, Dr. W. R. G. Baker, Syracuse general manager, announced that 3010 voted against the strike and only 262 in favor.

But on Thursday night at a mass meeting the strikers—voting by secret ballot—voted 1,860 to 1,137 to stay out on strike!

We could ask some pointed questions about the kind of vote GE conducted when the secret ballot showed seven times as many employees favoring the strike as Management's "poll."

But we think it is far more important that the public clearly understand the real meaning of this 1,860 to 1,137 vote to continue the strike.

It means one thing and one thing only . . .

There's something radically wrong with GE management and GE's labor relations in Syracuse.

Workers don't stay out on strike for four weeks over trivial issues. This strike was forced on GE employees as a result of two years accumulation of grievances and injustices. This is a Local strike on Local issues which GE aggravated to the breaking point. The Local Union tried and tried again to negotiate these issues without resorting to strike—but strike was forced on them. And GE, rather than settle these grievances, preferred to spend $125,000 to break our Union.

We ask the public to understand the meaning of our vote to remain on strike. The vote proved that the accumulated resentment of employees against management was so great that it could not be overcome by a $125,000 anti-union propaganda barrage and four payless weeks.

We ask the public to support our strike—which is designed to make Syracuse a better place to work in and live in.

As usually occurs during strikes, the local issues of difference got little exposition in the press. Not until the strike was almost a month old was there any comprehensive statement of the eight issues which now alone were credited with prolonging the strike. Here they are, with management and union comment on each, as they were printed in *The Post-Standard* the morning of the secret balloting:

1. Apprentice training program pertaining to layoffs and ratio of apprentices to journeymen.

Union: That pertains to a better pay progression schedule for apprentices and to the ratio. We want them to get better pay faster. There is one case where they have 32 toolmakers and 30 apprentices. That is too many. We want one apprentice for every 10. That is standard practice throughout the country. The company is exploiting both the employees working with the apprentices and the apprentices themselves. The apprentice boys are in our bargaining unit, but the company refuses to negotiate on the ratio or make changes.

Company: Apprentices are being trained to fill future needs. It is impossible to attempt to maintain any fixed ratio of apprentices to journeymen because of the ever changing conditions which may dictate considerable variation from time to time, both in the number of journeymen and in the number of apprentices.

2. Average earnings for employees when the breakdown of machines occurs.

Union: We want average earnings for piece workers to cover anything not the fault of the employee. In case of a breakdown, engineering change, company-stopped job, or any time the halt is not the employee's fault we feel the employee should have his average earnings. The company feels it should be able to put them on another job if one is available and pay the day rate with no incentive or let them remain on waiting time and pay them the day rate.

Company: A piece worker's extra earnings, over and above his hourly day rate, are based on his production. The union is demanding that a piece worker be virtually guaranteed these extra earnings at all times, even during periods when for some reason his job may be held up and he may be doing no work at all. It is the company practice to pay the employee his regular hourly day rate under such circumstances.

3. Engineer trainees, salaried employees and those not under

the bargaining unit of the union, performing work of employees under the bargaining unit.

Union: This involves a group of apprentice engineers. The company had been insisting that they come into our bargaining unit and displace other employees. We want something in writing to assure us that that would not be done. We are not against such a program. We don't want our people injured by having them. They took our leaders and instructors out and put student engineers in their place. The company has, however, offered to take out the permanent position they had and has agreed to put it in writing [that] it would be only a temporary deal.

Company: The company has agreed to a clause in the local agreement limiting the extent to which supervisors and others not in the bargaining unit may perform duties normally done by employees in the bargaining unit. The union is objecting to wording which would prevent this clause from interfering with the essential and long established practice of temporarily assigning employees on training courses to factory jobs to get factory training and experience.

4. Seniority protection for sectional stewards in cases of layoffs and back-to-work orders.

Union: This is not a strike issue. It's something we want for protection of our people only. It is not only for the protection of the stewards themselves, but to make sure there would be a committeeman in that section in time of transfers to police the contract.

Company: The national contract specifically sets forth the union representative who will be accorded seniority preference. The union is requesting an extension of this preferential treatment beyond the group specified by the contract.

5. Seniority protection for workers with longer service during lack of work periods.

Union: That involves transferring from one foreman to another within the same job classification. Our position is that it should be done as always at Electronics Park until recently, on the basis of seniority. For example, say you have 20 people and lack work for five. We want them to transfer the five in accordance with seniority. The company maintains it should be a lateral deal, that it should put them where it wants and pick who it wants regardless of seniority. That involves payment of average earnings.

Company: The union is insisting that the movement of employees between different jobs which are in the same classification and which carry the same rate be done on the basis of seniority. In many cases this movement of people would work to the disadvantage of the employees as a whole and would seriously interfere with efficient operation.

6. Revision of progression schedule, a clause in the national contract, providing for an extra step in the schedule equal to those of other GE locals, and also providing for an intermediate step in the schedule.

Union: Our national contract covers skilled workers. We have a progressive schedule for people up to $1.55 an hour in the national contract. There are skilled workers with a progressive schedule. In between there are hundreds of people with no progressive schedule. We feel those semi-skilled people should have a three-months progressive pay schedule. The company says it will review them at the end of six months. It won't agree to give any set increase.

Company: The company has offered to include in the local agreement a provision under which the rates of all employees who are not on an automatic progression schedule will be reviewed at least every six months. We firmly believe that on the intermediate and higher skilled jobs which are involved here a general policy calling for a rigid review at intervals of less than six months does not allow sufficient time for employee improvement between increases, and furthermore is not in keeping with the six months pattern established by the national contract for certain other employees.

7. Upgrading of trade's helpers according to seniority and ability.

Union: Following a recent communication from the company this now involves all upgrading. Earlier the company had offered what might be considered a fair upgrading program. They have modified it now and leave it strictly to the foremen. That involves everyone that works at GE.

Company: The national contract provides that "in general the higher rated jobs will be filled by upgrading." We are bound by this clause in the national contract and it applies not only to the upgrading of helpers but to all other employees in the bargaining unit.

8. Walkout clauses in union-management contract.

Union: The company has agreed to withdraw that. It wanted us to notify them 10 days in advance if there was going to be a legal walkout. They also wanted us to agree not to represent anyone that took part in an illegal walkout. That practically covers all hourly workers and affects their pay one way or another.

Company: No statement offered on this point.

The union said that, in addition to these eight points, it was asking for a wage increase of 10 percent at the start. Union officials pointed out that, based on figures supplied by the National Association of Manufacturers and the New York State Department of Labor, the national average GE pay was $1.84 per hour, whereas the average GE pay in Syracuse was $1.56. The average pay for comparable industry in Syracuse, the union said, was $1.83.

To this the company answered: "It is the stated policy of the company to pay what is right in any particular area, all things considered, for the type of work involved. We believe we are doing so, but, as we have told the union repeatedly, whenever it is determined that this is not the case, we are ready and willing to take . . . corrective steps. . . ."

This chronicling of the issues they were striking for may have influenced some members to vote that evening for going back to work. It is difficult to conceive that the eight issues by themselves could have stirred 7,000 people to eight weeks of striking and taking the pay losses daily tabulated in GE's ads. It seems improbable that many strikers could have described more than several of the issues, even following their discussion in the newspapers. The "more money" demands (which got little mention, either, in any very specific terms) probably had more appeal to strikers.[5]

Following the War Memorial meeting, with its revelation

that at least 38 per cent of the strikers (and management's estimate was 75 per cent, based on its own version of the balloting) were willing to return on the basis of the company's offer, the GE ads changed in character. They no longer attacked union leaders or stated management's position with their former typographical intensity. They became, instead, educational in presentation, restrained in tone, and informative in content. This change in tone resulted more from community and, indeed, from in-company pressures than from any event in the strike's progress. Nevertheless, the issues now were given comprehensive exposition, from the company point of view, yet with more than a show of objectivity. These ads were signed by Dr. Baker, not with the GE emblem.

Here are two examples:

A lot of people have been asking me "What are the issues in the GE strike?"

Letters and telephone calls have been flooding in to me. Not only our own people but many others affected by the strike want to know—What's the argument all about? Is headway being made in settling the strike? What are the issues now?

Yesterday on the radio I did my best to explain some of the reasons why the bargaining committee and GE haven't gotten together, as well as the reasons why our management has taken the positions it has. Anyone interested in getting the full story is welcome to a copy of the broadcast. In turn, comments and questions will be appreciated.

Some Progress Made: The 48 areas for discussion originally presented by the union have been narrowed down substantially by very patient examination of all the facts both by the company and the union.

What seems to be left falls in the following groups:

Issues Covered by the National Contract: As I said on the radio, GE has national bargaining with the IUE and local bargaining here in Syracuse with Local 320. Four issues that have been discussed locally are part of the national bargaining. These four— progression schedules; seniority preference for union representatives; upgrading and payment of average piecework earnings for idle time, we have explained to the union, aren't legitimate strike issues in our opinion, and don't really belong in the current discussions to settle the strike.

Three Issues of Plant Procedures are Bargainable Locally: These stack up as follows: [the issues and company statements are here given as above].

Money Issue: In this area, we have to distinguish again between what is bargainable nationally and what is bargainable locally.

In our national bargaining, covering all GE plants, a small increase has been offered. This *increase in pay* has been offered at a time when many thousands of workers in the auto, tractor, textile, rubber industries and on the railroads are taking a *pay cut*.

More than 30 of the unions representing GE employees have accepted this offer and have been getting a pay increase since April 15. IUE has not yet accepted our offer.

In our local bargaining the union has asked for an increase to bring our rates up to those paid by others in this area. The union has said that we pay less than the average. On our side of the bargaining table we pointed out two things. First, that we are confident, even on the basis of overall averages, that our rates are comparable. But second, we emphasized that it isn't just the averages, but also the kind of work people do that counts. For example, a plant with only highly skilled toolmakers would have a high average. A plant such as ours, with over 3,000 simple, light repetitive jobs obviously might be expected to have a lower average. But the fact of the matter is that our overall average compares favorably. Many, and I'm personally inclined to think, most of our GE people will agree that we're very much in line with the companies in this area.

What next? This I wish I could answer. But of one thing I can assure you. We will continue to the very best of our ability, patiently and carefully to examine the facts with the union bargaining committee until eventual agreement is reached.

In discussing the GE training program as one of the strike issues. Dr. Baker said in a subsequent ad:

The union points out that we are assigning test engineers to regular factory jobs. This raises such questions as: why does an engineer with a college degree work in the factory? for how long? —and why?

Let's get some background, first. Electronics—as an industry—is actually in the infant stage. Like all infants, it is growing rapidly. Unless a company in electronics has a viewpoint five—ten or even twenty years ahead of its nose, it's going to be left behind. And what helps GE keep ahead of the procession and thereby has made so many jobs available in Syracuse?

Almost as long as General Electric has been in existence, and we are this year celebrating our 75th anniversary, engineers have been contributing to our success. Out of our world-famous Research Laboratory in Schenectady, out of laboratories throughout the company, come the developments and ideas which are then translated into consumer products.

Every year, General Electric recruits college graduate engineers to enlist them in the never-ending job of developing new products and making old ones better. Right here in Syracuse, we have almost a thousand engineers at work. One engineer for every 11 employees. The union points out that we are taking the young engineering graduates and assigning them to jobs in the factory. The union says, too, that in assigning engineer trainees to the factory we are taking jobs away from hourly-paid workers. But let's look at the facts.

We do assign engineers to the factory. There is no other way that we know of to give our engineers practical experience in our type of work.

In order to temper their new developments with the requirements of modern manufacturing methods, our young engineers must know how the factory operates.

But does this program really deprive hourly workers of jobs? In the first place these engineers are assigned for a short period, usually not more than three months. Second, the company relies on these engineers, after getting practical experience, to come up with new developments that create thousands of new jobs. Over a period of years these engineers make jobs, they don't take them away.

When a GE research scientist announced the development of television in 1927, the efforts of hundreds of engineers, untold hours of work were behind him. With his announcement was born an industry which has given employment to millions of workers.

When we broke ground for the Park, there were a lot of people who thought we were too big for our britches. They said we could never be able to make a go of it.

Today, we have almost twice as many employees at the Park as we had ever planned for. That means twice as many jobs. Furthermore, we've had to build new plants in Auburn and Utica and in Anniston, Ala.

Believe me, we're not trying to be difficult in settling the issue— we are just trying to do what makes sense.

This message was accompanied by a coupon for a copy of Dr. Baker's radio broadcasts explaining the GE strike. The notice on the coupon, reading "It would be appreciated if you would print your name," was in keeping with the tone of the entire ad.

Efforts to compromise union-company differences developed, too, during the second month of the two-month strike. Local 320 and plant management talked a full day early in May, without much progress. Other meetings, before and after, ended similarly.

The Local requested that Mr. Lemuel Boulware, then GE's vice-president and head bargainer at headquarters, "enter the Syracuse picture." This strike concerns local issues, Mr. Boulware is said to have replied, and such issues should be settled locally.

The union next got prominent local people to agree to serve as arbitrators: two professors, an advertising executive, a civic-minded housewife, a rabbi, and the editor of *The Herald-Journal*. Management said it regretted that prominent Syracusans had been thus "embarrassed":

This is a well-worn technique that . . . we must decline. When all possible concessions have been obtained from management through collective bargaining, it is then usual for the union to propose arbitration. The hope of the union leaders is that the arbitrators, who are well-meaning people, will then go ahead and split the difference.

In mid-May James Carroll of the Federal Mediation Service arrived to mediate the eight issues. The union said it was glad to have him, but added that they would not agree to discontinue the strike pending outcome of discussions.

About mid-May, too, GE's ads took still a different tack; and rumors circulated that the company planned reopening the plant soon. Another rumor had it that manufacturing operations involving 4,000 jobs were being moved from Electronics Park to other GE plants.

The first ad in the "new" series, which reverted to signature by the GE emblem instead of Dr. Baker's signature, was a montage of letters from employees deploring the strike. The ad of May 15, illustrated with pictures of simulated checks, was titled "Today Should Be Pay Day."

The strike at the General Electric plants now has run a full six weeks. The loss to the workers and the community has reached the staggering total of over $2,800,000—or over $400 average for every affected worker.

This loss would have stopped today if union leaders had accepted our suggestion, that the workers be permitted to go back to work while Federal mediation discussions were going on.

In refusing to do this the union leaders have assumed further responsibility for continuing this serious loss of nearly $500,000 per week to the 7,000 workers who are being kept from their jobs.

Mediation can take many days—perhaps weeks. It could be a long procedure. Nothing more can be gained by keeping the workers out than by orderly and thorough mediation with the workers back in the plant and on the payroll.

The union leaders can still change their minds—if they are concerned for the welfare of the union members and the others who are being kept from their jobs. A word from them today would enable the company to get the plants ready for work over the weekend and have a large majority of workers back on Monday.

A "newspaper poll" (without precise tabulations) taken by four *Post-Standard* reporters found that 75 percent of the strikers wanted to go back to work, although one-half of this 75 percent thought that the company should not open the plant gates because of the danger of injuries. The poll also reported "considerable criticism of the company over work practices and conditions, particularly the 'pressure' put on the girls, that prevailed before the strike. . . ." [6]

Then, next day, on May 22, GE called back its salaried workers. Dr. Baker's letter to them was carried in the press:

. . . Obviously there comes a point of time when our engineers, administrative, purchasing, sales and other salaried personnel must pick up the loose ends and attempt to hold our operation together in anticipation of the day when the union calls off the strike, or the plants otherwise are back in normal operation.

It is absolutely essential that long-range development and research work continue, and that contact be maintained with suppliers and customers. Unless much advance planning is done and a minimum of essential administrative work is accomplished, there may be no jobs whatsoever six months from now regardless of the end of the strike. . . .

As you know, under the law the employer has an absolute right to continue to operate his plant as effectively as is possible, regardless of the existence of a strike. Furthermore, employees who are asked to report for work have an absolute right to free access to the plant. It is illegal for pickets to interfere in any way with an employee's right to enter or leave the plant at his will. Our county law enforcement officials have assured us they will do everything possible to insure that your legal rights are respected. . . .

The union's answer was that it "wouldn't allow hired thugs to push us around. . . . Our picket lines have been instructed to defend themselves if strike breakers lay hands on them. . . .

We are disappointed that GE has chosen to scuttle the services of the Federal mediators."

On the Sunday before the dreaded Monday reopening, both company and union ads appeared. GE's ad declared:

. . . Each week of the strike has caused irreparable damage to the business which our Syracuse plants had created. It is now time to avert what could have been an economic disaster for all. . . .
Legal Rules of Picketing are Clear and Well Defined: Here they are in brief: (1) Picketing is protected only as an expression of an individual's right of free speech . . . (2) Attempts to persuade other employees to join the strike *cannot* be accompanied by threats or actual interference. (3) Picketing can be illegal without violence or threat of violence. Physically blocking an entrance so that returning workers must push and jostle their way against the pickets to gain entrance is illegal. (4) The number of pickets must be small enough so that size alone does not present intimidation. (5) A striker has no special immunity from our criminal laws. . . .

Headlining its message "This Is Strike Breaking!", an IUE ad said:

General Electric Management has published a shameful proposal to break the seven-week old strike. . . . This is a desperate zero hour attempt by Dr. Baker to break the strike and break our union. . . . It is desperate because: Dr. Baker has failed in previous strike breaking attempts. Dr. Baker has failed in his expensive and phony back-to-work "ballots." Dr. Baker has failed in his 200,000 dollar propaganda campaign of full page ads and five daily radio programs. Dr. Baker has failed in numerous other strike breaking and union busting attempts just as he has failed over the past three years to establish amicable labor relations in his plant. Dr. Baker will fail again Monday morning if he attempts to bring in strike breakers. . . .

Five deputies and nine pickets were injured, and four union officials were arrested that Monday. A woman picket jabbed a deputy with a hatpin. One picket was injured by a car. About 1,500 workers got through the lines.

On Tuesday, some 3,000 entered the plants by showing up at 6 A.M. ahead of the pickets. Cars of later arrivals were roughed up, two deputies were hospitalized. Seven pickets and a "company official" (charged with leaving the scene of an accident) were arrested.

The union offered to give free access to the plant if a union committee were permitted to see that only salaried employees were inside. The company's answer was that the union "had no legal right to prevent anyone from freely entering and leaving the plant as they pleased."

Although violence continued on Wednesday (four deputies and six pickets hurt), more people came to work.

The violence of these few days electrified the city into action, whereas eight weeks of unemployment by 7,000 workers had failed to generate community pressures strong enough to end the strike. The fact is that the two-month strike which idled 11,000 GE employees had not disrupted the Syracuse economy. Shortly before the strike, hourly and salaried workers in Onondaga County totaled 65,100; and weekly earnings had decreased a few cents to $76.40 in mid-February. Several of the larger employers were advertising for both skilled and unskilled help. The strike caused little statistical change in this picture of community prosperity.

Paychecks received during the strike for previous work carried the strikers for a while; and 4,000 salaried workers (of 11,000 total work force) received checks throughout the eight weeks. Some strikers took temporary jobs elsewhere.

Department store sales continued a moderate climb begun well before the strike. They were up 10 percent the week ending May 2, for example. In mid-April, it was reported that not even the stores in areas where most GE employees lived had suffered a drop in sales, although restaurants in these sections reported some loss of business. Banks had few withdrawals of savings, although some people were cashing savings bonds. The city's two largest savings banks showed deposit increases in April of $2,547,060 over the previous month.

Following the violence, however, the pressures from all local industrial, civic and governmental bodies in town proved to be efficient and quick-acting. City leaders recalled that some years earlier a major company had moved its plant from Syracuse following strike violence, and they united in their determination that law enforcement agencies prevent such disastrous violence from occurring again. Before the Governor had a chance to react to the appeals being made to him, IUE President Carey arrived to talk with Dr. Baker. Their conversation is reported to have lasted all day and all evening.

The next day violence on the picket line vanished. The union would hold a vote next Monday, it was announced, on whether the agreement drawn by Mr. Carey and Dr. Baker was acceptable to the membership.

As Mr. Carey left town for the weekend, he thanked everybody: GE, the community, church people, the radio and newspapers for their help in "clarifying issues."

GE's brief report on the session with Mr. Carey was that the agreement they had reached was "a redraft [of the previous offer] incorporating such limited modifications as have been agreed upon."

At the Monday, May 29, meeting, an estimated 90 percent of the 2,500 union members attending approved, by standing vote, of accepting the agreement.

The changes in the agreement from the original offer two months before, it is obvious, were minor ones;

1. Rewording of a clause on upgrading; no change in substance.

2. Recognition of a journeyman machinist as liaison man to the company committee administering the apprentice course.

3. A clause which confirmed in writing the established practices for use of trainees, and the assignment of employees to jobs both in and out of their classifications.

4. Four clauses covering minor procedural items.

5. Addition of another step in the automatic progression schedule which would affect an estimated 50 people out of the bargaining unit of 6,500. The change did not increase "job rates" or "job values" but merely resulted in making it possible for some few employees to progress to the step rate of $1.595 automatically and a little sooner than before.

Strong community pressure to end the strike did not develop until the last few violent days. Arrests and injuries apparently had more effect on public opinion, to the end of terminating the strike, than had an eight-weeks schedule of General Electric advertising.

Nevertheless, GE seems to have calculated its communications about the strike to achieve the purpose of teaching the workers, the hard way, that strikes against GE's decisions "in the balanced best interests of all" can be painful and useless. Further, the company made the point that union leaders who lure employees into such painful futility are to blame for it all.

The stern, albeit just, disciplinarian, though he may be guided by "what is right," may not be regarded as a lovable character. The respect he engenders, one might think, would be as much for his whip-hand as for his righteous unswerving character.

Just what effect did the strike have on GE's long-term community relations? Here let the facts, as gathered by Opinion Research Corporation in 1951 and in late 1955, speak for themselves: [7]

Question (as asked of a community sampling): Which company is the best place (in Syracuse) to work?
Answer: General Electric. (24 percent thought so in 1951, and

27 percent in 1955; next highest ranking company's percentages were 21 percent in 1951 and 20 percent in 1955.)

Question: Which company has the best working conditions:

Answer: General Electric. (32 percent thought so in 1951, and 34 percent in 1955; next highest company, 17 percent in 1951 and 15 percent in 1955.)

Question: Which company pays the best wages?

Answer: General Electric. (22 percent thought so in 1951 and 29 percent in 1955; next highest ranking company's percentages were ten percent in 1951 and 12 percent in 1955.)

Question: Which company has the best employee benefits?

Answer: General Electric. (21 percent thought so in 1951 and 27 percent in 1955; next highest ranking company's percentages were 6 percent in 1951 and 10 percent in 1955.)

Question: Which company do you know most about?

Answer: General Electric. (27 percent in 1951 and 34 percent in 1955; next highest ranking company's percentages were 15 percent in 1951 and 18 percent in 1955.)

Question: Which company does most for the community?

Answer: General Electric. (19 percent thought so in 1951 and 32 percent thought so in 1955; next highest company's percentages were 10 percent in 1951 and 11 percent in 1955.)

In answer to the question: Which company has the most interest in workers? GE also rated high, although not tops.

These public opinions certainly did not grow out of the strike; it is much more likely that they resulted from the company's personnel and community relations programs. The interesting point is that the strike presented no insurmountable handicap to the long-range community relations program; and the inference seems justified that unfavorable opinions about a company's labor trouble are not necessarily transferable to other areas of judgment. To the question: "Which company has the most labor trouble?" the answer was "General Electric" by 52 percent in 1951 and 75 percent in 1955. The closest competitor was given 16 percent in 1951 and 7 percent in 1955.

And how about the union?

These same surveys asked the question: Who do you think is to blame for the trouble—the union, the company, or what? Here are the answers:

	1951	1955
Union to blame	31%	38%
Company to blame	13	16
Both to blame	35	25
Other answers	9	3
No opinion	12	18

If, as some industrial communicators maintain, evaluation of a program makes sense only when stacked against *results*, GE's strike-time communications appear to have paid off. Consider the IUE-GE contract of August 1955: a five-year contract for three percent annual wage increases and improved benefits, but without any supplementary unemployment benefits. It was a contract which the company, as one company representative put it, "could live with."

GE was in a strong bargaining position in 1955; no doubt the 1953 Syracuse strike and its accompanying communications program helped to put it there.

7-
Strikes and
Community Relations

Part Two

The public reacts to strikes to the degree that it is hurt. Public relations programs of the company and union involved, to the extent of their expertness and consistency, can modify this reaction,

When it feels no pain, the public's interest may be inclined, as John Kenneth Galbraith put it, to be "responsive to any relief from the tedium of an excessively peaceful existence. It [the public] has come to look to collective bargaining for some of the belligerence of a prize fight or an election." [8]

The 1953 GE-Syracuse strike was a constant piece for conversation. But only the newspapers and the people who worked for GE in one capacity or another seemed really perturbed by the strike until violence made it a kind of community crisis. The reason was that the local economy did not suffer, although Syracuse had nine work stoppages in 1953, involving 487,000 man-idle days. Nationally, industries were setting production records; and locally Syracuse's diversified commerce and manufacturing were busy enough to keep total savings bank deposits and department store sales growing rather than diminishing.

Public pain and reactions to it vary with circumstances. Size of the striking force relative to the size of the community is one of the factors which determine how much onlooking townspeople will be hurt by a strike. In towns where one company supports a majority of the residents, public pressures to end a strike will be real ones. Strike issues will get more public attention in smaller towns, too; but even so the pressures will be directed toward settlement *per se,* however achieved. A one-company town is likely to sympathize more with strikers than with management, since city officials and local merchants recognize their dependence upon the employees for their living. In highly unionized towns, too, merchants and law enforcement bodies are likely to act in the interests of strikers during the time of trouble.

Another affector of public opinion, at least to a minor degree, is the size of the company, irrespective of the size of any of its plant communities. According to a *Fortune* poll in 1946, people are more inclined to believe government should be called in to intervene in a strike against "big business"; 54.3 percent would support government intervention and 33.6 percent would oppose it in such a case. In the instance of a strike against a small company, 37.3 percent would favor compulsory government intervention, and 51.2 percent would oppose it. The inference seems justified that the public's concern for strikes against big business is greater than its concern for strikes against smaller businesses.[9]

The nature of the industry struck—whether or not it relates to defense production, or to public health or welfare—also affects public opinion about the strike; in most strikes which endanger or strongly inconvenience people, the public will be more sympathetic with the company, less sympathetic with the union, but, as always, primarily interested in getting the strike ended, one way or another.

Neil W. Chamberlain and Jane Metzger Schilling have

devised an "impact rating scale" for strikes, which they say reveals the "real basis" for public opinion. This rating scale takes account of the strike's effect on:

1. Household consumers of the struck product.

2. "Direct" producers, including non-party members and families of all members of the struck unit, commercial users of the struck product, suppliers of the struck unit and its members.

3. "Indirect" producers.

4. Household consumers patronizing indirect producers.[10]

Professor Chamberlain and Mrs. Schilling are talking about national affectors of public opinion rather than community affectors. Their own applications of the formula were to steel, coal and rail strikes. Applied to the 1953 GE-Syracuse strike, only the second group above (direct producers and their families) were seriously affected.

But whether or not a community is sufficiently aroused for various personal reasons, to exert pressures to end a strike, the people in town always have opinions about a strike; and these opinions may favor the company or the union, or, as is often the reaction, neither. A plague on both their houses, is a phrase that comes readily to the community bystander's mind.[11]

A long-term study of public opinion polls containing questions about strikes has convinced Professor Chamberlain that "Of all aspects of the union-management relationship, strikes are the *only* issue which has been designated not only as a major problem of that relationship itself, but as a major *national* problem." [12]

Some local union leaders in Syracuse and elsewhere have admitted they are resigned to the fact that the majority of the public, excluding union people, will lay the lion's share of blame for strikes onto the union.[13] They say they are also resigned to the fact that community newspapers at least editorially will take management's side. Faced with such handicaps, they maintain there is little to be gained in spending the union's money in competition with management's large budget for strike publicity.

In the 1953 GE-Syracuse strike, IUE largely concentrated its communication fire on its membership with printings of its own: handbills and the local's own newspaper. The object of this communication was short-range, while the company communication had strong elements of the long-range—that is, to make a point about GE's negotiations policy. The average striker lost more than $500; GE's communications let him know it. The union's messages had only the immediate end of keeping out the workers until an "acceptable settlement" might be made.

A union's best strike-time communication medium to this end is a spirited picket line; and much of the union's energy goes into maintaining picket morale. Usually other unions in town will join in to add numbers and zest.

Characteristically, strikes begin with high spirits. At first workers think they will be out only a few days, and strike leaders usually tell them so. With the passing of payless paydays, however, restlessness increases. Only after pocketbooks become empty and nerves grow frayed, in most cases, does violence occur. Some management people have said they suspect violence is sometimes engineered by strike leaders to bring about renewed "group unity" feelings which always are engendered by crisis situations. Actually, violence can also unite a community to break a strike.

Strikers' wives are unhappier even than their husbands about cashing bonds that were being saved for Junior's "college education." If wives are not convinced that the strike will pay off in wage increases, so that those bonds can be replaced, they may strongly advise their husbands to go back to work.

The importance of wives during times of strike is recognized by both company and union. Though hard to prove, GE's letters to workers' homes probably had more influence than the daily ads in ending the strike. Through family visits and the union auxiliary, the union did its best to keep the wives on its side.

Unions refer to company representatives who call on the homes of strikers as "missionaries." Companies which have used this device think it effective as "two-way communication." If the caller, who might well be the worker's own supervisor or foreman, talks to the family, and especially to the wife, about maintaining benefit programs during the strike and only incidentally about the futility of the strike, he may be effective. Blatant missionary messages, obviously, would do more harm to the company's position than good.

This matter of management communicating directly with employees both before and during strikes on "controversial issues" is subject to a divergence of opinion. Some management people believe that supervisors generally are confused about the amount of freedom of speech they have under the Taft-Hartley Act. They report instances of supervisors evading workers' questions, like "How do you feel about the strike threat?" or "Frankly, do you think we'd win more than we'd lose by walking out?" There is even a suspicion that such reluctance to speak up sometimes stems from lack of conviction as much as from a plethora of caution.

Top management itself is by no means agreed on when or how much or what kinds of communication are desirable in matters of union-company controversy. Increasingly, they are assigning trusted, able writers to cover negotiations sessions and to circulate their reports, without prolonged clearances, to the whole management force at all levels and plants. These letters get to their readers in some cases in a matter of hours, rather than days.

Fred Rudge, Inc., of New Canaan, Conn., in its continuing study of "Controversial Communications and Their Effect on Employee Relations" interviewed fifty-six companies in 1954 for their viewpoints. The as yet unpublished series of case histories, developed later as a part of the study by Mr. Rudge, makes revealing reading on "when and how much communication with employees (and their families and neighbors) had a measurable effect on the outcome of negotiations."

Here, in an abbreviated form, are the findings of the 1954 Rudge survey:

Ninety-five percent of the companies communicate directly with their employees—or are prepared to—in event of an impasse in negotiations or actual work stoppages. Companies . . . communicating directly with their employees report a high degree of success. . . .

Approximately [one-fifth] . . . have . . . programs designed to influence attitudes and actions of employees and their representatives at the bargaining table. However, about half communicate with employees only through union committees and representatives, [but these] report highly satisfactory relationships with the unions and rely on an accurate portrayal of the company position to the employees. . . . Another third . . . use house organs and supervisory meetings to talk economic facts and "sell" the management viewpoint. . . . Two companies reported complete lack of confidence in local union leadership . . . and communicate directly by word-of-mouth with their employees, purposely bypassing the union. They say [this is] effective because employees are the stabilizing factor at the bargaining table.

Approximately [four-fifths] . . . do not have programs designed specifically to influence employee thinking and actions at the bargaining table. Reports indicate that few companies have studied the potential value of such programs [but several plan] . . . to institute communications programs related directly to the economics . . . involved. About half report "comprehensive employee communications programs" . . . to keep employees informed, [saying] that such programs, while not specifically addressed to negotiations, have good effect on the attitude of the bargaining committee. . . . About one-third of this group carry on no employee communications, beyond those of an operational nature. . . .

Four out of 10 of the companies interviewed have operations that currently are not unionized, and either have just passed through representation elections or are now confronted with them. Sixty percent of this group openly resist unionization efforts by communicating directly with the employees on the subject. Only one . . . reported the union won a representation election in the face of a direct employee communications program. The balance of this group have made no effort to resist unionization. Their sole interest, communicated to the employees . . . was to encourage all employees to vote. Six out of 10 companies do not communicate . . . because they prefer union operation, are in an industry where they have no choice, or for other reasons.

Ninety percent of the companies do not discuss the Taft-Hartley Act with their employees. Philosophies of the 10 percent who did . . . were expressed as follows:

"We pass along any material on the subject we consider worthwhile. Others are propagandizing our employees, why shouldn't we give them ammunition to combat those points of view?"

"As a part of our over-all employee communications program we have employee conference-type meetings . . . (where) we toss the Taft-Hartley Act on the table for discussion. We have had no kickbacks, and . . . we have been complimented by the union on our method of handling the subject."

"We do not distribute literature or discuss the Act academically. But—if a problem arises out of the administration of the Act, we discuss it. The employees and union committee have 'brought' this method of talking about it."

Consider now the publicity aspects of "labor trouble."

Newspapermen with labor beats say that international union officers are more cooperative than management representatives in giving them information during times of negotiation and strike. Management, they say, is inclined to clearing of statements with lawyers and a succession of top executives, with the delayed result a weasel-worded release of little news value. Unions, less hampered by "policy" and less concerned with exactitudes, usually come up with headlines; and during nationally important strikes, the international's public relations man, often a capable professional, is on hand.

The situation is reversed at plant community levels, where local union officers and plant managements are primarily concerned. Plant management very likely has had a long, friendly association with the local press; local unions characteristically stay away from newspaper men, and distrust them. Plant management often includes a professional community relations expert; local unions have no public relations help of their own, and get little assistance from the international.[14]

Newspaper reporters, by and large, want to cover completely both sides of a strike, whatever may be their publisher's editorial position. Many local union people fail to understand this circumstance, and persist in transferring their resentment against a paper's editorials to the reporter covering the strike. Reporters react to this treatment according to their individual devotion to the ideal of objective coverage; but it boils down to the fact that managements at the local level generally have better press relations than local unions do.

In talking about coverage of negotiations and strikes, newsmen refer to public relations men as "press agents." In other contexts they are willing to call them by the more dignified term; but in their coverage of labor strife reporters want to talk directly with the principals of both sides without interference and delay from "press agents." It is the wise public relations man who abets this wish, rather than defeats it. It is the wise "principal" negotiator, too, who agrees to be so available.

The device of giving information (which the reporter could get from other sources) as "off the record" statements is also resented by reporters. They say management is more frequently guilty of this than is labor.[15]

Community relations, including local press relations, traditionally is labor's weakest area of public relations. Internationals have proved themselves expert in working with federal and state legislative bodies, and in achieving friendly coverage by the "labor specialists" from the larger newspapers and magazines. But union community relations, although improving, remains frequently defensive and self-conscious, sometimes inept or non-existent.

Union members, by and large, are not much interested in serving as public relations ambassadors for unionism, and indeed find it more socially acceptable to discuss other subjects with their neighbors. The potential of 17 million union members vocally crusading for labor continues, nonetheless, to intrigue the AFL-CIO executive bodies at Washington.

Labor leaders, too, want community acceptance as well as member acceptance. A. A. Imberman, a Chicago public relations man who surveyed 249 labor leaders, found they had much less social acceptance than management people had; and were classified by fellow townsmen as workers in whichever occupational group they represented—plumbers, electricians, or whatever.[16] This situation, Mr. Imberman believes, results in union leaders' antagonisms toward management in particular and toward the community in general. He says management would find union leaders easier to work with if management would accept them socially. Mr. Imberman may be right, but union leaders known to hobnob socially with business executives would be viewed with suspicion by their members. As a holder of a politically obtained office, he must always talk to his constituents even when he is talking with management, with the press, or with the community at large.

Even before the AFL-CIO merger, union battles for recognition of the part labor plays in community chest and Red Cross drives were being won. The unions' aim here is that contributors to in-plant solicitations be listed as "union members" as well as "employees of company." More union people are sitting on civic and agency boards; and they are learning to serve in such capacities "on their own," without having to consult union leaders about every board decision before they vote or express themselves. Unions are learning belatedly that they will better their community relations if they expect no overt accountability of members serving in community organizations.

Unions perform more community service than they get credit for, due to poor press relations. Sometimes local labor's attempts at community service fail because union people don't understand how the community and its organizations work.[17]

With all this, union people still are not as active in their communities as they might be, or, to be prophetic, as they will be. The AFL-CIO Community Services Committee, with Joseph A. Beirne, president of the Communication Workers, as chairman following the merger, has made this his Committee's platform:

1. The union member is first and foremost a citizen of his community.
2. The union member has a responsibility to his community. He must cooperate with his fellow citizens in making his community a good place in which to live, to work, to raise children. He must be concerned about the availability of adequate health, welfare and recreational services for the whole community.
3. Unions have a responsibility for the health and welfare of their members and their families which extends beyond the place

of employment. This responsibility includes not only the emergencies caused by the strike, unemployment or disaster, but extends to helping the employed member meet his personal or family problem.

4. The community has a responsibility to its citizens. It must be prepared to meet those social needs which individuals or families cannot meet or meet adequately with their own resources.

5. Generally speaking, unions have elected to support and participate in existing community social service agencies rather than to establish direct social services of their own. To the degree that the personnel and facilities of social agencies serve all the people, they serve the men and women of organized labor.

6. Government has the basic responsibility for meeting the broad health and welfare needs of the people.

7. Voluntary or privately-sponsored social agencies and facilities occupy an important position in meeting the social welfare needs of the community. Major responsibilities falling within the scope of voluntary social work are the fields of character formation, child guidance, family counseling and youth activities, as well as in the area of experimentation and pioneering research.

8. It is the responsibility of organized labor to cooperate with other community groups in improving the quantity and quality of social services, while at the same time educating union members about available health and welfare services and how to use them.

9. Assistance in whatever form should be given on the basis of need regardless of the cause of the need and without regard to race, color or national origin.

10. Prevention of social problems is preferred to the best treatment of social ills.[18]

CSC work [said George Meany, president of AFL-CIO] can be characterized as good business for labor because it gets us closer to our neighbors, shows them that the people in the trade union movement are neighbors and citizens like any other group. . . . If the citizens of a democracy do not work together to help those with problems and difficulties, it becomes the job of government to discharge all the duties that the CSC people have taken on their shoulders. . . . It is this approach that I consider the most important—not that it's good business for the trade union movement to do this, but that the trade union member must recognize it is his duty to take care of the people in his community who need help.[19]

Although managements have expressed themselves privately as not enthusiastic about the prospect inherent in the AFL-CIO Community Services Committee, perhaps increased community activity by union people in the long run will not be as unfortunate as they think. A union is an institution with an innate desire for the expansion of its influence; and although unions recognize that their future is bound to the success of the plants they have organized, union leadership also recognizes that it has grown largely because it has opposed management—a tradition it cannot altogether afford to abandon.

Management is concerned that greater union prestige will mean greater union power in plant cities. If, however, unions achieve sufficiently in the area of community services, their craving for expansion may be partially satisfied. With the decrease in numbers of company dragons available for slaying —and whatever the consequences—unions in the future will be more active than they are in community relations.

A few internationals already have accepted the job of educating their locals in the more mundane aspects of community relations, in training them to work in friendly, positive ways with the community press, in organizing speakers bureaus, in persuading members to wear union buttons and to put union decals on their cars and lunchboxes. The Machinists Union's very able public relations man has observed that, "Basically, of course, the job is to obtain publicity for the union in its popular activities and peaceful moments so that we have some reservoir of good will to draw on when we do get bad publicity." Again, he said, "Our slogan in every story about negotiations is: 'We're trying to negotiate a settlement, not a strike.' " [20]

UAW's monthly *Ammunition*, loaded with verbal buckshot for use by local union officers, advocates that local publicity committees be appointed, that local education committees add publicity to their responsibilities, and that members be educated to talk unionism to all the people they know. One of the best press relations booklets to be had from any source is called *Public Relations Manual for Local Unions*, issued by the American Federation of Musicians. The Teamsters Union also has a pamphlet, *Your Community and the Teamster*, on the flyleaf of which former President Dave Beck has inscribed, with perhaps unintended irony, "We do not want it said that our only interest is labor, because that is not true."

Oddly, unions sometimes apply the basic public relations principle—i.e., that communication is effective only when in terms of the groups addressed—more successfully to other publics than they do to members. They have had some success in their relationship programs with clergymen (and have enlisted them even in organizing drives) and with farmers (with union exhibits at state fairs to dramatize the interdependence of the farmer and the wage earner). A booklet called *Public Relations for Texas Labor*, published by the Texas State Federation of Labor, advocates that members talk about unionism in such ways as these:

To the movie theater operator: "If we still had the 70-hour week, nobody would ever have time to go to the show. . . ."
To the automobile dealer: "I can remember, and you can too, when the average working man in our town made $1 a day. Figure out how many cars you would have sold here in Houston in the last twenty years if the average wage was still $1 a day."
To the doctor: "In 1913, when the medical association and my union were both weak, the average income of doctors was about $1400 a year. Your income has gone up because mine has, because I can now afford to provide my family with the medical attention they need. . . ."

And to the community at large: "Your welfare is wrapped up with ours because we're all part of the free enterprise system. The merchant goes hungry and the farmer goes ragged when the union man is out of a job."

The success of union public relations will depend on its ability to reach the new kind of union member and to interpret unionism to him in his perspective and in terms of present-day industrial life.

Some students of organized labor believe that union members are inclined to regard their union in the same kind of way that they regard their insurance company. One pays union dues "just in case"; dues are "an investment." It may or may not be true that members now commonly regard their union with no more sense of personal identification than they feel, say, for Metropolitan Life.

I doubt that the union's decreasing opportunity to protect workers from villainous managements will ever turn the union into a kind of job and pay insurance policy. It may be that a strong union emphasis on security from inflation and from possible supervisory injustices, presented with the calm helpfulness of a life insurance company's "service representative" would be in keeping with the wishes of the "new" security-minded members.

I have heard an official of the UAW international refuse to sing the verse of *Solidarity Forever* that goes:

> It is we who plowed the prairies, built the
>   cities where they trade,
> Dug the mines and built the workshops,
>   endless miles of railroads laid;
> Now we stand outcast and starving 'mid the
>   wonder we have made,
> But the Union makes us strong.

Under their latest contracts, he said, UAW members aren't starving, and it's ridiculous to say so even in a song.

The old union role as the protector of the working man from the villainous, ruthless company becomes impossible when the company is recognized both by its employees and by its community neighbors as an organization with honest interest in its people.[21]

At the local levels particularly—due perhaps to cultural lag —the twin weaknesses of union communication: exaggeration and emotionalism, continue to be most prevalent. Together they weaken union acceptance and believability as more "security consciousness" and higher average levels of education are achieved.

From this point of view, the company management "unfairly" and emotionally attacked, may actually gain by the attack, relatively speaking, provided that the exaggerations are apparent or readily pointed out, and provided that the emotionalism is greater than the circumstances warrant.

Viewed charitably, local union newspapers are the last stronghold of the early American tradition of virulent, personal journalism. According to one estimate, unions in 1954 produced 650 weeklies and semi-weeklies, plus 250 monthlies, with a total circulation of 15 million.[22] With a double handful of exceptions (notably at the international levels where productions are first rate) they are not well written or edited. Most local papers are examples of unpaid amateur talent working at a labor of love.

A 1955 "content analysis" of union papers, including those of the internationals, found overwhelming emphasis put on "political action" and on federal and state legislation.[23] Relatively little space was given to wages, hours, and working conditions, which university-conducted surveys consistently find to be the members' principal interest in their unions.

Unions no doubt will always be able to command some emotional attachment from their members by skilled references to history. Two outstanding examples are the ILGWU film, "With These Hands" and the Machinists' LP recording, "Boomer Jones." No doubt, too, they will be able to command some members' emotional detachment from the company with the playing of such phonograph records as "A Pin for Your Lapel" and "Talking Union." Old timers at the local levels, nevertheless, delude themselves that these emotional attachments and detachments are today stronger than they really are.

There are indications that unions increasingly will use a "new" approach, too, in the organizing of plants. Companies will find, not the bellicose old-time organizer at their gates, but a younger man with a neat hair trim, perhaps wearing glasses. He will be a well-paid, well-schooled salesman. He will be a poised, sincere, likeable talker, and not the haranguer of yesteryear. He will know how to start friendly discussions at the tavern across the street from the factory, and how to talk pleasantly with wives about the high cost of living and the problem of educating children at present wage levels. He will be invited into workers' homes for an evening of beer, or maybe coffee and cake, and some light talk interspersed with serious conversation about the company and the union. He will not be excited, or try to excite anybody. No name calling; just helping families look to their own futures, and to consider what kinds of protection they're going to need from inflation, from unjust supervision, from unmerited dismissal which might occur even after considerable seniority is achieved. "These things can happen . . . new management might take over . . . no point in *not* protecting yourself with a union in the plant. . . ." The organizer will make a comprehensive study of big and little causes of employee unhappiness, and will play them deftly at opportune times.[24]

Certainly for managements, which might prefer not to be organized, meeting this new approach presents problems. Most companies faced with organization are (1) finding out in detail how their employees feel and what they are unhappy about, (2) removing causes for unhappiness, and (3) conducting intensive educational programs via letters, supervisors, house organs and meetings on every advantageous aspect of working for the company as it is.

In the first quarter of 1956, of the 1,152 representation elections held, the unions won only 64 percent. In 1945, the unions were winning 83 percent, and even in 1951 they won 74 percent. This, no doubt, is partly due to the fact that the easily won plants already have been organized, and only the hard-to-win operations remain. I think it is also because the old emotional approach to organizing no longer works as well as it did.

It is sadly true that publicity goes naturally with labor trouble, and not easily with labor-management cooperation. At one Cornell conference for labor news writers, reporters admitted that the cases of good labor-management relations included in the well-known National Planning Association study, *Causes of Industrial Peace*, just would not make many newsworthy stories for the local press.[25]

Reporters' efforts to get stories of "constructive" rather than combative labor-management relations are sometimes thwarted by one side or the other. Union leaders don't want to appear to be too cooperative with management; management people think that "building up one's negotiating opponent just doesn't make sense." [26]

The degree of union-management cooperation in plants

varies all the way from the Scanlon Plan to armed truce. The wartime labor-management committees have largely disappeared, or have limited their concern to matters of plant safety and in-plant solicitations. This, too, has come about with the consent of both parties: management wants the union's nose out of its remaining bag of prerogatives; union leaders think there might be some company confusion between "increased productivity" and "speed-up."

Professor William Foote Whyte, in his study of labor relations at Inland Steel's Chicago plant in 1947, found "symbolic values" being elaborated out of minor points in company-union negotiations; but that such symbolization of the relatively unimportant disappeared as union and management "developed a general understanding of their individual functions and of the way those functions may be fitted together." [27]

Some cities, impatient with waiting for local companies and unions to mature together, have organized committees to reduce conflict. Establishing communication between the community and the local companies and unions, it has been argued, cannot be put off until times of crisis. The Upjohn Institute for Community Research believes:

> There is evidence that . . . communities have a consciousness of unity and realize that by cooperative action they may control their destinies. This realization is evident in the rapid growth of community chests, of councils of community agencies, of community improvement programs, and of other local campaigns. A comparable community pattern for communication and cooperation in industrial relations has not been widely adopted, but there is reason to believe that one is needed.[28]

Toledo's Labor-Management Committee, and other plans based on it, concentrate on the voluntary settlement of local disputes. Toledo's Committee has eighteen members (five management, five labor, eight public) plus twenty-four associate panel members and an executive secretary, all charged to represent the community and not one faction, and to do so with minimal publicity. It has no powers, never arbitrates, never judges "right" or "wrong," takes no position on open vs. closed shop or matters of union organizing. Its sole job is to mediate: to make suggestions which may be approved or disapproved.

The Louisville plan, nearly as famous as Toledo's, operates on the same principles. New York City's "O'Dwyer Plan" operates under city government as the Division of Labor Relations, and will arbitrate as well as mediate; tri-partite committees are named anew for each dispute.

The Industrial Relations Council of Metropolitan Boston makes available both mediation and arbitration services to the unions and companies which are members; and via a "tickler system" it looks into negotiation progress thirty days before the expiration of every contract in the area. Boston's council also emphasizes keeping open the communication lines between labor and management at all times, through informal meetings and discussions, conferences and forums, and a joint labor-management weekly radio program over a local station.[29]

Such plans can succeed only to the degree that local companies and unions use them; and the Toledo and Louisville plans have been successful because they have upward of 90 percent participation. Plans which have failed in other cities have done so largely because managements were skeptical of them on several grounds:

1. They suspect that unions will, as a matter of course, use the plan to increase their gains with a mediated compromise *after* they have bargained as much as they can from the companies.

2. They suspect that the unions would publicize any

management refusal to mediate, and so would use public opinion to force companies into second or mediated compromises of their offers.

3. They suspect that large industry, which relies in good part on national bargaining, would not be so much affected by the local plan; and so would be in better labor-cost positions.

To these objections, the successes of labor-management committees in preventing strikes in Toledo, Louisville and elsewhere make effective rebuttals, at least from the community viewpoint. Citizens at large, it seems clear, are even more interested than unions and managements are in developing peaceful relationships in town.

The authors of the monumental study, *Labor-Management Relations in Illinois City*[30] found that union-company peace in a plant city correlates with favorable public opinions of both company and union. Other studies, as the private surveys by unit companies of the Bell Telephone System, find that strikes temporarily worsen public opinion of both company and union.

The fact that General Electric was well regarded in Syracuse three years after a strike there does not contradict these findings. It does seem to indicate the potency of a professionally conducted community relations program such as GE's.

Unfavorable opinion following a strike may be offset by able, continuous community relations efforts. If Syracuse had suffered more than it did from the 1953 strike, however, adverse reaction to GE might have been stronger and might have lasted longer; and offsetting the reaction might have required more community relations effort and more time.

Here are some further hypotheses, not offered as conclusions but rather as summary thoughts with application to the operation of industrial community relations programs:

Community people may think badly of a company's strike record, and at the same time think well of it in other matters. In Syracuse, GE in 1956 was believed to have the worst strike record in the area, yet the citizens thought rather highly of it as an employer and as a community citizen. Perhaps the community relations professional should seek, not a neutralizing of bad attitudes but rather the outweighting of a bad opinion with the construction of good opinions in different contexts.

A futile strike seems to discourage future striking. Management communications can emphasize this discouragement. IUE probably could not have struck GE-Syracuse if it had tried in 1955. No one can say, of course, how long such a restraining effect will persist; nor, for that matter, can any one say how long the disruptive in-plant tensions that always follow a strike will persist.

Industrial community relations men may find unions in the future operating much as they themselves do, with emphasis on rational, unemotional, people-centered services to workers and community. Because accepting community responsibilities is a sobering, maturing experience, unions of the future may be better respected than they now are in the nation's industrial cities. One incidental result of this circumstance may be further expansion of community relations aspects of managements' public relations programs.

Labor-management committees have reduced industrial conflict in cities where unions and companies have given their cooperation. Whatever reservations some managements hold, such committees usually have come into being following community histories of devastating strife. The public interest cannot long be neglected; sooner or later the public will force its interests upon those who become forgetful of it.

FOOTNOTES

[1] *The New York Times*, Jan. 24, 1953.

[2] *United Press*, April 4 (1953) dateline. In correspondence with the author, a company representative stated that GE was "firmly convinced that the Syracuse strike was planned by the top IUE officials as the first of what was intended to be a series of 'local' walkouts which would culminate in a company-wide strike to exert pressure on national negotiations. The facts show that subsequent to the premature Syracuse walkouts, IUE tried to get strikes over allegedly local issues at a number of other key General Electric locations, but in each case the union failed and the Syracuse local was left standing alone."

[3] In late August, 1950, 9,500 Syracuse workers were among the 40,000 GE employees in eight states who were idled by a strike during an IUE dispute with the company over wages and pensions. A settlement reached Sept. 15 was ratified by all locals involved except Syracuse Local 320 which remained on strike until Sept. 23.

[4] The *Post-Standard* carried a story charging that the turnstile count of persons entering the War Memorial Auditorium was 737 lower than the number of votes the union announced as being cast. This discrepancy, the newspaper alleged, was so close to the 723 margin rejecting the Company's proposal to end the strike as to make suspect the validity of the results. The union's reply was that some members had entered the auditorium by other doors.

[5] During the period, escalator paycuts being taken by United Auto Workers in town were publicized in the local press—a circumstantial "assist" to management's local public relations.

[6] *The Post-Standard*, May 21, 1953.

[7] Replies are not weighted for "size of company." Hence, results are more favorable to GE than they should be—although impressive still.

[8] *Economics and the Art of Controversy* (N.J.: Rutgers University Press, 1955), p. 19.

[9] "The Fortune Survey," *Fortune*, Nov. 1946, pp. 5 ff.

[10] *The Impact of Strikes: Their Social and Economic Costs*, Harper, 1954, pp. 9 ff.

[11] The degree of influence which public opinion has on strikes, and under what circumstances, is argued with academic give and take by: Edgar L. Warren, "The Role of Public Opinion in Relation to the Mediator," *Proceedings, Industrial Relations Research Association, 1952*, Chicago, pp. 34–42; Avery Leiserson, "Public Opinion as a Factor in Labor Disputes," *ibid.*, pp. 26–33; Allen Weisenfeld, "Public Opinion and Strikes," *Labor Law Journal*, July 1953, pp. 451 ff.

[12] *Social Responsibility and Strikes*, Harper, 1953, p. 64 ff. See also, Daniel Bell, "Industrial Conflict and Public Opinion" in *Industrial Conflict*, edited by Arthur Kornhauser et al. (New York: McGraw-Hill, 1954).

[13] The Opinion Research Corporation surveys in Syracuse bear them out.

However, people who held the company and the union together to blame (i.e., put some blame on the company) totaled 41 percent.

14 These newspapermen's reactions were obtained from discussions at the various Cornell conferences for writers of labor news, chaired by the author.

15 "Labor Leaders and Society," *Harvard Business Review*, June 1950, pp. 52 ff.

16 Under direction of Professor Alice H. Cook of the New York State School of Industrial and Labor Relations at Cornell, a two-year experimental education program, financed by a unit of the Fund for Adult Education, worked with union groups in three up-state New York cities to help them learn to work effectively as individuals in community service and civic affairs projects. See her *Labor's Role in Community Affairs*, published by the ILR School in 1955.

17 Serving with the Committee is a Health and Advisory Council made up of the executive heads of the twenty-five leading national health and welfare organizations.

18 *AFL-CIO News*, March 17, 1956.

19 Gordon H. Cole, editor and public relations man for International Association of Machinists, in *Machinists Monthly Journal*, May–June, 1955, Washington, D.C.

20 The author's speculations about future trends of union public relations are from his article of similar title in *Public Relations Journal*, Nov., 1956.

21 Joseph Pagano, management consultant and former editor, New York State Department of Labor, before a Cornell seminar on In-Plant Communications, 1954.

22 This analysis was made by the Employers' Labor Relations Information Committee, New York City, for member companies.

23 John Livingston, named AFL-CIO organizing director after the merger, had a staff of 320 professional organizers in 1956, located in twenty-two organizing districts. In 1956, UAW was reported to be paying men who attended its organizing school $115 a week.

24 Edited by Clinton S. Golden and Virginia O. Parker (New York: Harper & Brothers, 1955).

25 Wayne L. Hodges, "Newspaper Coverage of Labor-Management News," *Industrial and Labor Relations Review*, Oct. 1954.

26 *Patterns for Industrial Peace* (New York: Harper & Brothers, 1951).

27 Quoted in John B. Knox, *The Sociology of Industrial Relations* (New York: Random House, 1955), pp. 332 ff.

28 A similar program is run by the Committee for Industrial Harmony in the Paducah area of Western Kentucky. See L. Reed Tripp, et al., *Labor-Management Relations in the Paducah Area of Western Kentucky* (Bureau of Business Research, University of Kentucky, 1954).

29 Published by the Institute of Labor and Industrial Relations, University of Illinois, 2 v., 1953, 1954.

8-
Plant Sites and
Plant Communities

PART ONE: THE SYRACUSE CASE

CITIES compete for new business as vigorously as rival gasoline service stations at a highway intersection. Just as businesses, in keen competition with one another, strive for maximum service, efficiency and quality of product at minimum costs, so likewise do competing industrial cities strive to do better than their rivals.

No two companies in search of plant or office sites regard the same community factors as equally important. Each has its peculiar emphasis of interest. Yet, to varying degrees, all companies seeking sites will analyze the sociological and even psychological aspects of prospective communities—that is, those factors which permit or limit industry's freedom, productivity, and profitability.

Because these aspects of community attractiveness can be changed (if communities really want them changed), the result of this new emphasis is to heighten inter-city competition for new corporate employers and to make the people of these competing communities increasingly aware of industry's importance to them personally.

Some of this new emphasis just happened; some of it has

been the result of calculated and organized planning. But, un-planned and planned, the result has been to impose the very real virtues, as well as the stresses of free, competitive enter-prise upon our industrial communities as such.

The organized program behind this movement goes by the promotion phrase, "Better Business Climate," sometimes shortened to "BBC" or even "BC." This concept will be dis-cussed at length in Part Two of this chapter, but it is in-troduced here for its pertinence to the Syracuse program to expand its industry.

Industrial attention to "business climate" is considerably older than the phrase itself; likewise it is possible for com-munity relations men to hypnotize themselves with the phrase into believing that the physical and economic aspects of fac-tory sites no longer are very important.

Every company shopping for factory sites knows, as an initial top management decision, the section and perhaps the sub-section of the country where the plant is to be located. It knows, too, the limiting requirements of the industry, e.g., it may need large quantities of fresh water, or low humidity, or proximity to eastern highway networks, or whatever. There are few so-called "foot-loose" companies, although the myth of their plentifulness, as well as programs designed to attract them, persist in many chambers of commerce.

The first "case example" of this chapter to illustrate the selection process pre-dates the popularity of BBC as a phrase; yet the company concerned, Nationwide Insurance, certainly was aware, between 1952 and 1954, of those variable BC fac-tors which affect an installation's profitability.

Some companies prefer to keep their corporate identity a secret during their initial community explorations, particularly if substantial acreage is to be purchased. A few manufacturing firms, as Corning Glass, for example, insist, on grounds of

principle, upon complete forthrightness from the initial visit.
A good many identify themselves only to the staff executive
of the chamber of commerce or industrial council, because the
chamber can open all the needed doors, and will do so if it
knows the enquiring company to be a responsible and important one.

Leonard C. Yaseen of Fantus Factory Locating Service,
widely known as a practitioner in this field, thinks that . . .
"Perhaps the most important single element in the conduct
of a community investigation is the necessity for secrecy. A
slip . . . may cause troublesome labor turnover and allied
problems long before the manufacturer is ready to shift his
operation or establish a branch plant. Rumor can also result
in harmful competitive repercussions." [1]

Nationwide Insurance of Columbus, Ohio (then Farm Bureau Insurance) sought just the right city for its regional office
in upstate New York. Here, within the service area for its 110,-
000 policy-holders and related agents and claims adjusters, the
company identified six possibilities: Syracuse, Rochester, Utica,
Auburn, Canandaigua and Geneva. All were near enough to
the geographical center of the service area to qualify on physical grounds. In the fall of 1952, the company's vice-president
for operations wrote to the chambers of commerce at these
cities, frankly stating the reason for wanting detailed information about their communities.

The Syracuse reply was a twelve-page report, prepared by
Fred Norton, Executive Secretary, and his staff. Along with
the report went a carefully selected collection of maps, photographs, and printed materials on the community.

Over a two-year period of investigation (including a period
of inactivity due to changes in the company's decentralization
schedule) nine different representatives of Nationwide spent
varying times in Syracuse and the rival towns. The final survey

of all six competing cities by a crew of investigators, however, took only two weeks, from May 9 to May 16, 1954.

Nationwide's survey, which was the foundation of its final report, graded all six cities on a numerical scale on sixty-one community items, divided into six major categories. The importance to the company of each item to be investigated was pre-set with a numerical weight, and against this standard the community performance in that specific comparison was judged in each city. This pre-set or standard weight assigned to each item to be investigated represented the *relative importance* of that item to the company's profitable community relations. By adding together the numerical judgments for each city under each of the items of the six categories to be investigated, a final winning city was determined. The winner was Syracuse, with 1,443 points. Rochester was a very close second, with 1,418 points. Utica, Auburn, Canandaigua and Geneva followed in that order.

In the written part of the investigators' report, the strategic location of Syracuse was much stressed. Syracuse was easy to reach from all parts of the operating area which the new office was planned to serve; it was the point of intersection of important highways, including the East-West and forthcoming North-South Thruways; it was serviced by two railroads, three airlines, bus lines, plus the Barge canal and nearby connections with the Great Lakes and the St. Lawrence Seaway.

The diversification of the city's industry, and the economic stability so afforded, were mentioned next. The company also liked the Syracuse pay-as-you-go financial philosophy, and was satisfied with its "adequate" municipal services.

In the matter of schools, the investigators conceded Rochester's superiority.

Building expenses were estimated to be lower in Syracuse than in Rochester, although not as low as in the other cities surveyed. Syracuse's "experienced investors and builders" seemed "able to develop suitable office space quickly and efficiently."

Nationwide found Syracuse people helpful and friendly and making "a far stronger effort toward growth and progress."

They found the Syracuse labor market best in terms of quality and quantity, although not in terms of costs. Only Rochester rates were higher for the office skills needed.

The various items included in the survey, the standard (or "factor group points") assigned to each, plus the Syracuse score on each item are included in Appendix D for their usefulness as methodology to companies in making surveys for sites. A perhaps obvious precaution is that these items are pertinent only to Nationwide Insurance, and, even more specifically, to Nationwide in upstate New York in the year 1954.

Nationwide's Community Relations Department, headed by Edward Wagner, Director, and Will Hellerman, Assistant Director, brought professional knowledge and experience to the conduct of the survey. Under Nationwide's committee type of organization, over-all responsibility for the site location project was held by the Office of Operations and the Plans and Organization Committee, which latter body submitted the completed, fat, loose-leaf report to the Company's Operations Cabinet on June 3, 1954—a little more than two weeks after the investigators had completed their last interview. Following approval of the report by the Company's Operations Cabinet, it was re-submitted to the Executive Vice President's Cabinet Meeting on June 14. Public announcement of Nationwide's selection of Syracuse was made by Howard Hudson, Vice President of Operations, in November 1954.[2]

The site-seeking organization at Nationwide is not typical, for there seems to be no typical organizational structure for this function. Not even all companies with community relations departments or sections use them in their plant community investigations. Some companies use "real estate departments." Many companies rely heavily upon consultants. Some strongly decentralized companies do not utilize their decentralized divisions very much in explorations of various sections of the country; others, more centralized, do. Production men and engineers dominate most company site selection committees, although more frequently personnel and public relations men are being included.[3]

Where does the investigator go to get his unvarnished and un-whitewashed information in the community? The popular concept is that chambers of commerce rather specialize in varnishing and whitewashing; and the printed matter coming from chambers of commerce is, as a rule, professionally enthusiastic. Yet, salesmen though they are, paid executives of chambers of commerce and industrial development councils know that their long-term success depends upon their discretion and honesty. One plant community specialist for a large company said he always begins his investigation at the chamber office, as well as at the offices of all the other business-backed organizations in town, not so much for the information they passed out (which always was better than he'd expected) but rather for an insight into the community leadership and its willingness to cooperate and its ability to plan and execute community projects.

Leonard Yaseen of the Fantus Service is among those who disagree. He insists that "The fewer community pressures to which the investigator is subjected, the more successful the result. . . . Numerous instances can be cited where social pleasantries have taken the place of bedrock economics." "Surface facts," he says, "are easily available. It takes hard work and genuine probing to penetrate beneath the superficial and to determine the true 'climate' of the community." [4]

One of the early surprises of the depth interviewer working on community studies is the complete frankness often to be found in unexpected places. A surgical detachment frequently is encountered in public relations professionals, in the most devoted community-minded executives from local industry, and, sometimes, indeed, in chambers of commerce. Frankness of responses, in large part, depends on the skill of the interviewer.

Some company investigators, while maintaining anonymity, will talk with newspaper editors; some prefer the reporter on the business and labor beat; still others hold that walking into a newspaper office would be both unproductive and dangerous. Some like a sampling of the local clergy, particularly if it's a church-going town. Others always visit the high school principal. Some will talk with union officers at the local council or federation of labor; some would rather talk with the devil himself. Others think that the chief executive officer and/or the public relations man for the local community chest or united fund will provide more information and insight into the town than anyone else. One says that the mayor's executive secretary is a gold mine in most cities. Some believe that bus drivers and cabbies can give you the feeling of a town more accurately than anyone else. Others think that the most revealing worm's eye view of the city can be had from the bar and grill across the road from the largest factory in the area. One investigator reports that he spends all his evenings eavesdropping in the lobbies of local theaters.

Others, notably most of the consultant agencies, scoff at such "journalistic" approaches and adhere strictly to the scientific principles of area sampling.

The investigators for Nationwide Insurance fortunately kept a list of the people they interviewed in Syracuse; they did not, however, record their interviews with policemen, bartenders, barbers, cabbies, clerks, and bus drivers. Their list includes:

The mayor of Syracuse; six officers of Syracuse banks; six owners and managers of important Syracuse retail stores; the chief executives and staffs of the Chamber of Commerce and Manufacturers' Association; three investment house executives; two management consultants; two executives of the Telephone Company; four presidents of manufacturing companies; the executive secretary of Syracuse University; the field representative of the Empire State Chamber of Commerce; the regional manager of the New York State Department of Commerce; the president of a broadcasting company; and one rival insurance company executive.

In the case of Nationwide, the Syracuse Chamber of Commerce served as the official door-opener and introducer to the people on this list.

Of the various organizations interested in recruiting industry in Syracuse, the Chamber is unquestionably the most active. Yet Syracuse is fortunate in that its industry recruitment program is not the work of one man, or even of one organization. Perhaps in more cities than not, a single individual has shouldered this burden, and fellow townsmen willingly let him carry it, to the limitation of the program.

In Syracuse, both the Chamber and the Manufacturers Association have committees assigned this responsibility, and in addition there is a Mayor's Committee called the Industrial Sites Committee, plus an Industrial Planning Committee of the Planning Federation of Onondaga County Municipalities. The latter group completed a study in 1957 of land planning for industry in the county, which concluded that the area now had plenty of land suitable for industrial development, but advised that this suitable land be purchased in order to preserve it for future industrial sites.

Syracuse University, and especially its Maxwell Research Center, directed by Prof. Sidney C. Sufrin, probably has been more active in industrial development than any other university in the East. The University, the Chamber of Commerce, and the Manufacturers Association, operating together as the Economic Research Council of Metropolitan Syracuse, conducted a three-year study under a grant-in-aid to the University from the Committee for Economic Development and the Fund for Adult Education. The study resulted in two publications: *Business Stability and Opportunities for Growth in the Syracuse Area* (1954) and *Why Syracuse?* (1956).

In addition, Niagara Mohawk Power & Light, the New York Central Railroad, and the New York State Department of Commerce regional office all are active and experienced in recruiting new industry. It is remarkable, too, how frequently the Eagan Real Estate Company has been involved in the industrial development of the area. The Syracuse Industrial Park, 1,000 acres north of the city, constructed in 1953, and among the most successful industrial districts in New York State, was conceived largely as a project of the Eagan Company.

The New York State Department of Commerce was the original contact in the Sylvania Electric Products Company's search for a site for its contemplated data processing center, also in 1954. Here the decisive orientation was the communications accessibility, just as with Nationwide Insurance the decisive orientation had been transportation accessibility. To be processed in a Univac machine there, records would be sent to the center from forty-five plants and sixteen laboratories in forty-five states. In the site competition again were Syracuse, Rochester, and Utica, plus Buffalo.

In this case, likewise, the company made no attempt to hide its identity, at least in its exploratory Century Club sessions with men from the Chamber, the Manufacturers Association, the Department of Commerce, and Niagara-Mohawk Light and Power.

Sylvania's initial concern was to be absolutely sure that its installation would be welcomed; and in order to discover this they passed up the advantages of secrecy. Before answering, incidentally, the Chamber consulted General Electric to see if there would be objections for labor market reasons.[5]

Sylvania's choice of Syracuse was based primarily on these grounds: the presence in Syracuse of needed relay facilities of Western Union, available women workers of sufficient quality to take the necessary training, and a positive, cooperative community attitude toward local industry. During construction, the company expressed itself as amazed and pleased to be called upon by a representative of the Transit Company wanting to arrange bus schedules for the convenience of workers, and by a city representative wanting to discuss installation of stop lights near the center.

How enthusiastic *should* townspeople be about new industry? It is sometimes easy to confuse contrived enthusiasm for honest acceptance. After Nestle Chocolate located its headquarters in Colorado Springs, for instance, the company's executive and professional personnel sent there from the East were met at the railroad station by local residents whose job it was to help the new families to get located quickly and pleasantly. However welcome, this very probably was not a spontaneous gesture of generosity from the residents of Colorado Springs.

Probably no company puts more study, money, and professional time into community investigations to discover the *actual* attitudes of people in plant communities and prospective plant communities than does the General Electric Company.

General Electric's community relations specialists try to be as scientific as they can in their plant site selections. There is, they say, no alternative to thorough, objective investigation in a matter that involves the investment of millions in capital funds and that risks an enterprise that will affect the livelihoods of many people. Decisions must be based only on the documented analysis of all cost and competitive factors, and these analyses must end in complete conviction that the site will afford a profitable operation before the risk can be taken.[6]

In General Electric plant community explorations, all of these specialists are brought into the investigations: marketing, purchasing, traffic, engineering, industrial relations, manufacturing, and last but not least, community relations to appraise "the controllable cost factors," the elements which "provide the best business climate." These include:

Good laws and law enforcement
A good tax situation
Progressive community attitudes
Good employee attitudes, and a peaceful labor-management history
Good labor supply
Honest and efficient local and state government
Good schools, including vocational and technical training opportunities
Adequate housing at reasonable prices
Adequate utilities and business services
Adequate community services
A reasonable community wage and salary structure
An attractive social, cultural and recreational atmosphere
Favorable press, radio, and T.V.
Alert, active, constructive business-sponsored organizations and others which help to maintain and improve the business climate

General Electric keeps in mind certain "general guides" when appropriate areas are first being considered:

1. *Size.* In order that the new plant facility be compatible with the size and "balanced best interests of everyone in the com-

munity," GE feels that the employment level should comprise preferably no more than 15% of the total area work force or 6% of the total area population.

2. *Proximity to other GE plants.* In general, GE thinks it desirable that the new plant facility be separated at least fifty miles from any other existing GE facility "in order that it be kept completely separate insofar as the labor market is concerned."

3. *Dispersion.* Certain strategic war products should be manufactured in locations away from primary enemy targets, thus satisfying the criteria established by the National Industrial Dispersion Policy.

4. *Military Bases.* Generally, new plants should not be located in close proximity to large military bases, especially where personnel requirements fluctuate.

Stated very broadly, GE's plant selection steps are the following:

1. Establish the specific physical requirements of the new plant in detail.

2. Choose the general area most appropriate, "involving more than merely satisfying the plant's physical needs for raw materials, markets, transportation, labor, and utilities." The effect on the markets and production of existing facilities must be studied, and determination made of the area to be served. The proposed new plant's profit possibilities must be thoroughly investigated.

3. Screen the communities within the general area chosen, and eliminate those towns which are obviously unsuited to the plant's purposes, and arrive at those worthy of further consideration. A data sheet listing factors for comparison is prepared during this preliminary research. Every conceivable source of information is drawn upon to compare with acceptable "bench-marks."

4. By comparing the communities regarding which basic information has been developed, and by giving proper weight to each of the elements considered most important to the method of operation, including relative business climates, the final choice of a community can be "based upon a wealth of factual data assuring continued successful operation."

5. Select the specific site upon which the new plant is to be

built, subject to engineering tests to determine if construction is feasible, and providing that a reasonable price can be negotiated.

All these steps were taken at the time, after World War II, when General Electric was planning a large-scale installation in the rapidly developing television industry. Meanwhile, both government officials and the Syracuse business and industrial leadership were hard at work to land GE's contemplated Electronics Park plant for Syracuse.

At one point of crisis in the ten-months negotiations, thirty-five of the city's most important men got together on twenty minutes notice. The variety of GE's guests at just one of many early planning luncheons at Schenectady indicate something of breadth of participation in the community's plant recruitment project: The Mayor of Syracuse, Secretary of the Chamber of Commerce, President of the Real Estate Board, the City Engineer, and a prominent GE appliance dealer from Syracuse. Availability of water at the property line was a major problem of negotiation, but was solved by the city's construction of a water main, with the consent of the New York Water Service Corporation and the State Water and Power Commission.

One great attraction of General Electric to Syracuse was its centralized transportation advantage, located on the then-planned Buffalo-New York City Thruway, connecting GE facilities at Schenectady, Auburn, Utica and New York City. One of three Syracuse entrances to the Thruway, built after the plant was constructed, is at Electronics Park.

The presence of Syracuse University's School of Engineering was another strong attraction for the company. Because many women assemblers would be needed, the plant also had to be near a sizable labor market. Perhaps, too, the fact that the then Chairman of GE's Board had spent some of his younger days in this upstate area may have had some relevance.[7]

Syracuse grows while some other Eastern industrial cities decline. Companies entered Syracuse for various attractions. The most consistent appeal has been the city's location as a kind of upstate crossroads "astride a Northwest Passage," as a Commissioner of Commerce once put it. Another principal attraction has been the city's community-wide, intelligently organized interest in recruiting new industry and keeping old industry.

At one period, early in the century, textiles dominated Syracuse. Unlike some other cities, Syracuse was lucky enough to diversify its industry long before the textile companies began their southern migration. Syracuse prosperity, nonetheless, cannot altogether be ascribed to luck. To my knowledge, only one major company has left Syracuse in recent years; and that was Remington Rand which moved to Youngstown, Ohio, early in 1949. Loss of 1,100 jobs and a $1 million-plus payroll had its effect upon the psychology of the city.

The industrial leadership of Syracuse has given more time and spent more money to take the community's pulse than any city I know. In 1955, eight companies jointly sponsored a community-wide survey by Opinion Research Corporation of attitudes toward local industry, a project conceived by GE and organized by the Manufacturers Association. The survey made it apparent that Syracuse is, more than the average city, sympathetic to industry's points of view.

Twenty-six percent of Syracusans thought that the "American free-market business setup" was "very good" and 46 percent that its good features outweigh its bad; whereas comparable percentages from the U.S. public were 14 and 47. Thirty-one percent of Syracuse people held that raising wages raised prices also; whereas 27 percent of the U.S. population thought so. Owners do not get most of machinery's production, 34 percent in Syracuse said; as against 25 percent in U.S. Machines do not mean fewer jobs, 59 percent think in Syracuse; only 43 percent in the U.S. think this way.

As often happens, the survey included some startling paradoxes of public thinking. The survey as a whole nevertheless provided ample evidence that future investigations by site-seeking companies in Syracuse will also discover that the community's attitudinal business climate is well above average.

(Responses to sections of the community survey which do not relate to particular companies are tabulated as Appendix E.)

Then in the spring of 1957, also under the aegis of the Manufacturers Association, a task force of local public relations professionals as members of the Association's "PR Policy Committee" undertook a "business climate" appraisal. This group persuaded 275 business and industrial leaders to appraise the community in 127 aspects. Most of these 275 businessmen considered Syracuse to be "the bright spot" of New York State, the seventeen-page summary report stated; "it has a business climate which we believe is favorable generally to the continuation of dynamic economy, based on manufacturing, in the Syracuse area."

The bulk of the criticisms were directed against the state's business climate rather than the community's. Of twenty-two questions related to New York State aspects of business climate, the survey found seven bad, ten doubtful, and five good. The report added: ". . . the survey shows that not only state laws, but interpretation of the state laws and administration of these laws all added to the high cost of doing business in New York State."

The questionnaire was divided into two sections: (1) Community services and facilities, and (2) Social, cultural and educational institutions. Parking facilities were called "bad"; and under the "doubtful" listing were exhibit facilities, hotel space, airport limousine service, and most especially, hospitals. These criticisms were made more in terms of lack of planning for future needs rather than for present inadequacies. The city also needed more museum and library service, the respondents said, as well as better garbage disposal, arterial highways and traffic control.

This broad concept of business climate is more community-centered than most appraisals have been throughout the country.

"The lack of adequate and forward-looking, long-range planning, financing and action on a metropolitan basis," the report said, "has a marked and serious adverse effect upon the business climate of the community and upon the ability of the area to attract new business, new industry, new jobs, and new residents."

The report's emphasis upon metropolitan planning (as contrasted with city and county planning) is an indication of the future direction to be taken by the non-political leaders of the community:

"Current political boundaries have no relationship to the needs of the growing Greater Syracuse area . . . Problems created by fractionalized government create one of the most serious deterrents to the progress of the community." [8]

Better Business Climate, at least in Syracuse, can include More Intelligent Community Planning.

8-
Plant Sites and
Plant Communities

PART TWO

TRADITIONALLY, the dismal and implacable science of economics has supplied the reasoning behind the more logical determinations of industry's plant site locations. Certainly economics has distributed our industries within broad geographical sections of the United States. There are definable belts of cities in which certain industries—"city-forming industries"—are located; and these cities in turn attract "city-serving industries." Economics of freight rates, raw materials, labor markets, and product markets—the pricing of goods in space—as the economists say it—is forever painting and repainting the nation's industrial map.[9]

In time, advancements in automation, transportation, synthetics, and sources of energy, plus migrations of labor, will repaint our industrial map in still different patterns. Automobile and farm machinery manufacture, meat packing, textiles, rubber and aluminum no longer are anchored solely in the regions they occupied a decade or two ago. In the future as in the past, steel mills will locate as near as possible to their sources of ore and energy; but fuel economies and even new fuels may alter the traditional Great Lakes-Pittsburgh-West

Virginia matrix of the steel industry even more than it has been altered already. Chemicals, too, locate plants near the sources of their bulky, inexpensive raw materials and near the abundance of water they generally need; but the development of petrochemicals and synthetics has shifted some of the chemical industry, and some of the rubber industry as well, to locations that would have been thought unlikely a quarter of a century ago. War and the threat of war have permanently altered the industrial nature of some cities, e.g., aircraft manufacturing begun before World War II started a new era for southern California; but even stable old cities like Philadelphia developed both taste for and skill in war-centered manufacturing.

Labor markets stand still hardly long enough to be categorized. The population center of America moves ever west by southwest, causing industry's markets and hence industry's factories to move with it. Because people at the same time represent both consumer market and labor market, this moving of factories westward is mutually acceptable to both personnel and marketing departments.[10]

Inter-regional shiftings of our industrial geography can cause real unhappiness in the towns and in the state capitals of areas vacated. There is some long-term consolation, however, in the fact that more than one town which lived through such decline has emerged with a much healthier civic psychology and a more diversified industrial pattern than it had to begin with.

Both parts of this chapter, as the reader will perceive, largely concern themselves with those criteria for plant city location which can be affected by community relations programs. As progress and innovations make our industrial geography ever more flexible, these community relations or business climate criteria of plant location will become increasingly influential.

Business climate may be defined as the collective attitudes

of people about business or the conditions that result from these attitudes, which, overtly or covertly, make the community or area attractive or unattractive to companies. Business climate factors in plant city selection are those factors which by and large have stemmed from attitudes of local people and their elected representatives. Indeed, business climate in the broad sense, as understood in Syracuse, for example, includes all plant site selection factors except those which concern distance from raw materials and market centers, available transportation routes, electrical power, and water, and such other physical factors as climate and topography.

Business climate factors are those, hopefully, that can be influenced if community relations activities are aimed at improvement of specific conditions. They represent the company-centered reasons for community relations programs. A community's business climate derives from the historical and present community relationships—good or bad—of all business and industry in town. The Link Audit [11] has found that good and bad public opinions about one company reflect more or less upon all other companies in the audit; the same principle applies at the community level in terms of a common business climate.

Among others, three organizations at this writing are promoting the business climate concept most vigorously: the Chamber of Commerce of the United States, the Employers Labor Relations Information Committee, and the General Electric Company. All stress what they term the two-way, "something-for-something" relationship between communities and their resident companies. In his introduction to the U.S. Chamber's widely circulated booklet on the subject, Harry Bullis, chairman of the Board at General Mills and chairman of the Chamber's Committee on Economic Policy, writes:

". . . What must a community do to attract and keep good employers? What must employers do to merit the support of the community?

"Building a favorable community-employer relationship is clearly a two-way job. The employer must strive constantly not only to provide steady jobs at fair wages, but also to be a responsible citizen in every respect. Community leaders, in turn, must do their part to provide a climate which stimulates continued and expanding profitable operation for deserving employers." [12]

Genealogically, the business climate idea is son and heir to the "economic education" emphasis of the early 1950's, of which General Electric was (and is) also a strong proponent. It is, however, more than economic education wrapped in a new semantic cloak. Its application is in company selection of plant communities; it concerns also companies' determinations to move or not to move their plants from certain communities. As developed by the Chamber of Commerce, "Elric" and General Electric, it involves comprehensive studies of cities on comparative bases. Further, the business climate idea, at least as held by these organizations, includes "a decisive program of corrective action." All three organizations stress that business climate is more than a philosophical concept; that it is "an action program" as well.

But, though the plight of the depressed areas is most dramatic and pressing, it should not blind us to the need for a better climate *throughout the country*. Efforts of business and organization leaders throughout the country to assess and improve the climate in their communities will help meet the needs of our dynamic, expanding economy. Such initiative and action by community leaders will add strength and vigor to our competitive enterprise system.[13]

Business climate, obviously, would provide some competi-

tive motivation for the prodding of industry-hungry state and
community governments.

The business climate concept has matured considerably
since its beginning.

> Business climate [says General Electric consultant Clayton P.
> Fisher, Jr.] is determined by economic, political, and social in-
> fluences in and on the community. Business climate affects the
> profitability and growth of a community's employers because it
> influences their ability to compete successfully with concerns
> located in other cities and states. Good business climate helps
> create and stabilize jobs in the community. A bad business climate
> causes or contributes to economic deterioration.[14]

General Electric is known to have rejected one town as a
plant location because it had too many taverns and too much
juvenile delinquency—although in such matters as taxes, legislation, and labor relations the town scored high. Cities that
are not trying to improve their slum conditions, GE contends,
are not good prospects for plant sites.

One area of community questioning in the General Electric
business climate appraisal concerns the Community's social,
cultural, and educational institutions because GE wants "a
social and cultural atmosphere that will attract and hold good
professional employees, including good and adequate schools,
an enlightened press, radio and TV and an abundance of
healthful recreational opportunities." [15]

General Electric's "Business Climate Plan" has four steps:

> 1. Make a business climate appraisal of the community: a ques-
> tionnaire of 187 questions to be answered by management, divided
> into eight categories—Community progressiveness; Government;
> Labor Relations; People (adequate labor market of educated,
> healthy productive workers); Labor costs; Community services and
> facilities; Social, cultural and educational institutions; and Business
> citizenship (activity of local businessmen in civic and political
> affairs).

2. Determine long and short-range objectives from the appraisal.

3. Program and schedule company and employee activity to achieve the objectives. (Meaning: get started with a business climate type of CR program.)

4. Work cooperatively with other employers and civic leaders who are interested in taking the same approach to business climate improvement.

General Electric plant managers find that making the survey is in itself an educational process with more than academic significance. If business climate factors are important in locating plants from a potential cost standpoint, then these factors are even more important to plants where the company already has invested millions of dollars and many years of effort.

For further emphasis, General Electric's President Ralph J. Cordiner adds:

Let us have no doubt about our right or our responsibility, as businessmen, to improve the climate in which our companies operate. Through specific action, company-by-company, we can exert a constructive influence on all the outside conditions that affect the cost and ease of operating a business in the community. If we are successful in this, we will simultaneously increase the usefulness of the companies we manage, and improve the ability of the community to attract and hold desirable employers.

There is a whole new field to be explored in this matter of discovering and organizing the political resources of business. Perhaps in the past the manager has not felt that this was a part of his assignment. It is now.[16]

The Employers Labor Relations Information Committee, an employers' group with headquarters in New York City, calls its appraisal a "Community Inventory." [17]

... It is an outline calling for basic facts about employees, government, community's opinion-molders and management practices— the assets and liabilities shared by most of the businesses in your community.

Putting these fundamental facts on paper will help reduce

generalizations to concrete, specific factors. Opinions may be expressed with a shrug, but it takes accurate words and figures to describe facts that cannot be contradicted.

The headings and subheadings of Elric's "Inventory" [18] indicate its comprehensiveness:

> I. OUR EMPLOYERS
>   A. Our Labor Supply
>   B. Our Unions
>   C. Our Strikes and Work Stoppages
>
> II. OUR GOVERNMENT
>   A. Our Schools
>   B. Our Community Planning
>   C. Our Taxes
>   D. Our Laws
>   E. Law Enforcement
>   F. Our Voters
>
> III. OUR COMMUNITY'S OPINION-MOLDERS
>   A. Our Mass Communication Media
>   B. Our Unions as Opinion-Molders
>   C. Our Community's Morale-Builders
>   D. Our Business-Sponsored Organizations
>
> IV. OUR PRACTICES: The Potent Factor
>   A. Our Employee Relations
>   B. Our Civic Participation
>   C. Our Political Participation
>   D. Our Community Relations

It should be borne in mind that these are not surveys, but only appraisals, or, as Elric puts it, inventories or *guides* to management's evaluation, planning and remedial action programs in community relations. The appraisal tallies the community's score in terms of actual conditions. The community survey—with interviews of an adequate sampling of the population—alone can take attitudinal aspects of business climate evaluation out of the realm of speculation. After local managements have had the inspirational stimulation of making a business climate appraisal or inventory, a community survey is then needed to supply the accurate and realistic bases upon which to build community relations action programs. Nevertheless, the collecting of information and comparative statistics in such fields as taxation, man-days of lost time from strikes, social service expenditures per citizen, etc., represent the *overt* aspects of business climate. As such, they have not only educational potency for managements which need educating but also real significance in setting the sites of an action program.

The local public opinions and attitudes to be discovered via a real community opinion survey represent the *covert* aspects. The two approaches are complementary, as recognized by those companies which participate both in community surveys and business climate appraisals in plant cities—as they have at several larger installations, including Syracuse.

Some colleges and universities regularly study the communities in their areas, often in cooperation with citizen groups or local governmental bodies. The Metropolitan St. Louis survey made by St. Louis and Washington University in 1954, for example, found the city growing more slowly than its competitors, and presented some reasons why this was so. A comprehensive picture of Utica, N.Y., which went much deeper into social aspects of business climate than most companies as yet think necessary, resulted from a 1957 survey by public relations students at Utica College, taught by Professor Ray Simon.

The New York State Citizens Council has developed a "self-survey" technique for studying communities, a series of "citizen committee workshops" to take on the study of specific problem areas. A number of New York towns have been so studied, among those most thoroughly investigated being Auburn and Gloversville. These studies have the strengths and weaknesses characteristic of most grass-roots citizen groups themselves: Deep-rooted participation, plus "recommendations" which all too seldom result in successful action programs.[19] They do, nonetheless, supply some valuable information to companies interested in New York state communities. But since the studies emphasize *problems* of cities, their content by and large lacks very much treatment of the communities' good points.

Industrial interest in social aspects of business climate has grown markedly in recent years, and the importance of social aspects of community relations will be recognized by industry even more in the future. City planning bodies need to mature, also, and to recognize that maintenance of local employment is part of their responsibility. Studies of Planning Commissions are useful supplemental documents—one of the classics being the Berkeley, California, Master Plan, the result of four years of intensive study.

How good need a city be? Standards vary; and standards rise, too, rather quickly. The "good" city of twenty years ago might be thought behind the times today. E. L. Thorndike once devised a "goodness index" against which he rated cities of over 30,000 population (referred to as the "G Number").

His thirty-five categories included park acreage, teachers' pay, syphilis rate, etc. Pasadena, California, with a G number of 62, had top score—and Syracuse, incidentally, was well above the average with 44. California cities, Chicago suburban towns and New England cities generally were in the higher levels; southern cities were lowest. Thorndike's ratings, it should be kept in mind, were of the 1930's.[20]

Yet Pasadena obviously is not the ideal city for the location of all new industry—nor, equally obviously, is the South the worst possible place.

The organizations most enthusiastically behind the business climate approach to community relations are the first to caution against taking all information got from the community business climate inventory or appraisal at face value. Community services of all kinds are paid for by taxes—and one can't hold both extensive community services and low tax rates to be "good" without some contradictions. Perhaps, too, they point out, a record of no days' work lost because of strikes may indicate only complete domination of local companies by local unions.

The need for thoughtful caution is great, too, when comparing business climate analyses of states. At General Electric headquarters in New York, one of the most used reference volumes is a collection of statistics from federal and state sources on various factors relating to business climate. But the community relations service men who have compiled them emphasize that careful judgment must be applied in using the statistics. The statistics do not necessarily represent a complete picture of a state's business climate. Differences that show up among the states on some counts are not significant. Moreover, local communities within a state can vary widely in relation to certain averages. Some sixty measurable items are studied and compared to provide a statistical business profile for each state. Examples of these items for interstate comparison include: administration of unemployment compensation, workmen's compensation, taxes, labor laws, educational standards, etc.

One result of business' growing interest in the business climate concept is to pit city against city and state against state in competition for new industry, and in competition for industry now located in town but which might be lured away. Proponents of business climate see in it a dramatic educational device of influence upon the attitudes of state governments, state and local officials, and on the people who elect them.

Michigan was subjected to such education in 1956 and 1957.

In 1956, the Michigan Manufacturers Association surveyed its membership for the state's business climate—and got back 300 completed appraisal questionnaires. The printed report of the survey said that "a rather high proportion (of returns) indicated that they (the companies) were planning, considering, or contemplating, transferring operations outside of the State." (Exhibit I, in "Report to Members," dated Aug. 15, 1956). The stated reasons, relatively high taxes[21] and labor costs.

A University of Michigan study in the spring of 1957 acknowledged that industrial taxes were unusually high; but reported that it did not fear present industry would leave the state. But Harlow H. Curtice, then head of General Motors, held that his company was being forced to locate new plants in other states. The Detroit Free Press devoted much of its edition of Sunday, April 28, 1957, to making points like: Chrysler located six plants and Ford located ten plants in Ohio and Indiana since World War II's end. By 1957 more automobiles were being manufactured outside of Michigan than were being made in it.

A good many auto workers—particularly unskilled workers—were out of work in their preferred (because better paying) industry. Meanwhile, Governor Williams, with the support of organized labor, presented figures to prove that Michigan was not losing industry, but if anything was gaining, particularly in the chemical industry.

"As bold an attempt to dictate government from the offices of corporation management as the country has ever seen," said Governor Williams about the Michigan Manufacturers Association survey.

Fantus Factory Locating Service of New York, in testimony before the New York State Joint Legislative Committee on the State's Economy (with a mandate to determine what New

York State should do to retain and attract industry) described some difficulties in gathering comparative information on state taxes: "New York has a franchise tax based on income. Pennsylvania has an income tax which is really a franchise tax—and a franchise tax as well." Further, as stated in *Business Week*,[22] "the problem with most previous studies below the federal level has been that they don't cover all these factors. Some compare only state income and franchise taxes. Others take on local taxes, too. But most ignore workmen's and unemployment compensation taxes. So, to compare the forty-eight states and communities within them by any table is precarious, at least . . . Because states differ in how they divide services and funds with cities, New Jersey can have the lowest per capita collection of state taxes, but be second only to New York in local taxes. Conversely, Louisiana is near the top in state collection, but near the bottom in local per capita revenue. And by adding per capita state and local figures, California comes out on top, with New York in second place.

"Per capita figures, of course, aren't the whole answer to a manufacturer's question. He is even more concerned—aside from quality of governmental services—with whether taxes are slapped disproportionately on business or whether they are more broadly based."

Again, Leonard C. Yaseen of the Fantus Service says on the subject of taxes: "Perhaps, most important in any discussion of state taxes is the net debt now being incurred by many states, which eventually cannot help but be detrimental to its industry and other business interests. At the close of fiscal 1951, the total state debt rose to an unprecedented high of $7,824,000,000.

"Since the net debt of a state is at least a partial indication of future revenue needs, the finances of a state should be investigated prior to plant location." [23]

As did the Michigan Association, the California Manufacturers Association conducted a business climate survey of its membership in 1957, and gave every state legislator a copy of the results. The key to the report was that 37.9% said that capital investments by their companies had been lost to California because of high cost of doing business there. As a result, the California legislature passed a resolution setting forth factors inherent in business climate and asking that all bills be examined in the light of the state's industrial future.

A similar resolution was passed by another body, the Conference of Mayors and Municipal Officials of New York State, meeting in Syracuse in the spring of 1957: "Therefore, be it resolved that this 48th Annual Conference of Mayors and Municipal Officials, meeting in Syracuse, New York, on June 16–19, go on record in favor of the establishment and the maintenance of a good business climate in the State of New York . . ."

Business climate campaigns against high state and local taxes, it seems, will be perennial. State taxes change drastically from election to election.

Campaigns for the tax-reduction have been notably more successful at city levels than at state levels. Esso Standard Oil Co. in Bayonne, N.J., and Otis Elevator in Yonkers, N.Y., both forced city budget and tax reductions by threatening to move out. Esso's Bayonne taxes rose $1 million, to $2,786,000, between 1947 and 1956; and the city wished to raise the tax rate an additional $6 to $12 in 1957, in order to compensate for the tax loss caused by the move-out of Tidewater Oil in 1954. Tidewater, incidentally, had moved because of high local taxes.

Esso's achievement was no overnight operation, but, rather, preparations for it began in the early 1950's with the Economic Research Association, a carefully selected citizens' group. A "committee of ten" met weekly; its budget was $25,000 a year. As "Project A," it hired municipal consultants to survey the town and list its problems. The committee also hired a full-time researcher and secretary for fact-finding. His results, given broadside to the community, had a good press. Projects were begun next in four areas:

1. A sub-committee was named to visit and report on *schools*—planning a ten-year program of school maintenance.
2. *Public safety program*, in cooperation with the police chief was begun—with information of latest police methods given wide publicity.
3. *Vocational education program* was developed.
4. *Housing and planning*—to tackle problems of sub-standard areas—was undertaken.

Finally, thirty projects were in prospect. The committee worked closely with the Chamber of Commerce, and Esso's plant manager was active on both.

Meanwhile, the executive committee met weekly. All this kept the businessmen informed, involved, and prevented them from getting frightened of political dangers. They stressed constantly that they wanted the community to achieve wiser spending of tax money before becoming concerned with getting new industry into town.

Esso felt all this was good for the company and good public relations. In both conception and execution of the plan in all of its parts, Esso management was definitely the leader. When the time came to be decisive, the city was both educated and organized to accept reduction in tax spending.

General Electric, as a large employer in Massachusetts (40,-000 in 1957, with an annual payroll of $197 million, largely at its Lynn River and Pittsfield plants) protested increases in Massachusetts taxes and the state's indebtedness. The Lynn Chamber of Commerce and "Elric" jointly ran a business climate appraisal, with five major committees and numerous subcommittees operating under an eleven-man steering committee; the result was that more than 100 community leaders educated themselves anew on city and state shortcomings— and organized corrective programs.[24]

Much of Massachusetts has seen better industrial days; and, quite naturally, is loath to trim its living standards to meet its present income. Migration of most of New England's textile industry to the South, however, cannot wholly be blamed on the North's "bad" business climate—nor on the South's "good" business climate. Certainly, the South's poor schools, poor roads, poor housing and the drab, unprogressive nature of a number of southern communities, can hardly qualify as elements of good business climate. The fact is, textiles historically have been "labor oriented," or, better put, "cheap labor oriented." After wages rise in the South, textiles eventually will move even farther south—perhaps into Latin America.

The National Planning Association's study of *Why Industry Moves South*, discovered that, among eighty-eight plants newly located in the South, 45 percent said *good markets* were primary reasons for their choice; 30 percent said *available materials* were the primary reason; and 25 percent said *labor supply per se* (not necessarily cheap labor, but low labor costs) was the determining factor. These labor-oriented companies were generally of small size; less than one-third represented investments of over $1 million. By comparison, two-thirds of those oriented to markets and materials represented investments of more than $1 million and some over $10 million.[25]

As for labor factors, manpower supply and sympathetic attitudes are more important than cheap labor, the NPA report says. Some industries were induced to expand to the South to relieve the risk of strike shutdowns. The South's low labor turnover and lack of competition for workers were attractive, as was assurance of a continued labor supply.

The NPA reported that new companies customarily pay only slightly more than prevailing wages, thus avoiding local business antagonisms while recruiting workers. Once established, most are then willing to pay more.

Companies expecting their southern plants to be unionized prefer towns with good labor-management relations. A few apparel and textile plants try to avoid union towns.

All companies surveyed by the NPA said worker productivity is at least as good in the South as in the North. Perhaps the key to the difference between northern and southern workers is the willingness of southern workers to accept time-study methods of rate-setting without bitterness.

The AFL has criticized the South for employing such devices as roving teams of public officials to pressure northern industrialists and offering of financial subsidies to new firms, including tax exemptions and informal token assessments, free municipal services and outright grants of property holdings and equipment. The AFL charges that such subsidization may lead to further concessions, and gives the new firm an unfair advantage over old companies in the community, and that it tends to attract small, poorly-financed firms, and drains communities' financial resources needed for schools and roads.[26]

Even the casual reader of business magazines is aware, however, that some northern states have their own business development corporations to assist in the long-term financing of new enterprises; a few of them offer concessions of the same kind.

Too, it should be added here that—although some southern towns did use the lures described by the AFL (and already have come to regret it in some instances)—there is no denying the appeal of certain areas of the South for a number of industries. The Mississippi River between Baton Rouge and New Orleans holds physical and economic attraction for the chemical industry, among others. Further, the entire Ohio River Valley contains the irresistible lures to heavy industry of water, coal, salt, climate, space, and cheap transportation. Managements agree that southern green labor—ex-farmers, for example—adjust quickly to industry and outproduce more sophisticated northern workers. Textile firms which have moved South have, indeed, enjoyed better labor attitudes and have benefited from lower absenteeism, decreased turnover, and from absence of restrictive state laws.

Racial tensions that sometimes accompanied attempts at integration on inter-state carriers and in public schools have slowed the industrial growth of the South somewhat. A few companies put off their searches for southern sites. But because of the well-known CIO and AFL campaigns against discrimination, union organizing has been hard hit, a compensating circumstance to the managements of companies with cheap labor orientation.

At this writing, skilled labor costs in the largest cities of the South offer few bargains to the comparison shopper among industrial employers. Smaller towns increasingly are being selected as preferable sites in the South, and indeed throughout the country. In part this represents the companies' disinclination to become involved in the big city problems described in Chapter III. In part, the phenomenon represents recognition that unions generally are weaker in small towns than in cities, and that wage rates are lower.

A Princeton University study of *The Influence of Plant Size in Industrial Relations* in the Trenton area found that a higher proportion of plants in the suburbs or rural sections were union organized than in the city of Trenton. The study also found that where the incidence of union organization was high, all of the organized plants were small (under 500 employees). When small plants were organized, the union leadership was apt to be more conservative and less militant; and strikes were less prevalent in small plants.[27]

All human institutions, including cities, have an innate impulse to grow. Chambers of commerce across the land have assumed that bigger communities mean better communities. Local industrial development programs, egged on by Better Business Climate programs, encourage city growth, and so foster a multiplication of social tensions and community problems. And then, sardonically, industry chooses for its own reasons to move future plants into small towns just because they are small.

The important conclusion to be drawn from such philosophizing is that industrial development cannot be isolated from planning on a metropolitan area basis, as Dade County in Florida, Onondaga County in New York, and a few others, are slowly coming to realize.

Community planning means also the exercise of some discrimination on the recruiting of new factories. Just as companies have their Business Climate standards for judging communities, so should communities have standards by which to judge companies. A few basic questions to ask might be:

1. Is this company community-minded in its branch plant towns (not always the case for firms even with outstanding community relations programs in their HQ cities) and community-minded in terms of deeds and money as well as in words and publicity?

2. Will this company fit the community's standards and practical necessities in terms of wage rates, employee relations, and union relations?

3. Will this company supplement the employment oppor-

tunities of present companies, in terms of both (a) kinds of jobs, and (b) timing of its highs and lows in local hiring?

Industrial managements in many cities are not notably active in community programs in recruiting more local factories. But despite some examples to the contrary, industrialists no longer fight admission of new industry as inflationary influences upon labor costs. Nonetheless, the businessmen—bankers, realtors, merchants—most frequently are the hardest workers to bring in new industrial employers.[28]

Regularization of employment in the community is the most important end to be achieved by an industrial development plan, and an end important not only to local businessmen, dependent upon the spending of local payrolls, but also to industrial men concerned with reduced turnover, unemployment tax payments, and overtime payments, and with improved employee relations and community relations.

The town where too many people are dependent upon government contracts, and hence upon political whim, had better be looking for stabilizing companies that manufacture items used in products for sale. In Syracuse, the Manufacturers Association has to some extent capitalized on the area's diversification by serving as the center of information regarding coming layoffs and new contracts, so that some to-be-laid-off employees, if they like, can avoid the intermediary services of the State Employment Service.[29]

One can recognize and appreciate the community benefits of industrial diversification in Syracuse and other cities, and at the same time be realistic in recognizing its limitations. Gladys Palmer in her *Philadelphia Workers in a Changing Economy* [30] points out that the considerable industrial diversification of Philadelphia had not protected that city from the nation's various depressions and recessions, and she wonders whether or not the virtues of diversification have not been overstressed.

Unhappily, also, economic regional specialization is logical. Companies that use steel are those which followed U.S. Steel's Fairless Works into Bucks County, Pa. Chemical plants that use the products and by-products of other chemical plants locate in the neighborhood with them. Among industries, like seems to attract like; an airplane factory attracts a pool of specialized professional talent which in turn attracts other airplane factories. Diversification sometimes becomes academic, to be sure; nevertheless when possible it is a worthy community ideal.

Somewhat in contradiction to company preference for the small town is company reluctance to dominate a community. General Electric executives have said that they "don't want another Schenectady," and that GE plants of the future, hopefully, will be limited in size to 15 percent of the area's labor market. Some newer installations in the South, however, have little alternative to dominance in their small communities: Kaiser Aluminum at Ravenswood, W.Va., Lockheed Aircraft at Marietta, Ga., etc., not to mention the extreme case of A.E.C. at Oak Ridge, Tenn.

The non-diversified "company town," meaning specifically company-owned housing and company-owned retail stores, is now a rarity. Where they exist, in Latin America and a few in the United States, the companies which own them find difficulty in getting rid of them. People like to have their employer as landlord; the rents are low, and they suspect that their roles of tenant and employee may be mutually protective. Not until 1957 did Kennecott Copper rid itself of ownership of its last 2,000 homes in Utah, Nevada, Arizona and New Mexico, by selling them to the John W. Galbreath Company.[31]

Justly apportioning the credit for recruiting a new factory to a community is difficult to do; most agencies concerned have no modesty at all in claiming the hero's role. More than 2,000 formalized industrial development organizations exist, most of them allied to local chambers of commerce, a relatively few of them tax-supported. All major railroads and utility companies and some banks have advertising programs and specialized personnel devoted to recruiting industry to their operating areas.

Although no company or company executive, to my knowledge, has ever admitted locating a plant as a direct result of any advertising or direct mail sales program, the existence (and indeed the spirit and efficiency) of a local industrial development organization is highly important to companies. Its methodology communicates more about the community and its leadership than does the content of its formal communications. The obvious lesson here for the community is: don't begin an industrial recruitment program until ready to do so successfully, with thorough planning and with cooperation and work assured from everybody. A failure will damage a city more than the absence of a program.

Some of the soundest advice to communities to be had anywhere is in a six-page mimeographed manuscript called *Some Observations on the Establishment of Industrial Development Commissions*, produced by the Massachusetts Department of Commerce.[32]

Some points it makes:

1. Let the Industrial Development Commission (or Council or Corporation appropriate Chamber of Commerce Committee or whatever it may be called) concern itself with all economic resources in the community, and especially not forget industry already located in town. Never put old companies at a disadvantage in efforts to attract new companies.

2. The Commission must remember that it is a service organization, not a regulatory body. It should consider itself as a kind of board of directors working in the interest of community progress, and that the citizens are the shareholders of the community.

3. The Commission will be more effective if entirely autonomous, with no dependence whatever on city government, planning board, or any political body. (Its membership may, however, include people knowledgeable and active in city planning and in city and county government).

4. Employ a paid professional executive, and provide a reasonable budget, including an adequate travel and expense account. Confidences between this professional executive and his industrial contacts must be respected.

5. Base the promotional program on sound research and planning—in which the community's liabilities as well as its assets are taken into account and presented honestly to the prospects. (Working cooperatively with planning bodies jealous of prerogatives and jurisdictions is, in many cities, the most difficult part of the whole program.)

6. Keep the community constantly informed—and constantly sold on the work of the organization, yet without premature breaking of information to the press.

7. Present the collected background on the community in factual, well-organized, thoroughly indexed fashion, with all relevant statistics included. Maps, tables, and charts are more effective in influencing companies than are flowery phrases.

Either as part of this over-all developmental organization, or as a separate "development credit corporation" or "development foundation," the community must have some unit to supplement financing in order to meet the existing competition. Some such bodies are profit-making, more are non-profit; some providing that profits shall go to a local charity or community chest.

The great virtue of an Industrial Development Corporation, too, is that it *is* organized; it has money, information, sites and buildings ready for prospects. "It's prepared to do business,"

as John Rentz of the U.S. Department of Commerce's Office
of Area Development puts it; "it's in a position to close a
deal." [33]

The majority of such community corporations and foundations are willing to erect new buildings for lease to new industry, with the rent providing the return (unless the organization
is non-profit) to the investors. Some community corporations,
but not so many, are willing to build for sale; and in some cases
leases provide for option to buy or for amortization of building
costs by the company.

A few will lend money outright to companies for the purpose of buying land and buildings, with security being a first
mortgage on the land and buildings. A few, too, will buy stock
in a newcomer company as an inducement, in the hope that,
as the company prospers locally, the investment likewise will
grow in value.

The development credit corporation at the state level, to
provide risk capital for new business, be it noted, is a New
England invention. Maine's was begun in 1950, followed by
New Hampshire's, Rhode Island's, Massachusetts', and New
York's, among others, feeling the need to offset offers from
the South of tax-exempt, utility-free, municipally-financed factory buildings.[34]

Community sponsored "industrial districts" or "industrial
parks" are sensible post-war devices to attract new factories.
Although the device is to be found all over the nation, some
New England ex-textile towns, Lowell, Mass. and Woonsocket, R.I., for example, have found them particularly successful in helping to keep the wolf from the community door.
The district or "parks" are characteristically near main highways, railroads or water transportation, are serviced for waste
disposal, water, power, etc., and are attractively landscaped and
spacious for the accommodation of modern horizontal facto-

ries and parking lots. They make honest sense from the point of view of master planning and zoning, since they discourage industrial dispersion into scattered, small sites that eventually and inevitably would become blighted areas. Because they are community-originated and usually politically independent, most industrial parks are flexible; they will lease or sell either land or buildings or both, or will arrange financing to suit the case. At Lowell, profits from the industrial park go to community welfare agencies after investors have received their 6 percent.

The technique for forming an industrial development corporation or an industrial park, or a combination of both, is the old familiar community organization plan:

1. Collect a committee of able, respected community leaders to do the spade work and basic planning.

2. Conduct a series of "participation" meetings with all related important groups to discuss the town's future and what can be done about it.

3. Finally, at a tuxedo meeting of all important people in the area, get pledges of supporting money (most pre-arranged, of course) and elect officers of the organization.

4. Incorporate.

As a fifth step, the corporation may wish to raise additional money from the community public-at-large, in part to establish the sense of public participation in the project; to this end, no-dividend stock, with par value unstated or as low as $1.00, may be sold.[35]

The popular magazines carry inspiring small articles from time to time on how depressed cities, which had lost an important employer or industry, now are "on the come-back trail" due to a local industrial development council and to the faith of the people in their town. Investigations of these featured cities indicate that conditions sometimes are not as sanguine as described. Top-drawer corporations don't like ninety-year-old abandoned mill buildings any more than the former tenants did; and New England's gains in durable goods, electronics and apparel have *not* offset the decline in textiles there. As another example, Scranton, Pa., has achieved some justified fame with its triad of organizations to gain industry that would replace bituminous mining, at one time the area's major industry. The "Scranton Plan" had indeed brought in plants from General Electric, Chrysler, Trane, Daystrom, among others; but with the exception of U.S. Hoffman's plant to make artillery shells for the Army (which in 1957 laid off 1,100 of 1,400 workers in a Congressional economy cutback) most recruited plants have under 500 employees. Publicized as it is as a "come-back town," at this writing Scranton is also listed as a "distressed area."

It seems inevitable that closing of plants in a town always put many older people out of work. It was true in the Alexander Smith Carpet Company closing at Yonkers, N.Y., true in the hat works closings at Danbury, Conn., true in many of the textile mill closings of New England. The average displaced New England male textile worker was between fifty-six and sixty-five years old, and his age has been the greatest barrier to his re-employment elsewhere.[36] Professors Leonard Adams and Robert Aronson in their study of the aftermaths of the International Harvester closing at Auburn, N.Y., also noted that I-H workers unemployed more than twenty-six weeks were the older workers without highly developed skills.[37]

When it is finally and fully determined that a plant will lose money in its present location, no matter what steps management takes, then the company has no alternative but to move or close the plant, despite community unhappiness that will result. There have been attempts to pass state laws forbidding companies to close plants. Some union contracts in the garment and hat industries will penalize managements with "damages" to be paid to the union for work diverted out of local union's jurisdiction.

It is asking a lot of the northern worker to think of plant moves in terms both of the old town and the new town: both of Yonkers, N.Y., and Greenville, Miss., in the case of Alexander Smith; or of Auburn, N.Y., and Memphis, in the case of International-Harvester. The northern worker can hardly be expected to be magnanimous enough to recognize that, for the good of the nation, the South must (as per the Mississippi slogan) "balance agriculture with industry," even if this raising of living standards in the South is partially at the expense of northern living standards.

Yonkers was badly frightened at the announcement in 1954 that Alexander Smith Company was leaving to consolidate its carpet manufacturing in the then three-year-old plant at Greenville, Miss. Management's reason for moving, as usual, was inability to make money at the old site. The buildings were very old, crowded, outdated and cumbersome; and labor costs and wool prices went higher each year. The company decision to move was reached and announced while the local union of the Textile Workers, CIO, had the 4,000 workers out on a lengthy strike. The company publicly placed a good part of the blame for the plant move on the union. The union, in turn, took ads in the Yonkers *Herald Statesman*, asking for laws to protect workers and communities from runaway industry.

The Yonkers Community Council for Economic Development did a conscientious job in finding employment for Smith workers (the company had pensioned workers who were at least fifty-seven years old) and in finding new tenants for the old buildings, which were re-named the Westchester County Industrial Center. The former Smith property had been bought by a syndicate headed by a local real estate broker. New tenants, some of whom bought space, some of whom rent, included a plastics manufacturer, a tea packer, a display designer, a furniture factory, a battery maker, and an automotive warehouse.

Another classic example of a plant closing is the case of International Harvester's withdrawal from Auburn, N.Y. in 1950 because of obsolete plant and market shift. The company gave the community eighteen months' notice and the plant itself was sold for one dollar, plus liberal severance pay to the 1,500 work force. Under the aegis of the Chamber of Commerce, an Industrial Development Committee (later changed to an Industrial Development Foundation) was formed with a local utility manager as chairman. It raised nearly $50,000 to advertise Auburn and to remodel the I-H buildings. After a time the community's work brought in, first, the Remington Company (room air conditioners), then New Process Gear (later to be a Chrysler unit), U.S. Hoffman (artillery shells), and General Electric (which built its own plant rather than occupy abandoned I-H quarters). With the impetus of the Korean War, Auburn for a time was employing more people than before Harvester moved away.

The Adams-Aronson study of the aftermath of the study nevertheless concluded:

While the Auburn experience represents only one case of local efforts to promote industrial expansion, it raises some questions that may be of general interest. For one thing, the loss of ten small business concerns between 1953 and 1955 shows that the job of industrial development is a continuing one that calls for constant analysis and effort. The history of the area provides many illustrations of the rise and fall of industrial concerns. In the past, as in the case of the Harvester shutdown, no agency or group has had responsibility for keeping constant watch of the economic status of local business. No one, for example, seemed to be able to explain why the ten small concerns failed, moved away, or shut down during the post-Korean war period, but the loss of 1,000–2,000 jobs was enough to offset much of the gain achieved during the preceding two years by bringing several new concerns into the area. An effective industrial development program would seem to depend on having a realistic evaluation of the advantages and disadvantages of the area for different types of business concerns. Some agency needs, therefore, to be fully informed on both business vital statistics and their significance.

Another question concerns the responsibility to the community of a business concern to provide information about its local operations. Harvester management waited until they were ready to make a definite announcement that the plant would be shut down before telling the people of Auburn that local operations were no longer profitable. Yet there is evidence that this situation was not new. If the plant had not shifted to war production in World War II and had not been needed to help meet the pent-up demand for farm machinery after the war, it would probably have been closed down earlier. No financial statements of local operations were issued, however, and since the company was showing profits in its consolidated statement, most people assumed that local operations were also profitable. The fact that the company gave warning considerably in advance of the shutdown was not an adequate substitute for providing accurate information on the status of its local operations. This inference is based on the evidence of shock and surprise with which the shutdown announcement was received and the subsequent unsuccessful attempt by representatives of the community to persuade management to change its decision. Keeping the community informed concerning the financial status of local operations might also prove to be in the company's interest by helping to provide better understanding and hence a more ready acceptance of drastic changes if these should be needed.[38]

Techniques for leaving town gracefully are beginning to develop with practice. Turning the old plant over to the community is not always financially possible, but perhaps the company can pay the rent for a replacement, say for eighteen months, as Westinghouse did when it left Sunbury, Pa., in 1954. Long notice periods before moving ease the pain, experience indicates. Westinghouse was the first to engage, at company expense, the Fantus Factory Site Locating Service to find a company to fit the community.[39]

When Blaw-Knox left Nunda, N.Y., company officials took on the job and the expense of a program to find a replacement. It is very common practice of late, too, to offer jobs and transportation to employees wishing to transfer to the plant's new location. (Experience is that in most instances not many accept, and many of these return shortly to the old home town. In such offers, of course, are problems of transferring workers' seniority to the local union at the new plant and of explaining to the new community why you are importing labor instead of hiring locally.)

A plant move into a community may not be met always with undiluted joy by the townspeople. The Massena, N.Y., citizenry, for example, viewed construction of the St. Lawrence Seaway and of a new aluminum plant, plus miles of trailer camps, with mixed feelings. The town of Ashtabula, Ohio, on Lake Erie west of Cleveland, found itself to be a chemical industry town, with most plants outside the city limits requiring services but not paying city taxes. Waving the banner of "research center," some companies are putting their feet into the doors of suburban residential cities, as the towns of Wilton, Conn., Princeton, N.J., among others, are aware. Perhaps, indeed, residential communities would be well advised to recruit carefully selected industry to help pay the tax bill.

No company wants to locate where it is not wanted, or at least where the community cannot be educated to want it. Most companies will locate only where they will be welcome by the majority of the people as well as by the business and governmental leadership.

Nevertheless, the process of moving into a community is

sure to result in a community relations program, with all stops out: a series of institutional ads, open houses, dinners, movie showings, ceremonies and celebrations of various kinds which in public relations circles fit under the euphemistic heading of "special events." The purpose of all this is to tell the residents of the town about the company and its people.

One example of the establishment of an industrial plant should suffice. U.S. Steel's Fairless Works replaced fields of spinach on 3,900 acres in Bucks County, near Morrisville, Pa., some six miles below Trenton, N.J., about one hour distant from New York City and a half hour from Philadelphia. Although a modest operation in comparison with the Company's Gary Works, the nearly half billion dollar Fairless Works employs 6,000–8,000 workers and can produce more than 3,000 tons of iron and 6,000 tons of steel a day.

The increased market for steel, the area's proximity to much of the steel-using industry in the East, plus the cheap transportation afforded by the Delaware River, were economic reasons for the Fairless Works' location. Likewise, an ample labor pool surrounded the site, although the immediate area was at the time of its purchase strictly agricultural. The site, according to Richardson Wood, "represents a perfect equilibrium between coal, ore, and market competition." [40]

It would have seemed unlikely that a recognized giant of American industry—a steel company, at that, with steel's reputation for labor trouble and air and water pollution—could ever gain acceptance from Bucks County residents, a people known to be a society unto themselves. But as soon as the land was purchased (options on the acreage were picked up by the Manor Real Estate and Trust Co., and not by U.S. Steel, to prevent land prices from skyrocketing) the company began an extensive education program. Movies, teacher aids, and company speakers explained the steel industry, its importance and processes, and especially the Fairless Works, to everyone who would listen. Even during the construction period, plant tours escorted 75,000 local people through the site.

To counteract the "industrial giant" stereotype, much stress was placed on the importance of small businessmen and independent contractors in constructing and operating the plant. Residents of Bucks County and their elected officials were encouraged to discuss effects—present and anticipated—of the installation on local schools, traffic, stores and hospitals. Financial support was given to community projects in Morrisville and also in Trenton and nearby Bristol.

Bucks County people are strongly conscious of historic traditions of their area; so the Company moved four eighteenth century houses to Mount Vernon, there to be added to the historic buildings on the George Washington estate. Much was made of the fact, too, that in Revolutionary days the area's furnaces were among the principal suppliers of iron to General Washington's army, and that steel now was returning to its historic home on the banks of the Delaware.

The experience here as elsewhere indicates the wisdom of keeping hands off the provision of homes for employees. Private builders experienced some criticism from occupants of homes in their mass-produced residential tracts, but little of this ill will rubbed off onto the U.S. Steel Company.

The young plant had its community relations problems, with a local school board leading a campaign to increase the tax levy against the Fairless Works. It has become embroiled, also, in a promotion campaign to deepen the Delaware River channel between Philadelphia and Trenton. In both instances, the management showed itself to be fair, rational and helpful.

The company has had its critics, one of them complaining publicly that industrial companies of the area "have not taken responsibility for providing leadership to the residential communities that are being created around these industrial plants."

Nonetheless the company by and large has demonstrated the good sense to leave to the community those responsibilities which belong to local governments and to popular decisions and effort—when it would have been all too easy to be the dominating social force of the area.[41]

Companies and communities are learning to respect one another's requirements and problems, and to plan together for the future needs of both.

For the complacent community relations man, there is in the files of General Motors a dramatic pair of photographs. The first is an aerial view of a new Chevrolet assembly plant, set in the middle of miles of farm land. The second photograph, taken only three years later, shows the same plant now completely engulfed by the houses of a city.

Too few communities are yet willing to restrict areas most suitable to industrial development exclusively to industrial development, or to do so in terms of acreage demanded by modern factory building requirements.

Local planning is "very weak in defining and holding industrial lands for future development," in the experience of the Western Pacific Railroad's director of industrial development, Mr. F. B. Stratton:

> There has been little thought displayed looking forward to the long-range needs of the state (Calif.) for industrial lands. We have foreseen a need and, in light of the inadequacies of local planning efforts, have had to spend over $6,000,000 in the postwar years to buy up potential industrial lands to protect them from subdivision and to establish the base for future industrial development.[42]

The fact is that industry's building standards are infinitely higher than most communities' standards, and higher even than the communities' standards in present planning stages. In her *Space for Industry*, Dr. Dorothy Muncy cautions that:

> Before the public surrenders its freedom to build homes on land needed for future factories, it must be convinced that such sacrifice is in the best public interest. If the standards a community sets for new industrial developments are not as good as those set by responsible industry, it will *not* be in the best interest of either the community or the manufacturer. The key word is "industrial," not "development."
>
> The community must not find, twenty years hence, that the crowded industrial lofts cleared out of central areas by redevelopment have sprung up in new form in the suburbs. We need not build horizontal industrial slums today to plague us in the future.[43]

I would add that communities might well be thinking also in terms of industrial parks and of planning for their whole metropolitan regions.

Companies, on the other hand, too frequently locate where they do because of immediate and, no doubt, transient advantages offered as bargain premiums by certain cities and areas.

Dr. John A. Garwood of Fort Hays Kansas State College studied "the orienting factors of location" for 116 new manufacturing plants in Utah and Colorado from 1946 to 1951. He discovered that sites for buildings, or buildings located by the municipality, or built by a local development and construction corporation, was the single most influential factor in managements' decisions. In some instances, Dr. Garwood found, property was given outright to incoming firms. Instances of cash payments were not uncommon, mostly in the guise of meeting moving and settling expenses.[44]

Accepting such gratuities from a city obviously weakens the company's position in all future relationships.

Plant managements with unhappy personnel relations, union relations, and community relations have been heard to yearn for the opportunity, as they put it, "to make a fresh start" in a new plant location. Seldom does it occur to these managements that there may be some need to improve their basic policies in order to prevent matters at the new location eventually from becoming as bad as they were at the old location. Wherever its plant may be located, the company has responsibility for the community that surrounds it. As the plant manager studies the plant's future more intensively, he finds himself planning for development of the community, too. The community likewise in its long-range planning is discovering that the area's success in good part depends upon prosperous local industry. The phrase "business climate" has an unfortunate crass sound; but as it is interpreted in Syracuse and as it ought to be interpreted everywhere it is used, it means simply "better community."

FOOTNOTES

[1] See his *Plant Location*, Business Reports, Inc., Roslyn, N.Y., 1952, p. 97.

[2] The following year the modern office building was constructed on West Genesee Street, some blocks from the center of town, the company's first choice of location having been disapproved by the mayor's planning committee despite a plea from the mayor. The Syracuse office of Nationwide employs about 200, mostly women. Some of the supervisory force was transferred from Columbus, Ohio. Annual payroll at the time of opening was announced at $1,340,000.

[3] Some examples of community plant site location organizations can be found in the National Industrial Conference Board's *Techniques of Plant Location*, by Malcolm C. Neuhoff, Studies in Business Policy No. 61, New York, 1953. This study includes in its appendix a plant-city questionnaire developed by Monroe Calculating Company for evaluating communities, and a check list of factors affecting plant location, prepared by the Fantus Factory Locating Service of New York and Chicago.

[4] *Ibid.*, p. 97.

[5] The site selected after an eight-months search was a thirty-acre hillside tract in the town of Camillus outside of Syracuse. The Center employs about 300.

[6] The following quotations indicate phrases taken from correspondence with GE community relations staff men at the company's New York headquarters.

[7] Construction of the plant and landscaping of the 155 acres with lawns, trees, flower beds and a lagoon, began in 1945. GE is now Syracuse's largest employer, manufacturing TV tubes, transistors, plus electronic equipment for the military; the workforce averages over the years more than 10,000.

[8] *See* Chapter III.

[9] *See* Richardson Wood, "Where to Put Your Plant," *Fortune*, July 1956, p. 100 ff.; Seymour, L. Wolfbein, *The Changing Geography of American Industry*, Industrial Relations Research Association, 1953; Gunnar Alexandersson, *The Industrial Structure of American Cities* (Lincoln: University of Nebraska, 1956); Walter Isard, *Location and Space Economy*, Wiley & Sons, 1956; and Melvin L. Greenhut, *Plant Location in Theory and in Practise* [sic]: *The Economics of Space* (Chapel Hill: University of North Carolina Press, 1956).

Greenhut studied locations of eight small firms in Alabama and found that the traditional economic theories of "least cost" and "maximum sales" were not always sufficient to explain location. The factor of "personal considerations"—the owner's personal contacts leading to loan capital or materials, etc., was the primary factor in five of these cases, and a "secondary specific" factor in a sixth case.

[10] A survey of location preferences among professional personnel of one major company listed these states, in order of preference: Arizona, California, New York, Florida. Climate, it seems, is important but only a partial explanation of this phenomenon.

[11] A continuing survey of public opinions about certain major corporations, conducted by the Psychological Corporation of New York.

[12] *Getting and Holding Good Employers*, Chamber of Commerce of the United States, 1956, p. 1.

[13] *Ibid.*, p. 3.

[14] Clayton P. Fisher, Jr., Consultant, Business Climate Development, General Electric Company, in a speech, "Improving the Business Climate of Massachusetts," before the 4th annual conference, College of Business Administration, Boston College, Boston, Mass., May 23, 1957.

[15] General Electric Company, *Guide to Making a Business Climate Appraisal*, n.d.

[16] Address by Ralph J. Cordiner, President, General Electric Company, "Managerial Skills for a New Age," before the Executives' Club of Chicago, March 8, 1957.

[17] Employers Labor Relations Information Committee, Inc.: *A Tool for Analyzing Factors That Help or Hinder Business: The Community Inventory*, New York City, n.d.

[18] *Ibid.*, pp. 1–11.

[19] Copies of New York State Citizen Council studies may be had from the Council, 613 E. Genesee St., Syracuse 2, N.Y.

[20] E. L. Thorndike, *Your City* (New York: Harcourt Brace, 1939). For the modern scientific approach—notably a statistical method of describing a

city's urbanization trends—see Eshref Shevky and Wendell Bell, *Social Area Analysis: Theory, Illustrative Application and Computational Procedures* (Stanford Sociological Series No. 1, Stanford University Press, 1955). The New York Citizens Council has simple city-rating charts, as do a number of civic organizations, including the League of Women Voters. *A Guide to Economic Base Studies for Local Communities*, by Edward K. Smith (Boston: Bureau of Business and Economic Research, Northeastern University, 1955) contains a "research outline" for the collection of data relating an area's economic resources and economic future.

21 Michigan has a "business activities" tax of $6.50 per $1,000 in gross receipts, plus a corporation franchise tax of $4 per $1,000 of net worth. Michigan has no state income tax, but is in part supported by payroll taxes.

22 "Where to Get a Tax Break," *Business Week*, July 13, 1957.

23 "Taxes, How They Affect Plant Site Selection," by Leonard C. Yaseen, *Management Methods*, Dec. 1956.

24 Other cities to run business climate appraisals include Akron, Bridgeport, Schenectady, San Mateo (Calif.). Results in most cases may be obtained from Chambers of Commerce in those cities.

Ford Motor Company runs its own Business Climate Studies in plant cities for its own guidance; it does not join city-wide appraisals or publicize results.

25 *New Industry Comes to the South*, National Planning Association, Washington, D.C., 1949.

26 *Subsidized Industrial Migration: The Luring of Plants to New Locations*, American Federation of Labor (Recommendations for Legislative Action by the Sub-Committee on Migration and Subsidy of Industry, National Legislative Committee), Washington, D.C., 1955.

27 Sherrill Cleland, *The Influence of Plant Size on Industrial Relations* (Industrial Relations Section, Princeton University, 1955).

28 An exception worth immortalizing in a footnote in this book is Mr. Frank H. Lee, a hat manufacturer, whose efforts and money have been fundamental to the industrial development of Danbury, Conn., following departure of most other hat factories from town.

29 Responsible companies, too, take great pains to equalize their own employment over the year: introducing new models when sales slacken, rather than at specified times during the year; engineering packaging and preservative qualities into perishable goods with seasonable sales (like photographic film and paper, for example); scheduling plant maintenance work for light months; advertising and researching of markets to improve sales during low-level months; developing supplementary products for off-season production, etc.

30 University of Pennsylvania Press, 1956.

31 One of Kennecott's ex-company towns, Hayden, Ariz. (pop. 1,494) quietly incorporated itself after Kennecott stepped out. The catch was that the city limits extended across a considerable extent of desert to encircle a company smelter, so that Kennecott might help, however reluctantly, with village taxes.

32 Boston, Mass., Oct. 1954.

[33] An address before the Montana Community Development Conference at Helena, Mont., April 20, 1956.

[34] Some companies scorn tax concessions because they don't want to be obligated. Some states, like New York, scorn them, too, because they say such concessions will result in a collection of less desirable companies. However, companies interested in comparing tax concessions offered by various states will find them listed in some of the annual reports of the New York State Joint Legislative Committee on Commerce and Economic Development.

[35] At Woonsocket, the industrial development foundation and the local industrial park are partly paid for by payroll deductions. In Fall River, $5 par value stock was sold. In Arkansas, thirteen insurance companies, at the behest of Winthrop Rockefeller and the Industrial Development Commission, bought 50 percent of bond issues floated by local industrial development corporations in the state, while the State Board of Finance, with authorization of the General Assembly, bought up the other 50 percent.

[36] William H. Miernyk, "Labor Mobility and Regional Growth," *Economic Geography*, October 1955.

[37] Leonard P. Adams and Robert L. Aronson, *Workers and Industrial Change, A Case Study of Industrial Mobility* (Ithaca: Cornell University, 1957), p. 137.

[38] *Ibid.*, pp. 159–160. A detailed account of preparation for, and execution of, this move was used as a case study, presented by the late Dale Cox, Director of Public Relations at International Harvester, to the Cornell Community Relations Seminar in the summer of 1953.

[39] Since then, incidentally, Fantus has gone seriously into the business of helping communities and areas and even states (Oklahoma and Iowa) to find the companies that they need.

[40] *Op. cit.*, p. 101.

[41] An unpublished, undated MS by public relations students at Boston University, based on material gathered by Prof. David M. White, describes U.S. Steel's program to inaugurate the Fairless Works.

[42] Before California Assembly Subcommittee on City and County Planning in California, Jan. 1955.

[43] Dorothy A. Munch (a planning consultant in industrial development), *Space for Industry, An Analysis of Site and Location Requirements for Modern Manufacture* (Washington: Technical Bull. No. 23, Urban Land Institute, July 1943). This pamphlet, although priced at five dollars, is a clearly presented compilation of information useful both to community planners and site seekers.

[44] Doctoral dissertation, University of Colorado, July, 1951. Summarized by Dr. Garwood in *The Management Review*, Sept. 1952.

9-
Conclusions

INDUSTRIAL community relations, as preceding chapters make clear, presumes a potpourri of knowledges about a variety of subjects: politics, sociology, zoning laws, fund-raising, labor relations, public education, agency administration, and air and water pollution, to mention only some. Occasionally, talent in news writing and public speaking, or a familiarity with depth interviewing and area sampling are also helpful.

There are, however, some general principles of community relations to be drawn out of the experience of industrial cities. These principles are as pertinent to the success of community relations programs of local government, schools, and health and welfare agencies as they are to the programs of plant managements.

The most fundamental community relations principle is that mutual understanding between organizations, e.g., between a locally operating company and various organized "publics" in the plant city, grows out of the establishment of common interests and projects, and thereafter out of the mutual development of these common interests and projects. This linking of fortunes in one area of endeavor implies mutuality of fortunes in other areas, too, although the contagion of public attitudes from one area to another may not be as common as once thought. We have seen that the community may be critical of a company's labor relations record, for example, and think highly of the company in other matters.

Every organization, and indeed every company, has its own special "publics." A community, like the nation, is made up of a cross-hatching of groups, racial, religious, occupational, avocational, educational, social, political, economic, etc. Collectively, the opinions of these publics constitute "public opinion."

Not every group in the city is of equal importance at all times to an organization; nonetheless, the essence of a community relations program ought to be the establishment of *bridges of agreement* between an organization and groups presently or potentially important to it, followed by the enlarging and strengthening of these bridges of agreement. The company which has built many such bridges with many groups and organizations in the city, and which sees to it that the bridges are in constant repair, has established a pattern of organized friendships which can be called into action if and as needed.

Public relations programming must begin with analysis of an organization's relationships. Conversely, public relations programming ought not to begin only with plans for publicity.

But the communications half of the public relations process is nonetheless important. Indeed, a corollary to the basic principle of establishing areas of mutual understanding and of common concern with various publics is the concept that this pattern of built-up relationships should be used regularly to carry communications between a client organization and its related publics.

The Syracuse company conceded to have generally the highest rating by the people of the area has a long-standing program of services to organizations in its operating area. Furthermore, this company has a professionally staffed program of community communication. Some companies, smaller ones, to be sure, have managements equally devoted to the community, but they make no special effort to communicate "to the groups that concern their profit and/or prestige." These non-communicators among corporations do not often suffer from bad reputations; they just are not very well known. Unlike the company in the case of the Solvay Process Division, described in Chapter 6, they have not needed a reservoir of good will for they have experienced no period of community trouble. Perhaps they never will. Nevertheless, their failure to communicate is depriving them of the very real community advantages which their social behavior warrants.

The "old family," locally-owned company often inherits its operational philosophy from an older day, when management's relationships with workers and community were more intimate. These companies have sought to maintain a feeling of closeness with employees, and in many cases have succeeded surprisingly. To the degree that their employees communicate for them, they do very well indeed. But the relations of these companies to the complexities of the new, exploded community are more baffling. Relatively, companies in this category gradually are slipping in community reputation, particularly in the face of the communications competition of the companies in the area which are heavily staffed with communications professionals.

Nevertheless, there needs to be re-thinking about the communications aspects of community relations. The "filtering down" theory of communication via organized groups cannot stand close, critical inspection, as indicated by various studies of organizational memberships. The Lazarsfeld-Katz thesis of "personal influence" further indicates that so-called "thought leader" lists in the community relations offices of industrial plants might well be restudied.[1]

Effective community relations is educational. The communications problem is to educate community communicators to carry information about the company, its philosophy and projects back to the community. Granted that word-of-mouth is the best way to communicate in a community, these communicators ideally would set in motion a geometric increase in the number of communications of the message.

Company information, as contained in publicity formally released to newspapers, is often unbelievably dull: standardized, routine stories that have been repeatedly carried in the press, with changes only in the proper names used. If the geometric communication principle is to be used, with employees acting as starting points for the communication, management has got to put its messages so strongly in the interests of the community that people will want to talk and will want to listen.[2]

The central lesson of the Lazarsfeld and Katz research is that each level of society in the community generates its own opinion carriers, since each level contains both relatively active and inert segments. This means that the influencer and the influencee for the most part are rather close together on the socioeconomic ladder.

This, in short, is a "sociometric" approach, a who-will-tell-whom approach; it is the technique of asking people on a social group level for their preferences of work-partners and social friends—and to consider that those most frequently named are the group's "natural leaders."

This concept has had some experimentation in the field of marketing, where it is discovered that consumers can become salesmen; but much needs to be learned before it can be fully applied to industrial community relations.

The 1955 community attitudes survey of Syracuse citizens revealed that Syracusans were better informed about industry and more acceptant of industrial points of view than is the average American. This state of affairs resulted in large part from the conversations of the employees of local industries.

As in other surveys by Opinion Research Corporation, it was found that community attitudes about companies are obtained chiefly from "someone I know who works there."

What this means, in summary, is that the most potent communications medium within a town is a grapevine: a grapevine with its roots embedded in the factory itself. What this also means is that the best possible basis for a good community relations program is a good personnel program.

Successful community projects of all kinds require that there be (a) able, influential leadership, (b) organization of that leadership (which bears remarkable resemblance to project organization within a company), and (c) early involvement and participation of all groups and individuals to be affected by a project.

Here is still another community relations principle; and in it lies the explanation of why some community projects succeed and why others, equally worthwhile, fail.

The absence or neglect of any of the three elements above can result in a project's failure. All groups and organizations (again, all "publics") that will be affected by a community project must be involved in the planning of the project. This is true whether the community project is a community hospital program or an air pollution reduction campaign.

The heads of the community's organizations—who become lieutenants or salesmen for various large-scale city, industrial or social activities—must be fully utilized to put over an important project. This is the principle of involvement, of utilizing the community's leadership structure in terms of both organizing and communicating.

A successful united fund campaign provides illustrations of many community relations principles: (1) that participation or "involvement" increases one's interest to the point of giving more of one's time and money; (2) that year-around commu-

nity communication and education is better than spasmodic
or at-the-time-of-action publicity; (3) that a people-to-people
drive can be the only successful one—e.g., people communicating with their peers, via a rather tightly controlled complex of
sub-organizations; (4) that failure, as well as success, can become a habit in the community; and hence the campaign must
be sure the goal set is a possible one; (5) that public recognition of campaign workers must be constant; and (6) that the
successful campaign must utilize the community's ultimate in
prestige and influence in its leadership, and that this leadership must have extensive preparation for those top positions
acquired via a "work-up" system.

Of all these principles, the last one (6) is key to the others;
for the exercise of all the principles depends on the community
leadership itself.

Representation of industry in the leadership of an industrial
city does not come automatically. Sometimes, by industrial
default, merchants, bankers and realtors exclusively constitute
the leadership even of strongly industrialized communities. It
is neither good business nor good democracy for company
managements to decline participation in establishment of the
community rules and the policies under which they will all
have to work. Chapter I lists some other reasons why companies ought, in their own interests, to be involved in the affairs
of their plant communities. There are reasons, too, why the
communities should do their best to recruit management participation in civic affairs.

Major metropolitan projects succeed or fail in proportion
to the cooperation they receive from industry. The phenomenon of a successful community rejuvenation, when it occurs,
is no mere spontaneous demonstration of civic-mindedness by
local managements. The impetus to success, you may be sure,
comes from the strength and power of the project's leadership.

You may be equally sure that a "leadership of leaders" exercised some rather rigid controls over all subordinate segments of the leadership structure.

An appreciation of the leadership structure in a community and a firsthand acquaintance with its members, obviously, are necessary to intelligent performance of the work of public school administrators, health and welfare staff, as well as the executives of locally operating businesses.

Some companies stress the point that their executives are active in the community solely as citizens: that community services are entirely divorced from the company. This is only relatively possible, depending upon the prominence of the man and upon the prominence of the community service under discussion. A foreman of a factory may sit on a village school board, and do so merely as a citizen of the community. On the other hand, a vice-president of the largest corporation in the city cannot direct the local united fund drive altogether outside of his industrial position; whether he or his company likes it or not, he will always be Vice-President Smith of the X-Corporation.

Some companies discourage their more prominent executives, particularly upper management, from serving on planning boards or boards of education, or from seeking office that must be got through public election. This may be one reason why community leaderships so commonly ignore basic social problems of American cities like substandard housing, metropolitan area unification, or the improvement of public school education.

Industrial cities and their surrounding villages and towns have become unbelievably complicated with a complex of inter-related problems. This is the basic concern of communities today, and hence should be a basic concern of the industries which are contributing to the difficulties in those cities. An approach to a solution of the fundamental urban problem, I am convinced, is to reorganize metropolitan areas into some new kind of unity, thus dispensing with the expensive governmental and service duplications of numerous overlapping political divisions. Such reorganization will not be easy; but none has a bigger stake in it than industry.

Few community projects of magnitude are completed without some controversy. But I do not know of a single company which did not gain in community reputation, over the long run, because its management had the courage to enter controversial projects of real value to the community. The Pittsburgh, St. Louis, and Miami stories of community progress all contain some hair-raising passages of conflict; and so has the recent social history of Syracuse.

Syracuse companies, indeed, have become so inured to controversy as to start a sort of COPE [3] for management there. The Manufacturers Association in the spring of 1958 began a multi-company program to put local management men into politics. Executives from twenty companies were given an intensive course in "how politicians operate" and in "the influence of voter reaction at the grass roots level." These twenty men were in turn to carry the course information into their own plants, presenting it eventually to some 300 managers, from line supervisors to vice-presidents. These in-plant seminars were eleven weeks long, and used an especially written text in "Practical Politics." A few of the assignments in the course are: to write a personal letter to Congressmen; to visit a city council meeting; to interview one's own political party election district committeeman; to break down and appraise local tax rates; and, finally, to ring twenty doorbells in a 1958 voter registration campaign. In view of top management enthusiasm for the program, it is likely that these assignments will be carried out as prescribed.

Organization is necessary to successful community projects; and for large-scale projects a veritable pyramid of organizations is needed to direct and perform the work, and, more than incidentally, to protect the constituent member groups, organizations and individuals from the attacks of opponents, if any. An organization of organizations can provide its members with protective insulation to a degree; but no one, and notably the community's more important people, are ever completely immune to the possibility of attack. "If you can't take the heat," Harry Truman once advised, "stay out of the kitchen." By remaining in the kitchen, on the other hand, one has some say about what he will have for dinner.

More positively, a project which has become institutionalized through organizations widely representing the community will have the public power to achieve its community goals. The success of Syracuse as an industrial city is due to its carefully planned organizational structure, consisting of

a) the local Manufacturers Association and Chamber of Commerce, to gather and to exchange information internally and, when helpful, externally; and to be the holding company, so to speak, for the more specialized organizations in the city's leadership structure;

b) the united fund, community chest and agency boards, to develop experience in community leadership, and to keep the leadership on top of all local problems.

c) the Research Bureau, to act as a watchdog over the public pocketbook; sometimes to take conservative positions that are unpopular; and in financial matters, to serve as an advisory unit to local governments.

d) the Citizens Foundation, largely to perform a communications and educational function.

Of these units in the Syracuse leadership structure, each has its planned purposes. The same men, or at least management men from the same companies, are involved in all four units. This total organization, and its potential for coordination of city projects, is in large part responsible for the community's high score in the various evaluation studies recently made there.

Another characteristic of the city of Syracuse responsible for its success and prosperity is the realization on the part of local companies and their managements that "business climate" problems and "community-centered" problems increasingly are becoming the same problems.

Syracuse industry, the Opinion Research Corporation surveys indicate, is better thought of at the time of this study than it was even a half dozen years earlier. The case studies of this book illustrate how community relations programs, and community relations thinking, have helped businesses to achieve this improved public opinion.

FOOTNOTES

1 Elihu Katz and Paul Lazarsfeld, Personal Influence: The Part Played by People in the Flow of Mass Communication. Glencoe, Ill., Free Press, 1955.

2 Several AT & T community surveys verify the finding that about three-fourths of the people interviewed got their opinions about the company from talking with employees. R. S. Callvert (of AT & T's Public Relations Department), "Employee Attitudes: The Key to Better Community Relations," Personnel, Nov., 1956, p. 242 ff.

3 AFL-CIO's Committee on Political Education.

Appendix A

SOME SYRACUSE COMPANIES
AND THEIR COMMUNITY
RELATIONS PROGRAMS

SYRACUSE, New York, an upstate city of a quarter-million population, is reasonably clean, well-managed, and generally prosperous. Its industry is diversified, its community conscience is fairly active, and its business climate is better than average. More than coincidentally, it is also a city with well-planned and organized industrial leadership.

Since the days when Hiawatha guided the Five Nations from his council fires near the city's present site, Syracuse has been blessed with luck as well as with leadership. It was born in the path of commerce and became a busy port city on the Erie Canal after 1820. Salt springs along the southeastern shore of Onondaga Lake gave it its first industry. Syracuse is still nicknamed the Salt City, and still honors its main street with the name Salina.

The great majority of locally operating companies in Syracuse and, for that matter, throughout the United States have no planned community relations programs at all; and their managements seldom think of community relationships, except, perhaps, when forced to it by a united fund solicitor. Most of the "old family" companies which have histories replete with demonstrations of corporate concern for their communities hire no public relations or community relations specialists. These managements may not think of their community service activities as "community relations" as such.

Locally operating companies in Syracuse employing professional public relations men include: General Electric, Carrier, Niagara Mohawk Light and Power, Solvay Process Division of Allied Chemical and Dye (all four of which have Syracuse staffs of at least three professionals), Brown-Lipe-Chapin (General Motors), and Crouse-Hinds. Several engage consultants for more or less extensive servicing.

In Syracuse, as in other industrial cities, community relations operates at two levels:

(1) At top management levels the concern is with company policy, with the selection of community projects for corporate support in cooperation with other top managements; this concern is centered on social aspects of the community, such as health, welfare, education, and the community's facilities in these areas. (2) At staff levels, community relations is largely concerned with public relations projects (open-house, B-I-E Day, press releases, mailings, etc.) to improve the community's attitudes toward specific companies.

Some executives of the top level in Syracuse think of community relations only in terms of their own and their company's contributions of time and money to community projects. Some community relations people think exclusively in terms of Community Relations techniques and press releases.

Certainly, top management must bear responsibility for policy-making; and certainly the community relations professional must take responsibility for company-centered community relations communications and techniques. Nevertheless, companies which push this dichotomy too far are not getting their money's worth out of either aspect of community relations.

Local companies often tend to see only the obvious advantages of bigness. It is true that the name of a large national company is a tremendous asset. Because people have heard it repeatedly all their lives, the name is likely to get initial discussion in any layman's conversation about any phase of business or industry. Just because the famous name comes first to mind, people first consider the big company whether they are talking positively about industrial advantages and virtues, or negatively about industrial disadvantages and sins. That is why operators of comparative industrial community relations surveys find it wise to compensate for this tendency in their evaluations of citizen attitudes toward smaller locally operating companies.[1]

Unless they have friends or relatives working at locally owned companies, newcomers to the labor market, whether from out of town or from the graduating classes of the public schools, are likely to think first of the big company as a place to work. Women's clubs, civic groups, or school teachers on B-I-E Day likewise are apt to think first of the big company as the place to visit.

The community relations professionals on the big company's local staff devote full time to heightening this advantage with a well-organized and publicized speakers bureau and with programs of local publicity, institutional advertising, and "thought-leader" mailings.

Nevertheless, the "first-to-come-to-mind" principle sometimes operates to a big company's disadvantage. Probably it will get more than its just share of blame for air and/or water pollution. Surveys may rank it high as a company with a poor labor record (while paradoxically it may also rank high as a good place to work). This, as described in Chapter 7, Part One, was true at General Electric in Syracuse.

In the smaller plant city, or in plant cities of companies which do not hire local community relations staffs, the

"committee system" as used by Ford, General Motors, and
Celanese, among others, can stimulate local managements to
community relations planning and programming. Such committees are effective only to the degree that the plant managers participate in them.

The service kind of business with offices in many cities
(communications and insurance companies, railroads, airlines,
big brokerage houses, etc.) have the handicap of spreading a
relatively small work force over many communities; the result
is that community impact is difficult. The salvation of the
thin-spread company lies in the fact that it is service oriented,
and as such it gets close to the lives of many people.[2] The telephone companies' emphasis upon employee service to customer and community is an example in point. The service
company, with no production processes to display, also finds
itself at a disadvantage in holding open houses and plant tours;
Nationwide Insurance uses its excellent collection of Currier
and Ives prints as an additional "something to come and see"
at its regional office "open houses."

Companies with headquarters located in a plant city, e.g.,
Caterpillar Tractor in Peoria, Eastman Kodak in Rochester,
Pitney-Bowes in Stamford, Corning Glass in Corning, among
others, supply the best models of community relations programs to be found anywhere. The reason is that managements
of these companies participate heavily in community affairs;
they make the community's problems their problems; and
they have the influence, the finances, and the honest interest
to do something about them. As national corporations, too,
they know the value of good communications, and hire top-
notch professionals to do the job for them locally as well as
nationally.

Every locally operating concern, however small and whether
a branch or locally owned, can have good community reputa-

tion if it works at it. Caterpillar's formal program (newspaper, radio and TV contacts, participation in civic activities, community discussion groups, assistance to local program chairman, direct mailings, plant visits, and contributions) is not as important or as fruitful of friends as is its "odds and ends" division, as Community Relations Manager Fred Jolly calls it. These sometimes unplanned, improvised and generally inexpensive opportunities to earn good will in Peoria are what really count, Mr. Jolly believes. E.g., Caterpillar throws nothing away, but obsolete materials are made available to anyone who has real use for them. School parade floats are pulled by Caterpillar vehicles. Even solicitors of legitimate "nuisance advertising" are given pleasant receptions and sometimes a payment for space.

This may seem like a small-time way to operate community relations, but community relations works best in an aura of the intimate. Community relations can't be seemingly big-time, or it ceases to be community relations. This is the real explanation, it seems to me, why some locally owned companies have better community acceptance than some branch plants of big companies do.

The locally owned company—characteristically unorganized, or at least organized by unions less troublesome to management—makes the point that community relations is closely tied with personnel relations. This is so because each employee has his average fifty to seventy-five friends outside of the company who will listen to, and believe, what he says about the company. Consider a few Syracuse examples:

Porter-Cable Company, which thinks of itself, with some reason, as "the Cadillac of the machine tool industry," is profit-sharing and multiple-management. Its "associates" (management does not use the term "employees") are working capital-ists, and they insist on knowing as much about the business as management does. Porter-Cable has the most thoroughly read bulletin boards I have encountered anywhere. The company has meetings galore; and uses a public address system for really hot information. Recently, Porter-Cable started a management newsletter, which naturally goes to everybody since everybody is management.

Porter-Cable is a small company; but when you talk to a man who works there you are talking with a man who knows, and with one who is interested in telling you, about his company.

Four Smith brothers began making "writing in sight" typewriters in 1903 in an eight-story building that is still part of the Smith-Corona factory in Syracuse. The Smith family has had a fondness for using their initials rather than given names ever since the days of L.C., W.L., M.C. and H.W., the four founding brothers. H.W., last of the brothers, died in 1951 following a long tenure as "Mr. Syracuse," a title earned by service (usually as chairman or president) on ninety separate community agencies and projects. The Seneca Indians made him an honorary member, and named him Hah-squi-sea (Man-with-tomahawk).

Smith-Corona's workers are on piecework, and are permitted to work at their own pace. It is a relaxed company, with many personal radios on the floor and a twice daily between-meals lunch wagon. Typical of the company is that the employees requested that there be no "build-up" of propaganda and meetings, etc., preparatory to the united fund drive; and then they came through with 90-plus percent contributions. There is no foremen's club, no suggestion system, no reading rack, and the house organ contains no "management messages" whatever. Smith-Corona employees include many twenty-five-year men and women, and colored girls are intermingled on the assembly line. The company just doesn't think much of "planned programs" for its people.

Onondaga Pottery has its own employee summer camp, and an impressive listing of long-service employees. The two plants in the city both have a strong family feeling about them, as though everyone were honestly concerned for the happiness of everyone else. The company holds regular family outings at nearby parks and family "open houses." The company has a successful production bonus program to point out to employees that "usable production is the source of all wages."

Both the family names in the title of Crouse-Hinds Company, which manufactures condulets, industrial lighting and traffic signals, etc., have had their tenures as "Mr. Syracuse." The company's management is the most community conscious, per its size, in the whole city. There is hardly an organization in the area even today without Crouse-Hinds representation on its board. Crouse-Hinds kicks off the U.S. Savings bond sales, holds an in-plant "lighthouse" sale for the blind, supports the local school for retarded children, and sponsors a Christmas toy fund. Its people collected material for the Cancer Society's bandage drive. The women workers in the company cafeteria decided that, rather than exchange Christmas gifts, they would buy hospital apparatus for polio victims. Its remarkable Saturday morning "good neighbor" contribution to the united fund is described in Chapter 5, Part One.

The company contributes heavily to employee recreation programs: An Anglers' Association, which holds fishing competitions and conducts courses in hunting and fishing for children; two softball teams for men and one for women; a twilight golf league, a tennis tournament, a camera club, both men's and women's bowling leagues, a thirty-man basketball team, and an inter-company bridge tournament. In addition to funds from management, the money put into all vending machines in the plant goes to employee recreation. At Christmas, the carpenter shop builds a "rocket" for Santa's transportation to the company family Christmas party, usually held at a downtown theater.

Carrier Corporation has developed a kind of democracy of its own, consisting of a seventy-member management Cabinet, which receives the same information as the Board of Directors, and an expanded Cabinet of all (about 1,000) supervisors, which meets with management twice a year for frank, informational sessions on profits and prospects. In addition, there is the Carrier Institute of Business, for all employees and run by the employees. During this affair, following an address by a visiting speaker, management and employees hold a question-and-answer session of the "how are we doing?" type. The Carrier benefits programs likewise are well above average, and the company is near the top among the most active companies in the community, in terms of both management time and corporate money. Carrier's own booklet about the city of Syracuse is a model of its kind, rivaled to my knowledge only by General Foods' booklet on Battle Creek and by Celanese's booklet on Cumberland.

Of these home industry companies, only the first and the last (Porter-Cable and Carrier) have unions—an independent, not associated with AFL-CIO, and a so-called "federated union," respectively.

Syracuse has a surprising number of companies in this locally owned tradition, a good many of them unorganized, all of them very conscious of their responsibility to employees and community. Also included in the category would be Will &

Baumer Candle Company, Lamson Corporation (industrial carrier systems), Aircooled Motors (successor to the famous Franklin automobile, now making airplane engines), Syracuse Ornamental (home accessories, advertising gadgets, etc.), Lennox Furnace, Oberdorfer Foundries, Pass & Seymour (ceramic electrical fittings), Precision Castings, Marcellus Casket, R. E. Dietz Co. (lanterns, torches, roadlights, etc.), and Engelberg Huller (processing machinery for rice, coffee, etc.).

Some local companies have been absorbed into national corporations. Sometimes this change results in greater community-mindedness, as was the case of Prosperity Company (laundry and dry-cleaning machinery) when it became a unit of a large holding corporation. Sometimes this change has resulted in seemingly less community-mindedness, as in the case of Easy Washing Machine, which before its absorption by a large corporation had been one of the outstanding leaders of the industrial community. Sometimes the result is a changed community relations policy and philosophy, although not necessarily a less responsible plant operation.

Those large holding operations which buy and sell companies as though they were marbles characteristically have no concern with community relations.

Among national corporations' branch plant operations in Syracuse, two of them, Solvay Process Division of Allied Chemical and Dye, and General Electric, have been discussed in earlier chapters. Both are typical of companies which adopted community relations as a defensive measure, to begin with, but which have now discovered that preventive public relations is a sound investment.

Solvay's in-plant concentration has been in large part on foremen. (Advancement to supervision is never given to a man who does not want to be a supervisor.) Solvay's program includes a Foremen's Council meeting, plus seminars for all supervisory levels, held in the evening and taught by company officers and division heads.

Solvay proves that all long service people do not work for the locally owned companies; at this writing it has 146 active workers with forty years' service, and 1,700 with fifteen years and more. Solvay ranks with Crouse-Hinds in providing the steadiest work in the area, thus having a definite employee-appeal advantage over companies tied to the automobile, electrical products, and air-conditioning industries.

A Solvay neighbor in the village of Solvay is Crucible Steel's Sanderson-Halcomb Works. Like many steel operations, this one is glad to see visitors, is frank in talking with questioners, and is hopeful that its employees at the mill will learn to pull their share of the united fund and other financial loads of the community. But it has no community relations staff, or even a community relations program as such. The same may be said for some other branch plants in Syracuse: Continental Can, U.S. Hoffman, Frazer & Jones, Auto-Lite Battery, etc.

At no other company studied is production-mindedness more dominant than at Brown-Lipe-Chapin Division of General Motors (metal-plated parts of cars). A good day's work is expected—and received—in return for some of the highest daily wages paid in the area. Skillful organization and supervision are apparent in the new and modern one-floor Town Line plant. Here is a well-trained, well-disciplined business-like relationship between local management and the U.A.W. local; management and workers know what to expect from one another. General Motors approaches community relations more cautiously than does General Electric, for example. Investigations of GM's size and its proportion of the automobile market have deterred management from seeking prominence in the power structures of plant communities. They want their people to be active in communities, but they don't want to dominate any activity, or even to seem to do so.[3]

Still another version of branch plant community relations is supplied by Bristol Labs, which has no community relations program or staff locally but which has been very active in the city, due largely to a community-minded plant manager. The result is that in many ways, the Bristol plant resembles the city's numerous civic-minded, locally-owned companies which have no formal community relations programs either. Bristol Labs, also, has no union, but does have a first-rate benefit program, including a pension plan based on common stock yields, so that pensions will increase for retired people just as prices rise and stocks grow in value. Only the limitations of its headquarters contributions policy distinguish this plant from locally owned companies. Bristol-Myers HQ does have a public relations department, and in some plant cities has earned a first-rate community reputation.

And, finally, General Electric is by far the most active company in the whole country in the area of community relations; but because its program already has been so thoroughly chronicled I will only refer to:

(1) the GE booklet series on various aspects of community relations (institutional advertising, open houses, and programs for specialized publics) which may be purchased from Employee and Plant Community Relations Service Division, General Electric Co., 570 Lexington Ave., New York 22.

(2) The book, *Community Relations for Business*, by John T. McCarty (GE's well-known community relations man) published by the Bureau of National Affairs, Washington 7, D.C., 1956.

FOOTNOTES

[1] Wayne L. Hodges, "Community Relations is Community Responsibility" pr, Jan. 1957.

[2] In the 1955 Opinion Research Corporation community survey in Syracuse, a utility, Niagara-Mohawk, was accorded outstanding community acceptance.

[3] See *How You Can Make Friends for General Motors in Detroit; GM Lives Here; Open House;* and *How GM Dealers Can Make More and Better Friends,* General Motors Department of Public Relations, Detroit 2, Mich.

Appendix B

ATTEMPTS AT EVALUATING COMMUNTY RELATIONS PROGRAMS

ONE of the few companies to attempt to evaluate community relations programming has been General Electric. GE's efforts are tied to what John T. McCarty calls "evaluative indicators," meaning indicators of relative success or failure of community relations programs in plant cities. Indicators, one might say, represent the payoff of a program—they are a means of judging a community relations program's success in terms of results.

At a Cornell Community Relations Seminar in the summer of 1955, Mr. McCarty posted on the blackboard the following list of "CR Indicators" which GE thinks may provide relative determinations of local reactions to plant activities.

Community Relations Indicators
1. Number of job applications (per size of the workforce and per size of the community).
2. Newspaper, radio, and television comments, stories and editorials (favorable or unfavorable—got at by the technique of "content analysis" perhaps).
3. Sale of company products in the area (if applicable).
4. Number of stockowners in the area (if applicable).
5. Leadership of company personnel in civic activities.
6. Audience response to company-sponsored radio, television or newspaper advertising.

7. Favorable or unfavorable treatment from city governmental officials in such matters as tax rates, police protection if needed during strikes, support of business and civic leaders in times of crisis. (This must be reduced to a statistical handling, of course.)

These indicators would be checked by attitude surveys, using:

1. Regular sampling techniques (the community questionnaire) and
2. Depth interviews of the following:
   a. Newspapermen
   b. Investors
   c. Church functionaries
   d. School teachers and principals
   e. Credit agency administrators
   f. Employment agency staff people
   g. Service club leaders
   h. Doctors

Later in the same day, a committee of participants in the seminar (all community relations professionals) reported on their evaluation of various possible "indicators." As a general answer, the group thought that the use of the term "indicator" was wise, because, very likely, no exactly precise formula or index can be developed. "Indicators can be found, but even these are applicable to, or carry different weights within specific communities."

To supply "before and after" information, each indicator must be examined: 1) before a CR program is started, and 2) afterwards. Among the indicators, the committee suggested the following, but with reservations, as their questions indicate.

(a) *Job applications.* Related to influencing factors: important, but labor market may change. When do applicants know of the company? Are applicants members of families who are present employees? What is the quality of the applicants? How did they decide to apply? Who told them? Why did the applicant select the company? All this cannot be applied to an absolute scale, but should be considered.

(b) *Newspaper, radio, and television comments, stories, and editorials (favorable or unfavorable)*: Situations change from day to day; qualitative (how treated and what kind of story); quantitative (how many stories and where placed?); character of news media; nature of competing news media; source of story (company or newspaper); is coverage regular or crisis? How does company fare compared to competing firms? What is the nature of editorial comment? What is the size and composition of the audience reached? How is the story displayed? Hence, the committee did not believe that this indicator, either, could be reduced to a formula.

(c) *Sale of company product in the plant area:* Is pride shown in the company name? How are sales and what is the knowledge of the company's products and services? This is not measurable by any hard and fast scale.

(d) *Stockholders in the plant area:* Are they members of the community and not employees? Are they new owners? How much do they hold? What is the general market trend? How long is stock held? (As a device against "absentee owners" regional stockholders meetings may be held.) This indicator is of some value but again is not an absolutely precise measuring rod.

(e) *Leadership of company personnel in civic activities:* What is the size of the plant and its relationship to the community? Do only the top people participate? (Beware of too much participation which tends toward domination.) How broad is the participation and how deep? Who participates and the nature of the participation are the most important of the factors to consider.

(f) *Audience responses to radio or television programs or advertising campaigns:* What is the type of program: Is it controversial? Music? When does it appear? What about ads appearing during crises? Each gets different kinds and amounts of response.

(g) *Treatment by the local governmental unit:* Does the company receive fair or unfair treatment from city governmental officials in such matters as tax rates, police protection if needed during strikes? Does the company have the support of business and civic leaders in times of crises?

(h) *Additional indicators:* What do merchants think of the company? What does the union think of the company?

In conclusion, the seminar committee advised that it believed the development of community relations indicators is feasible. Indicators do have a sales value to management, but it is dangerous to oversell indicators to management as representing solid, scientific proof. "Don't call them an index or formula," they warned, "because the facets of a community relations program may be really but just a portion of the total influence upon the indicated community result."

Other General Electric men have struggled with a similar program in their attempt to evaluate, on a comparative basis, the employee relations programs of various GE plants. They came up with these indicators of programs for hourly paid workers: (1) periods of absence, (2) separations (all types), (3) initial visits to the dispensary for occupational reasons, (4) suggestions submitted through the suggestion system, (5) actions incurring disciplinary suspension, (6) grievances submitted through the formal grievance procedure, (7) work stoppages, and (8) participation in the insurance plan. Their studies at forty GE plants showed that these eight indicators did fluctuate together, and furthermore, that the fluctuations bore a relationship with "the pattern of employee behavior that contributes to productivity, profitability, and the like." [1]

As the Cornell seminar committee noted, one of the great difficulties in evaluation of community relations programs is the social differentiation among communities: Obviously a good community relations program in City-A might not do at all for City-B, and vice versa. Yet, is it possible to work "community variables into an evaluative formula"? The answer, unfortunately, is that community relations is not a science, and cannot be reduced to an exact formula.

Evaluation of results can't altogether be separated from (a) Business Climate, (b) communications techniques, or (c) the various areas of Community Relations programming.

Let us think of community relations in terms of its various

aspects; perhaps we can break up the community relations program into a cross-hatched chart, and then see which aspects of community relations are susceptible to measurement.

There are, it seems to me, four basic areas of community relations activity: (1) Publicity aspects, (2) Plant personnel and economic aspects, (3) Social (or sociological) aspects, and (4) Political aspects. I have tried in the chart at the end of this appendix to show graphically the relationships to these basic community relations areas of (a) variables, (b) techniques, (c) indicators, and (d) factors of business climate.

For each area of community relations programming, there are one or more pertinent community variables. Including three variables which relate to all aspects (and so are termed "over-all variables") I have listed a total of twelve community variables.

Next, there are the community relations techniques (mostly communication techniques, of course, of one kind or another). Some of these techniques particularly fit one aspect of community relations (personnel, perhaps, or political aspects). Community relations techniques are legion; some collectors have listed as many as 150; I include sixteen here.

Community variables and community techniques are themselves closely related; for the ability to vary his use of techniques to fit community variables is the community relations professional's basic skill.

Community relations "Indicators" can be used to test certain community relations techniques, which in turn have been applied to certain community relations aspects under specific variable conditions. I include twelve "indicators." I am sure there are many more possible, especially indicators to evaluate community relations techniques that relate to social aspects of community relations. Here, I refer again to Thorndike's criteria for establishing his "G" index of city "goodness," or to

Angell's "The Moral Integration of American Cities," for his "moral integration" criteria.[2]

Finally, consider the factors of good business climate, and divide them into four categories, those that apply to each of the four aspects of community relations, respectively.

In many pertinent ways, it will be found, the factors of good business climate are indicators of good community relations.

All of the above, as placed in chart form at the end of this appendix, it seems to me, is community relations synthesized in its entirety, including (1) planning for coverage of various aspects in terms of community differences, (2) using appropriate techniques, and (3) conducting a double evaluation: (a) in terms of the community relations program's success or failure and (b) in terms of contributing to the community's business climate.

The chart does not, of course, solve anyone's community relations problems. It does not even take the problem of program evaluation out of its subjective approach. Hopefully, however, it will help companies to go about solving problems for themselves. No one should delude himself into thinking that there is any substitute for finding out the public attitudes and opinions, in considerable detail, that relate to a company. This means constant listening at proven listening posts around town—depth interviewing, if you will. It means, too, an occasional community survey of a more formal sort, perhaps sharing costs with other local companies.

Still another evaluative technique has been developed by James Rowan of Mellott, Thomsen, Pitnay, Rowan and Co., whereby, in depth interviews, he asks his respondents to evaluate the community (and the company) against what the interviewers themselves previously had established as their own criteria of excellence for a community and for a company's contributions in various community areas. Mr. Rowan has proved with a number of surveys in General Electric plant cities that an accurate evaluation can be got quickly and cheaply in this way.[3]

FOOTNOTES

[1] William V. Merrihue (of General Electric) and Raymond A. Katzell (of the consulting firm of Richardson, Bellows, Henry and Company), "ERI— Yardstick of Employee Relations," *Harvard Business Review*, Nov.-Dec. 1955, p. 91 ff.

[2] E. L. Thorndike, *Your City*, New York, Harcourt Brace, 1939; and R. C. Angell, "The Moral Integration of American Cities," *American Journal of Sociology*, July 1951.

[3] The expensiveness of large-scale scientific surveys has concerned many companies represented at Cornell Community Relations Seminars. One large company is experimenting with brief telephone surveys, at this writing, with undetermined results.

CHART C

INTER-RELATIONSHIPS AMONG COMMUNITY VARIABLES, COMMUNITY RELATIONS TECHNIQUES, COMMUNITY RELATIONS INDICATORS, AND BUSINESS CLIMATE, WITHIN THE FOUR AREAS OF COMMUNITY RELATIONS ACTIVITY

Areas of Community Relations Activity	Community Variables	Community Relations Techniques	Community Relations Indicators	Factors of Good Business Climate
	[Over-all variables: 1. City size 2. Regional customs, taboos, mores, traditions 3. Size, number and diversification of local industry]	[Techniques below, of course, affect all areas of community relations more or less—and their classification here relates to emphasis of effectiveness in particular areas]	[Over-all indicators: 1. Surveys—full-scale or panel—but with questions to evaluate success in each of the four areas of community relations activity 2. Local stock ownership 3. Product purchases locally 4. Community reaction to emergency situations]	[Over-all factors: 1. Diversified industry 2. Available and qualified workers, in town not dominated by one company 3. Cheap water, power, transportation]
I. Publicity Aspects	4. Size and number of media 5. Local journalistic traditions and standards	1. Paid institutional advertising (space and time) 2. Publicity releases with news value	5. Coverage (news and editorial) evaluated by technique of content analysis	4. Able and fair press, radio and TV

324

3. Media-relations program designed from their point of view
4. Sponsored radio and TV service programs
5. Regular but not overdone program of special (news-making) events

6. Public response to sponsored programs and events

II. Personnel & Economic Aspects

6. Community industrial traditions of human relations and corporate citizenship
7. History of union action and union power

6. Good personnel practices that give workers senses of belonging, of participation, recognition and security
7. Economic education—emphasizing the employee, his job, his plant, his company, his industry
8. A participatory program of in-plant communication, verbal as well as written

7. Turnover
8. Job applications ratio
9. Number and nature of grievances
10. Employee action indicating relative allegiance to company and union

5. Specific demonstrations of cooperation among locally operating managements and local thought leaders
6. Record of moderate union behavior
7. Reasonable local wage scales
8. Production-minded local labor force

CHART C (Con't.)

	Community Variables	Community Relations Techniques	Community Relations Indicators	Factors of Good Business Climate
III. Social Aspects	8. Existing social, religious, educational, cultural levels, groupings and facilities	9. Company's monetary contributions 10. Contributions of management time to community projects		9. Good schools, churches, hospitals and clinics, recreational facilities, etc.
	9. Racial and nationality groups 10. Socio-economic pattern	11. Employees' time given to community		
	11. Nature of local "social power structure" and leadership	12. Aids to school curricula, loan of facilities and apparatus to worthy organizations		
IV. Political Aspects	12. Quality and performance of locally elected officers and their staffs, in recent history	13. Management speakers bureau 14. Community-centered economic education 15. Openhouse and specialized plant tours 16. Regular mailings to thought leaders	11. Voting action of citizens 12. Executive action of public office holders	10. Honest government 11. Favorable laws 12. Police and fire protection 13. Reasonable tax rates

326

Appendix C
INTERNATIONAL HARVESTER
CONTRIBUTIONS

<small>POLICIES</small>

Procedures

To: OFFICERS
GENERAL MANAGERS
DEPARTMENT HEADS
WORKS MANAGERS
DISTRICT MANAGERS

THIS manual is addressed to management people in the International Harvester organization who are concerned with the handling of the numerous requests for charitable and other requests that are received at works, district offices and other Company locations. These requests are now received in such number and cover such a wide variety of organizations that the problem of handling them courteously, intelligently and with a maximum degree of uniformity has become an increasingly difficult management public relations problem.

You know, of course, that some years ago our management appointed a Contributions Committee in the General Office for the purpose of screening all contribution requests and making recommendations concerning them to top management. The committee has been functioning in that capacity for a number of years.

It has been increasingly evident that a printed guide or manual which would undertake to set forth the general outlines of our contributions policy, and which would establish procedures for the handling of contribution requests, would be helpful to management people in the field who receive so many such requests in their local communities. That is the purpose of this manual and we hope it will be helpful to you.

I wish to emphasize that the manual deals only with general rather than specific cases. Undoubtedly, there will continue to be requests of such unusual nature that their handling will have to be taken up as special cases with the divisional or sales organizations and finally with the Contributions Committee.

The management has approved the handling of contributions, if they conform to the policies of the Company contained in this manual, up to an amount of $100 by works managers and $50 by district office managers without approval of the Contributions Committee. Such contributions, of course, are subject to the budget controls of the divisions and the respective sales organizations.

The policies set forth in the manual have been approved by Mr. McCaffrey and will be in effect from the date of the receipt of this manual by the field organization.

/s/ Frank W. Jenks
Chairman, Contributions Committee

For many years International Harvester Company has contributed from its corporate funds to many worthy undertakings. It has not been alone in this policy, by any means. Most corporations today, large and small, give of their funds to many different kinds of charitable, welfare and other types of organizations.

Because the Company is requested to contribute to so many organizations, it seems desirable to have a written statement of policy concerning our contributions, for the guidance of those people in the Company who receive these solicitations, and particularly for the organization in the field.

General Policy

Certain considerations of general policy apply to all contributions. The most important of these considerations are:

1. Any contribution to charitable, welfare or other organizations which our Company makes comes from funds that belong to the stockholders. The theory under which such contributions are made is that they bring direct or indirect benefits to our business, and that corporations have a generally recognized responsibility to support such organizations when there are direct or indirect benefits.

2. The nature of our business has an important bearing upon our contributions policy. Ours is a national even an international business. Hence, there must be a general pattern that governs our contributions in all parts of the country. We have to consider precedents carefully. We cannot very well give to certain types of organizations in one part of the country and not give to them in another. So, while every contribution request should be considered on its individual merits, nation-wide consistency in our contribution policy is almost a necessity.

3. Because we must contribute in so many different communities, we sometimes cannot make local contributions as large as those made by the larger, purely local businesses.

4. We regard our first contribution responsibility as being to those approximately 200 communities in which we have manufacturing plants, parts depots, district offices and other operations. We seldom make contributions, therefore, in other towns or cities. To try to do so would spread our efforts too thin, and the businesses with operations in these other localities have a responsibility there that we do not have.

5. Company executives should bear in mind that if they accept important working assignments in fund-raising campaigns, the Company is very likely to be asked for a corporate contribution because of that connection. Harvester executives should exercise discretion, therefore, as to the fund-raising campaigns in which they participate as workers. Key management people should limit such participation to organizations where support would fall within the policy of the Company.

Summing up general policy, it must be remembered that since any contribution made by any unit of our Company is stockholders' money, the responsibility of justifying it is great. The first test, therefore, that should be applied to all contributions requests is: Does it benefit the Company directly or indirectly? Unless it can be demonstrated that it does, the contribution should not be made.

Types of Contributions Made

The contributions our Company makes can be classified into five main categories, as follows:

1. Relief and Health: Contributions of this type are made to Community Chest funds, American Red Cross, hospital building funds, cancer, tuberculosis, infantile paralysis, heart and other similar health campaigns, etc. We follow a definite policy of not contributing to the operating expenses of agencies that are members of Community Chests in cities where we have operations, since such operating funds are provided in large part from Community Chest funds. Such agencies, however, are given permission by their Community Chest organizations from time to time to seek capital funds, and in such cases their requests to us are given consideration on their merits, and in the light of our contributions policy.

Because of the large expansion of hospital facilities in recent years, it seems advisable to state in some detail the Company's policy on contributions to hospitals.

Contributions to hospitals are restricted to building programs, equipment additions, or for unusual medical research in which the Company may have a strong interest. Contributions are not made for hospital operating expenses. Hospital contributions are restricted, also, to communities in which the Company has works, sales offices, parts depots, or other important operations.

The first consideration applied to hospitals is the direct benefit which the Company's employes receive from use of the hospital. In works cities, this takes the form of industrial usage. This is the most important factor in extending support to hospitals, and in works cities would limit our support to the one hospital which our works physicians use for Company employes.

The Company on occasion contributes to other hospitals in works cities, however, either to help relieve the patient load upon the hospital which we use for industrial purposes, or for public relations reasons. Sometimes the Company gains an advantage in the hospital we use because one or more other hospitals, by increasing their facilities, make more beds available for Company use in the hospital we use. In every case where the Company makes a contribution to a hospital, it must rank high as a medical institution, and must possess high-grade business administration.

In district office cities and towns contributions are made to hospitals on occasion where the situation makes it advisable from a public relations or customer relations standpoint. These cases usually occur in the smaller cities and towns where the Harvester district office is an important business unit in the community. Amounts in such cases are quite modest.

The recommendations of Company physicians, both locally and at the General Office, are given important consideration in all hospital requests for contributions.

2. Public Welfare: These are many organizations which we classify under this heading, including taxpayers' association, Better Business Bureaus, civic federations, safety organizations, etc.

3. Social Betterment: Social betterment agencies include such organizations as the Y.M.C.A., Y.W.C.A., 4-H Clubs, Future Farmers of America, Junior Achievement, and many others.

4. Educational Institutions: Many educational institutions today seek corporation financial support. Such support to educational institutions, we think, can be looked upon as a proper expenditure of corporation funds where it brings direct or indirect benefit to the Company. We believe such support must be limited to assistance of specific research projects, scholarship and fellowship programs and loans of, or discounts on purchases of, machinery and equipment by these institutions, provided any crops that may be produced by the institution are not sold in competition with crops produced by our farmer customers.

We follow the policy of not making contributions to tax-supported public educational institutions, except in rare instances where public funds may not be available for some special project that is of great interest and potential direct benefit to the Company's business.

Consequently, such support as we give to educational institutions usually is to privately endowed schools, not supported by tax funds, and which are generally located in cities where we have large operations. We are in position to benefit from such support. Amounts of such contribution are related to the size of the Company operation in the community and the anticipated benefit.

5. Business Organizations and Trade Associations: These types of financial outlay are not strictly a contribution, but are in the nature of a business expense. They are included as a part of our contributions setup, however. Included in the list are such professional and trade associations as it seems desirable for the Company to support: Chambers of Commerce—local, state and national; service clubs in cities where we have operations; manufacturers' associations; etc.

Types of Contributions Not Made

The Company does not make certain types of contributions as a matter of policy:

1. Corporations are prohibited by law from making political contributions.

2. Because our stockholders, employes and customers represent all religious groups, the Company does not contribute to strictly sectarian or denominational religious organizations, such as churches, missionary groups, etc.

3. Generally, we do not contribute to war veterans' organizations, unless the undertakings for which they are seeking funds are for the welfare of all the people of a community.

4. Except in unusual circumstances, such as some clear evidence of Company support to so-called "courtesy advertising" in such media as fraternal programs, yearbooks, labor union papers, convention souvenirs, etc. Requests for advertising of this nature should first be screened at field operations, and if it is felt a request has some unusual merit, it should be referred to the Public Relations group in the General Office.

Many of these groups to which we do not contribute are very worthy. But worthiness alone cannot justify our contributing to them. There are too many worthy institutions for us to try to support them all. Many of them should be supported by individuals. We can justify corporation support only through direct or indirect benefit to stockholders, employes or customers.

Contribution Procedure

Works managers hereafter are authorized to approve local

contributions or business membership expenditures, if they conform to the general policies of the Company as stated in this document, in individual amounts up to $100, such expenditures to be charged against the local works operation.

District managers hereafter are authorized to approve local contributions or business membership expenditures, if they conform to the general policies of the Company as stated in this document, in individual amounts up to $50, such expenditures to be charged against the local district operation.

Since these locally authorized contributions are charged against local operations, they are subject to the controls of the annual budget.

Frequently, however, requests are received locally where the local management feels that the contribution should exceed the amounts authorized for local handling. In such cases the following procedure should be followed:

1. The works or district manager should first investigate the request and determine whether, in his opinion, the Company should or should not make a contribution, taking into consideration the same factors by which he would judge a request for an amount he is authorized to make above, and the factors applied by the General Office Contributions Committee as listed in the following section. If he is certain no contribution should be made, he should dispose of the matter finally.

2. If the works or district manager feels a contribution should be made in excess of the amount authorized for local handling, he should so advise the manager of manufacturing or regional manager as to the reasons why he feels it should be made. In all cases where he favors the contribution, he should state a recommended amount.

3. The contribution request is then considered by divisional or sales organizations in the General Office. The recommended contribution either is approved and passed on to the Contributions Committee for final action, or is referred back to the local operation for further study.

4. The Company contributes to many organizations with a single, national contribution, made at the Chicago office. Before local operations contribute any amount to any organization they should be certain no national contribution is being made in

Chicago. If they have a question about it they should write Frank W. Jenks, Chairman of the Contributions Committee.

5. Final approval is given by the Contributions Committee, except in cases of large amount or of an unusual nature, where approval must be had from the President or the Board of Directors.

Ordinarily, contributions and business membership expenditures are to be considered as a charge against the local or divisional organization. Exceptions will be made, however, in the case of larger contributions made for unusual reasons, where a charge back against the General Office is permitted with the approval of the Contributions Committee.

It will be the policy of the Contributions Committee, in deciding where the charge is to be made to take into consideration the size of the contribution, the size of the Company unit recommending it, and whether it is reasonable to charge the contribution against the local operation.

Contributions Committee

Responsibility for the Company's contributions rests with the Company's Contribution Committee in the General Office. This committee is appointed by the President of the Company. Frank M. Jenks is chairman of the committee. Other members of the committee are: Forest D. Siefkin, Ivan L. Willis, William R. Odell, Jr., Gerard J. Eger and Dale Cox.

If a contribution request involves special policy questions, the request is taken to the President, with the recommendation of the committee. Contributions of more than $5,000 also are taken to the President, and if these larger contributions are approved by him, they are then taken to the Board of Directors for final approval.

In considering whether a contribution should be made, the committee takes into account these things:

1. Will the contribution benefit the Company, directly or indirectly?

2. Does the Company's present business position justify it?

3. Will the request likely lead to other similar requests in the future?

4. Is the purpose of the soliciting organization a good one, and does the organization have widespread acceptance and support?

5. Is the soliciting organization efficiently and honestly managed?

6. Does it aid all kinds of people, or is it restricted in its operations?

7. Is the request consistent with the Company's place in the community?

8. What will be the public reaction if we give or do not give?

9. Are some of our large customers interested in the solicitations?

10. Are other companies in the community similar to ours supporting the soliciting organization, and if so, in what amounts?

11. Who are the people heading the organization asking our support? Are they first rate people?

12. Will the contribution advance the community and public relations of the Company?

If the committee decides the contribution should be made, it takes these factors into account, among others, in deciding what amount should be given:

1. What is the best measurable extent of the Company's benefit? Is it great or small?

2. What is the total amount being asked for in the campaign? What seems to be a reasonable share for us to assume?

3. What amounts are other businesses in the community giving? What are other businesses most similar to our operation giving?

4. What is the size of the community from which the request came?

5. What is the size of the Company's operation in the community?

6. What is the relationship of the size of the Company's local operation to the total life of the community? Is Harvester a big or a little factor in the community?

7. How many employes do we have in the community? Is there any relationship between employes and the amount we should give?

8. As a matter of policy, we will not accept suggested formulas prepared by some organizations as a means of determining how much we should give. We do not believe any such formulas can work equitably for all types of businesses in the community. We

will listen to suggested formulas, but all contribution solicitors should be frankly told the Company cannot follow them.

INTERNATIONAL HARVESTER CONTRIBUTIONS COMMITTEE
Frank W. Jenks, Chairman
Forest D. Siefkin
Ivan L. Willis
William R. Odell, Jr.
Gerard J. Eger
Dale Cox

Appendix D

Appraisal of Syracuse, N.Y., as a Location for Regional Offices of Nationwide Insurance Company

I. PERSONNEL FACTORS	FACTOR GROUP POINTS 330	FACTOR POINTS	POINT SCORE
1. Population		40	34
2. Projected Population—1960		40	38
3. Employed—Office Personnel		20	16
4. Employed—Other Personnel		15	12
5. Unemployed—Office Personnel		25	16
6. Unemployed—Other Personnel		15	10
7. Compensation Levels—Insurance Types		50	36
8. Availability of Local Personnel		50	40
9. Employment Services		20	18
10. Local Business and Industrial Pattern		30	26
11. Compatibility of Largest Employer		25	22
			268

II. COMMUNITY FACTORS (Company)	FACTOR GROUP POINTS 250	
1. Physical Environment	20	18
2. Business Environment	20	18
3. Meeting Facilities	40	38
4. Hotels	45	40
5. Quality and Type of Local Government	30	25
6. Municipal Finances	25	20
7. Police and Fire Department	15	12
8. Streets and Municipal Maintenance	15	12
9. Emergency Conditions	10	8
10. Attitude of Local Government and Business	30	30
		221

III. COMMUNITY FACTORS (Employee)	FACTOR GROUP POINTS 165	FACTOR POINTS	POINT SCORE
1. Rental Apartments Available		25	20
2. Rental Homes		10	5
3. Rental Rates		20	14
4. Homes for Sale		25	20
5. Sale Prices		15	10
6. Local Transportation		15	12
7. Educational Facilities		20	16
8. Physicians, Hospitals and Clinics		15	10
9. Cultural, Religious and Recreational		10	8
10. Personal Services		5	4
11. Social Environment		5	4
			123

	FACTOR GROUP POINTS	
IV. OPERATING FACTORS	385	

1. Existing Office Space for Lease	55	30
2. Existing Office Space for Sale	40	20
3. Office Rental Rates	35	25
4. Possible Development Office Space to Lease	60	50
5. Building Sites	35	30
6. Office Machine Maintenance Facilities	45	40
7. Banks	25	22
8. Other Financial Services	20	16
9. Tax Structure	30	20
10. Utilities and Municipal Services	25	22
11. Contacts	15	15
		290

	FACTOR GROUP POINTS	FACTOR POINTS	POINT SCORE
V. TRANSPORTATION AND COMMUNICATION FACTORS	320		
1. Mail Service		60	52
2. Telephone		40	40
3. Telegraph		35	35
4. Radio and Television		20	20
5. Railway Passenger Service		55	50
6. Highway and Bus Transportation		45	42
7. Airlines and Airports		45	38
8. Freight Service		20	16
			293

	FACTOR	GROUP POINTS
VI. SCHOOL SYSTEM FACTORS	300	
1. Elementary Schools	20	16
2. Number of Students Enrolled	20	18
3. High Schools	40	32
4. Number of Students Enrolled	40	36
5. Parochial Schools	25	20
6. Number of Students Enrolled	25	20
7. Enrollment Commercial Classes	45	38
8. Commercial Graduates— Female	35	28
9. Post High School—Business College	25	18
10. Colleges, University, Other Educational	25	22
		248

Total Points 1750   1443

Appendix E

Partial Report of a Community Attitude Survey, Made in Syracuse, N.Y., December 1955

The Free-Market System.

The Business Setup in this Country—	U. S. Public	Syracuse Workers 1955
It is very good, needs little change	14%	26%
On the whole, the good features outweigh the bad	47	46
The good features and the bad features are equal	24	15
On the whole, the bad features outweigh the good	5	4
It is very bad; major changes needed	5	5
No opinion	5	4

For or Against Government Ownership of—

Banks
Electric power companies
Railroads

Combined Average For Three Industries	U. S. Public	Syracuse Workers 1955
For government ownership	20%	22%
Against government ownership	72	71
No opinion	8	7

"Would you like to see labor unions grow larger and stronger, or do you think they have grown enough as it is?"

Grow larger	27	24
Have grown enough	53	56
Too large now	10	12
No opinion	10	8

How to improve the American worker's standard of living—produce more and get more?

	U.S. Public	Syracuse Workers 1955
Produce more	42%	35%
Get more	27	45
Both	23	13
No opinion	8	7

Disagree that—

"Owners get too much of the money companies make compared to what employees get."	41	43
"Most companies could raise wages 10 cents per hour without raising prices."	27	31

Disagree that—

"Consumers don't have much influence on prices since companies set the price and the customer has to pay it."	45	48
"Money invested in new machinery and equipment has increased output. The workers have got some of the increase, but the larger share has gone to the owners."	25	34

Disagree that—

"As factories put in more and more machinery, that means fewer and fewer jobs."	43	59

"You can't expect stockholders and employees to work together in harmony—
their interests are opposed." 62 62

	Syracuse Workers 1955
Disagree that—	
"From the company's standpoint workers should produce all they can. But from the worker's standpoint it is better to produce just about what the average man does."	43%
"Some people have said that the fairest economic system is one that takes from each according to his ability and gives to each according to his needs."	52

Syracuse Employers in General.

"If a friend asked you about the Syracuse area, would you say it is a good, average or poor place to work?"

	Syracuse 1955	Workers 1951
Good place	76%	78%
Average	21	18
Poor	2	2
Qualified	0	1
No opinion	1	1

"On the whole, would you say that Syracuse workers are treated very well, fairly well, or rather poorly by their companies?"

	City A Public 1955	Syracuse Workers 1955
Very well	31%	32%
Fairly well	65	61
Rather poorly	1	3
Qualified	2	2
No opinion	1	2

"Do you feel that most manufacturers in Syracuse really have the interests of their workers at heart, or not?"

	U. S. Public	City A Public 1955	Syracuse Workers 1955
Really have interests at heart	46%	60%	52%
Show some interest	17	18	15
Do not have interests at heart	19	8	17
Qualified	15	14	12
No opinion	3	—	4

"Some towns have the reputation for being high-wage towns, while others have the reputation for being low-wage towns. Do you think of Syracuse as being a high-wage town or a low-wage town?"

	City A Public 1955	Syracuse Workers 1955
High-wage	70%	34%
In between; average	26	50
Low-wage	3	13
No opinion	1	3

"In most cases, do you feel that workers in Syracuse today get their fair share, or less than their fair share, of the money their companies take in?"

	U. S. Public	City A Public 1955	Syracuse Workers 1955
Fair share	57%	66%	61%
Less than fair share	29	22	24
Qualified	7	4	7
No opinion	7	8	8

"At the present time, do you think most companies around Syracuse are making a reasonable profit, or too much profit?"

	City A Public 1955	Syracuse Workers 1955
Reasonable profit	74%	71%
Too much profit	9	17
Some large; some small	8	3
Small profit	2	1
No opinion	7	8

Syracuse Companies
(Names and statistics omitted).

Reasons Behind the Attitudes expressed by respondents

"Why do you pick that one (as best place to work)?"

Good wages and wage policies: wage scale is reasonable; they pay well.
Friends and relatives work there: sister works there; husband is there.
Steady work: never a layoff
Treat employees well: treat the men better; stand up for their men.

I work (ed) there: working there now and enjoy it; used
to be employed there.
Advancement opportunities: employee can move up.

"What do the men running that company do to show this high
interest in their workers?"

They have the human touch: treat employees as individuals; show keen interest in well-being of employees.
Benefits (specific and nonspecific): good insurance plan;
pension plan; bonus.
Recreational program: sponsor all kinds of sports; base-
ball and basketball.
Job security: don't have strikes; never out of work; no
layoffs.
Working conditions (specific and nonspecific): safety
measures; clean; good equipment.

"What have they done for this community?"

Products and services: provide goods or services to the
community.
Contributed to growth, prosperity and prestige of city:
put Syracuse on the map; helped town grow.
Have large payroll: provide employment and wages.
Civic-minded (nonspecific): active in supporting civic
enterprises.
Recreational activities: parties for employees; athletic
program.
Sponsor educational training programs.

Manufacturing Workers' Views of Their Own Companies.

"Aside from your own job—how would you rate your company as
a place to work—good, average, or rather poor?

	Syracuse Manufacturing Workers	
	1955	1951
Good	65%	71%
Average	26	22
Rather poor	6	4
Qualified	—	1
No opinion	3	2

"How do you feel about your own particular *job*—would you say you like it very well, fairly well, or not so well?"

	Syracuse Manufacturing Workers	
	1955	1951
Very well	67%	69%
Fairly well	27	25
Not so well	2	4
Qualified	1	—
No opinion	3	2

"What are the things you like most about your company as a place to work?"

	Syracuse Manufacturing Workers 1955
Wages and wage policies	18%
Steady work	18
Fellow employees	15
Treatment of workers: fair, courteous	12
Employee benefits	12
Type of work	11
Not overworked	8

"What are the things you don't like so well about your company
as a place to work?"

	Syracuse Manufacturing Workers 1955
Nothing wrong: no complaint	40%
Poor wages and wage policies	10
Poor working conditions	9
Location	4
Poor buildings and equipment	3
Management and supervision	3

"At the plant where you work, how do you get most of your
information about company operations and policies?"

	Syracuse Manufacturing Workers	
	1955	1951
Management sources		
Company publications	40%	29%
Bulletin boards	19	29
Management and supervision	16	18
Company meetings	11	12
Personnel Department	—	3

Information about the company

	Syracuse Manufacturing Workers	
	1955	1951
Other sources		
Hearsay: grapevine	13%	10%
Union channels	12	21
Personal observation	4	3
Fellow workers	3	5

Mention of supervisors or foremen—	New England Rubber Products Plant	Middle Atlantic Refinery
As actual sources of information to employees	30%	16%
As sources from which employees prefer information	70	40

Appendix F

Syracuse Board of Education Questionnaire

	Yes	?	No
Are you satisfied with the general school program of our Syracuse public schools?	14,002	1,192	1,151
Do you feel that you receive enough information about our schools?	11,248	1,256	3,577
Are our schools teaching your child how to get along with other people?	13,701	1,553	718
Is the school that your child attends well equipped?	10,791	2,372	2,078
Do you feel that our school buildings are being well maintained?	13,296	1,754	816
Are you satisfied with the type of report card being used?	12,523	942	2,303
Are you satisfied with the discipline in the schools?	11,879	1,880	1,972
Is your child given enough homework?	10,470	2,117	2,404
Do you feel free to visit the school about your child?	14,528	550	547
Should our present technical and industrial high school program be expanded?	10,497	4,013	958
Should our school encourage the discussion of different sides of controversial topics?	12,281	2,380	588
Do you think that you are getting value received from your school tax dollar?	11,873	239	1,429

Would you like to see more "school news" in your newspaper?	13,437	1,161	674
Do you feel that our schools are doing a good job in the teaching of the "Three R's"?	12,700	1,762	1,684
Do you like the type of information provided in previous school factographs?	12,684	2,177	605
Would you be willing to pay increased city taxes to provide higher pay for teachers?	10,322	2,951	2,226
Have our schools shown enough interest in your child?	13,619	1,293	889
Did you enjoy your visit to the school on "Open House" night?	13,367	1,187	384

Index

ACTION (American Council to Improve Our Neighborhoods), 41
AFL, see Labor unions
Aircooled Motors, Inc., 123, 313
Air Pollution Control District, Los Angeles, 172–173, 186
Air Pollution Foundation, 173
Air Pollution, Indianapolis Bureau, 170
Alexander Smith Carpet Co., 64, 282, 283
Allied Chemical & Dye Corp. (Solvay Process), 70, 156–164, 178, 183, 184, 297, 306, 313–314
Allyn, Stanley C., 3
American Airlines, Inc., 102, 103
American Can Co., 106
American Cyanamid Co. (Lederle Laboratories Division), 138–139, 140, 182–183
American Standard (American Radiator & Standard Sanitary Corp.), 106
Anchorage, Alaska, 168
Anheuser-Busch Inc., 55
Arlington County, Va., 63
Ashtabula, O., 286
Auburn, N.Y., 244, 245, 265, 284–285
Automobile, Aircraft & Agricultural Implement Workers of America (U.A.W.), 198, 231, 232–233, 240, 314
Automotive Manufacturers Association, 139

Baltimore, 36, 58, 60, 65, 168
Baker, Dr. W. R. G., 50, 193, 197, 200–202, 207, 208, 209, 210, 211, 212, 213, 215
Beck, Dave, 231
Beirne, Joseph A., 228
Bell Telephone Laboratories, 238
Bethlehem Steel Company, 167
Better Business Bureaus, 108, 113
Better Schools, National Citizens Council for, 41
Bien, William, 79
Blaw-Knox Co., 286
Boston, 168, 237
Boulware, Lemuel, 210
Bowery Savings Bank, 71
Branch plants, 15–16, 21, 26, 29, 42, 75, 97–100, 244, 308, 313–315
Bristol-Myers Company, 315
Buffalo, N.Y., 87, 116, 118, 250
Business climate, 243, 252, 256–257, 259–275, 291, 305
Business-Industry-Clergy Day, 39
Business-Industry-Education Day, 40, 50, 142–143, 148–149, 307
Burke, Gerald W., 79

California
    education, 135–137
    Industry Educational Council, 145
    Manufacturers Association, 270
California State Polytechnic College, 136
Capital Improvement Commission, Syracuse, 46

Cancer Society, American, 81, 82, 99, 311
Career days, 138, 139, 153
Carrier Corporation, 15, 20, 38, 71, 117, 306, 312
Carey, James B., 189, 190, 191, 194–195, 197, 199, 215
Carroll, James, 211
Caterpillar Tractor Company, 102, 308, 309
Celanese Corporation of America, 312
Central business districts, 61
Central Virginia Industries, 37
Chambers of commerce
  Rockford, Ill., 37
  Syracuse, 4, 19–23, 45, 120, 143, 161–162, 249–250, 303
  of U.S., 154, 260, 261
  Utica, N.Y., 127
Chappell & Sons, C. E., 117
Charleston, W. Va., 168
Chemical Society, American, 153
Chicago, 73, 168
Chicago Pneumatic Tool Company, 128
Chrysler Corporation, 139, 148, 268, 282
  New Process Gear, 117, 284
Citizens Council of New York State, 34, 41, 265
Citizens Foundation, Syracuse, 21–23, 39, 303
Citizens' groups, 17–19, 31–36, 39, 183, 265–266
Citizens League of Greater Minneapolis, 36
City-county coordination, 43–44, 48, 49, 64–67
City planning; see Community development
Civic Progress, Inc., St. Louis, 55
Cleveland, O., 36, 51, 56, 57, 59, 60, 87, 108, 110
Closing plants, 282–286
Communications Workers of America, 228

Community chests, 10, 18, 75–80, 104, 110, 228
  Syracuse, 38, 76–80, 84, 110, 303
  union role in, 79–80
Community development
  Allegheny Conference on, 55, 56, 61, 168–169
  Mahoning and Shenango Valleys Industrial Information Institute, 37, 129–130
  Syracuse, 43–51, 56
Community structure, 13–38
Commuting, 62–63, 88
Consolidated Edison Company of New York, 176–178, 183
Continental Can Co., 314
Contributions; see Philanthropy
Cordiner, Ralph J., 263
Corning Glass Works, 243, 308
Crouse-Hinds Company, 14, 50, 86, 110, 117, 306, 311–312, 314
Crucible Steel Company of America (Sanderson-Halcomb Works), 156, 184, 314
Curtice, Harlow H., 268

Dade County; see Metropolitan regions, Miami
Dade County Research Foundation, 36
Detroit, Mich., 31, 60, 81–85, 88, 94, 95, 110, 168
Development credit corporations, 279–280
Dietz Company, R. E., 313
Donations; see Management, community activity; Philanthropy
Donora, Pa.
  smog deaths, 167
Dorst, Joseph M., mayor, St. Louis, 55
du Pont de Nemours & Co., E. I., 6, 134, 167, 174

Eagan Real Estate Company, 250
Eastman Kodak Company, 308
Easy Washing Machine Company

(now Syracuse Industries, Division of Union Chemical and Materials Corporation), 14, 313
Economic education, 28, 39, 104, 261
  workshops, 143
Economic Research Council of Metropolitan Syracuse, 250
Economy League of Pennsylvania, 36
Electric Auto-Lite Company, 314
Electrical, Radio and Machine Workers, International Union of (I.U.E.), 187–217, 222, 239, 240
ELRIC; see Employers Labor Relations Information Committee
Employee relations, 25–26, 187–189, 309–315
  during strike, 197–198, 200, 223–225
Employers Labor Relations Information Committee (ELRIC), 260–261, 263–264, 271
Engelberg Huller Company, 313
Essay contests, 39, 138
Esso Foundation, 144
Esso Standard Oil Company, 97, 180, 270–271
Ethnic groups, 17, 18
Evanston, Ill., 63
Evansville, Ind., 37, 129, 151–152

Ford, Henry II, 82
Ford Motor Company, 84, 139, 144, 174, 268, 308
Foundations (corporate); see Philanthropy, corporate
Franklin, Herbert H., 13
Fraudulent soliciting, 107–109, 113
Frazer and Jones Company, 314
Freedom Foundation, 22

Garment Workers' Union, International Ladies', 60, 234
Gas Association, American, 139, 147
Gaylord Container Division, Crown Zellerbach Corp., 55

General American Life Insurance Co., 55
General Dynamics Corp., Convair Division, 153
General Electric Co., 50, 68, 100, 117, 128, 141, 147, 148, 153, 292, 306, 313, 315
  business climate, 260–263
  CR evaluation, 317–320, 323
  labor relations, 187–218, 219, 221, 222, 238–240, 307
  plant location, 251–255, 271, 277, 282, 284
General Foods Corp., 144, 312
General Mills, Inc., 147, 260
General Motors Corp., 173, 268, 289, 308
  Brown-Lipe-Chapin, 306, 314
Government services; see Municipal government
Government Efficiency and Economy, Baltimore Commission on, 36
Governmental Research
  Cleveland Bureau of, 36
  Institute, St. Louis, 36
  Syracuse, Bureau of, 21–23, 36, 40, 45, 48, 49, 122–123, 303
Greenewalt, Crawford H., 6
Greensboro (N.C.) Industries, 37
Grimm, Sergai, N., 44
Gulf Oil Corp., 144

Hancock, Stewart F., 14–15, 20, 77, 79–80
Harrison, Clyde, 193, 201
Hazard, F. Rowland, 13, 157
Hazard, Leland, 94, 96
Health Council, N.Y.C. Citizens, 8
Health and welfare programs, 8, 26, 43, 49
  agency funds, 80–81, 104
Heart Association, American, 82, 99
Hellerman, Will, 246
Hiawatha, 155, 305
Hinds, Will, 50

Home Improvement campaigns, 57–58
    cleanup campaigns, 58
Hospitals, 18, 26, 43, 44, 104
Housing, 18, 49–51, 57–60, 62, 70–71
    U.S. Housing Act, 60
Housing and Planning Council, Chicago Metropolitan, 73
Hudson, Howard, 246
Hughes Aircraft Co., 145

Indianapolis, 170
Industrial development committees, 56, 250, 279–280, 284
Industrial Editors, American Association of, 90
Industrial Relations Council of Metropolitan Boston, 237
Industrial Management Council, Rochester, N.Y., 20, 37
Industrial parks, 280–281, 289–290
    Syracuse, 250
Industrial waste; see Pollution
Infantile Paralysis, National Foundation for, 80, 81, 111
Inland Steel Co., 236
International Harvester Co., 101, 282, 283, 284–285, 327–336
Iron and Steel Institute, American, 139
Ithaca, N.Y., 131
Ithaca College, 145

Johnson, Roy W., 68
Jolly, Fred, 102, 309
Junior college, 135–136

Kaiser Aluminum & Chemical Corp., 174, 277
Kaiser, Henry J. Cos., 58
Kansas City, 58
Kennecott Copper Corp., 277
Kenosha, Wis., 37
Kiwanis, 18

Labor-Management cooperation, 235–239

Boston, 237
    Louisville, 237–238
    Syracuse, 79–80, 314
    Toledo, 236–237, 238
Labor unions, 117–118, 120, 151, 312, 314
    AFL, 273–274
    AFL-CIO Community Service committee, 228–230
    community relations, 227–231
    education programs, 230
    newspapers, 231, 233
    organizing, 234–235; in the South, 274–275
    strikes, 187–218, 219–223, 283
    Syracuse Federation of Labor, 117
    Texas State Federation of Labor, 231; see also Labor-Management cooperation
La Crosse, Wis., 136
Lackawanna, N.Y., 167
Laidlaw, Walter C., 82
Lamson Corp., 313
Lang, Dr. Edward H., 116
Leadership; see Management, community activity; Syracuse industrial leadership
Lennox Industries, Inc., 313
Life Insurance, Institute of, 139, 147
Lipe-Rollway Corp., 14, 117
Location of industry, 52, 54–55, 61–64, 242–291, 292
Lockheed Aircraft Corp., 277
Los Angeles, 168, 171–174, 176, 185, 186
Louisville, Ky., 56, 237, 238
    Louisville Area Development Association, 56
Lynchburg, Va., 37

Mallach, Aubrey, 8
Management related organizations, 19–25
Manufacturers associations
    California, 270
    Evansville, Ind., 37, 130–131
    Kenosha, Wis., 37

Michigan, 268, 270
National, 37, 38, 148, 153, 206
Racine, Wis., 37
Stamford-Greenwich (Conn.) Manufacturers Council, 37
Syracuse, 37–39, 45, 80, 89, 302, 303
    and community development, 249–250, 255–256, 276
    and schools, 114–120, 141–142, 143
    and pollution, 161–162, 184
Machinists, International Association of, 151, 230, 234
Management, community activity, 1–41, 77–78, 301
    as teachers, 145–146
    money, 86–87, 110–111
    time, 1–2, 96
Manufacturing Chemists Association, 138, 139, 166, 181, 182
    Air Pollution Abatement Committee, 170
Marcellus Casket Co., 313
Massena, N.Y., 286
Mead, Donald H., 46
Mellon, Richard King, 55
Mental health programs, 17–18
Metropolitan regions, 50–53, 301–302
    Chicago, 64
    Los Angeles, 172
    Miami (Dade County), 66, 275
    New York, 53, 74
    Pittsburgh, 36
    St. Louis, 64
    Syracuse, 70, 275
    Toronto, 74
Metropolitan Study Commission of Allegheny County, 37
Mial, H. Curtis, 34
Miami, Fla., 36, 51, 55, 58, 66, 302
Miller, Glen B., 159
Milwaukee, Wis., 58
Minneapolis, Minn., 36
Monsanto Chemical Co., 55
Moses, Robert, 54
Municipal government, 26, 36

duplication, 64, 66, 69, 302
financing, 39–40, 45–48, 53–55, 245
services, 49, 57, 245
see Metropolitan areas
Musicians, American Federation of, 231

Nassau County, N.Y., 63
National Association of Manufacturers
    see Manufacturers Associations
National Cash Register Co., 3, 86
    Adding Machine Division, 145
National Petro-Chemicals Corp., 174
National Standard Parts Association, 139
Neighborhood improvement; *see* ACTION
Nationwide Insurance Co., 243–249, 308, 337
Nestle Co., The, 251
New England industry, 271–272, 280, 282
New Orleans, La., 58, 65
New Voters' Forum, 39
Newark, N.J., 58
New York Central Railroad, 250
New York City, 53–55, 60, 61–62, 65, 71, 143–144, 168, 176–178
New York City Board of Transportation, 177
New York City Bureau of Smoke Control, 177
New York Port Authority, 65
New York State
    registration of fundraisers, 109
    Thruway, 245, 254
New York Telephone Co., 117
Niagara Mohawk Power Corp., 117, 250, 306
Nolan, James, 134–135
North Carolina fundraising permits, 109
Norton, Fred, 244

Oakland, Calif., 137–138

Oak Ridge Institute of Nuclear Stud-
ies, 144
Oberdorfer Foundries, Inc., 313
Onondaga Lake, 305
pollution, 155–164
Onondaga Pottery Co., 14, 311
Otis Elevator Co., 64, 270
Owens-Illinois Glass Co., 107
Oxford Paper Co., 134

Parking; see Traffic and parking
Pasadena, Calif., 266
Pas and Seymour, Inc., 313
Paterson, N.J., 63
Payroll deduction plans, 85, 88
Pearl River, N.Y., 138
Pendray, G. Edward, 616
Pennsylvania fundraising permits, 109
"People Act in Syracuse, The," 39
Peoria, Ill., 102
Petroleum Institute, American, 139,
147
Philadelphia, Pa., 31, 36, 65, 259,
276
Philanthropy, corporate, 25, 48, 75–
77, 87, 92–109
comparison, 100
foundations, 105–106
policies, 94–109, 111–112
Philanthropy, private, 13–14, 76
Pittsburgh, Pa., 36, 302
Pittsburgh Plate Glass Co., 94, 96
Pitney-Bowes, Inc., 308
Plant location, see Location of industry
Political activity, 23, 30–31, 33, 36,
69, 121, 302
Pollution, 155–184
air, 167–178, 180–181, 185, 186
cities compared, 168
community relations programs, 176–
184
expenditures, 173–175
regulations, 166, 167–171, 185
research, 171–175
self-policing, 168–169

water, 155–164, 165–166, 171,
174–176, 182
Population shifts, 52–55, 62, 71, 259
Porter-Cable Machine Co., 309–310,
312
Power-structure (community leader-
ship structure), 13–20, 25–28
Precision castings (Ainsworth-Preci-
sion Castings Co.), 313
Press relations, 298
during strikes, 225–227, 228
rel. pollution abatement, 160, 175,
176–177, 182
Procter and Gamble Co., 144
Prosperity Company Division (Ward
Industries Corp.), 313

Radio Corporation of America, 145,
153
Race relations, 56, 72, 274
Racine, Wis., 37, 146
Railroads, Association of American,
139
Ralston Purina Co., 146
Real Estate Boards, National Associa-
tion of, 58
Recruitment of industry, 44, 127–
128, 249, 255, 275–276, 278–
282
Red Cross, American, 80, 82, 228
Remington Co., 284
Remington Rand Division (Sperry
Rand Corp.), 255
Rochester, N.Y., 20, 37, 116, 118
competition for industry, 244, 245–
251
Rockford, Ill., 37
Rotary Club, 128
Roth, Carl F. B., 123
Rumford, Maine, 134–135

St. Louis, 37, 51, 55, 60, 64, 168,
265, 302
Sales taxes, 47–48, 70
San Francisco, Calif., 60, 65
Sarnoff, General David, 145
Schools, 26, 102, 114–151; see Voca-

tional counseling, Vocational education, Teaching aids
financing, 122–124
gifts, 104
improvement, 43, 44, 46, 48
School boards, 10, 39, 48, 148–149, 301
Scranton, Pa., 282
Sears, Roebuck & Co., 57, 72, 147
Foundation, 105
Slums, 43, 44, 53–60, 72, 73, 262; see Urban renewal
costs of, 59
to industry, 69
Smith-Corona, Inc., 14, 50, 310–311
Smith, H. W., 50, 310
Smith, L. C., 13, 310
Smith, M. C., 310
Smith, W. L., 310
Smoke Control Bureau, New York City, 177
Smoke Control Ordinance, Allegheny County, 168–169
Social Agencies, Councils of, 38, 40, 79
Solvay Process Division; see Allied Chemical & Dye Corp.
Southern industry, 272–274, 277, 280, 283
Southwestern Bell Telephone Co., 55
Spokane, Wash., 136
Standard Oil Co. (Calif.), 147
Standard Oil Co. (Indiana), 10
Standard Oil Co. (New Jersey), 107
Stanford Research Institute, 173
Steelworkers of America, United, 117, 198
Strike Advertising Campaign
General Electric, 192–200, 207–213
I.U.E., 201, 213
Strike, effects of, 189–190, 214–215, 216–218, 219–223
Sunray Mid-Continental Oil Co., 140
Sylvania Electric Products, Inc., 250–251
Syracuse
attitudes, 255–256, 298, 304

Board of Education, 114, 117–120, 122, 139
business climate, 266, 270, 291, 337–349
Citizens Foundation, 21, 23, 39
CR programs in, 305–315
Economic Research Council, 250
fundraising in, 75–91, 97–98
General Electric in, 187–218, 238–239, 254–257
industrial leadership, 5, 13–24, 28–29, 43, 50, 77–79, 254–255, 303–304, 305
Industrial Park, 250
labor dispute (GE-IUE), 187–217, 238–239
Long-Range Capital Improvement Committee, 46
Municipal Research Bureau, 40
Nationwide Insurance Co. in, 244–246, 248–251, 337–351
Postwar Planning Council, 44, 56
Retail Association, 139
Sales Executives Club, 89
Solvay Process pollution dispute, 155–164, 183, 184
vocational education, 114–126, 133–134, 139–140
United Fund, 78–91, 110
Syracuse Bureau of Governmental Research; see Governmental Research
Syracuse Community Chest; see Community chests
Syracuse Chamber of Commerce; see Chambers of commerce
Syracuse Manufacturers Association; see Manufacturers associations
Syracuse Ornamental Co., 313
Syracuse University, 39, 50, 70, 118, 141, 143, 249, 250, 254

Taft-Hartley Act, 198, 223, 225
Taxes (see also Sales tax), 26, 40, 47–48, 52–53, 57, 58–59, 262–271, 288, 293–294
duplication of, 64

excess profits, 92, 105
industry's share, 63–64, 69, 167
Teachers, 39, 40, 142–148, 153, 307;
    see also Teaching aids
Teaching aids, 147–149, 154
Teamsters, Chauffeurs, Warehouse-
    men and Helpers of America,
    International Brotherhood of,
    231
Textile Workers of America, United,
    283
Thought leaders, 27, 75, 297, 307
Tidewater Oil Co., 270
Timken Roller Bearing Co., 144
Toledo, O., 108, 236–237, 238
Tolley, William P., 44
Toronto, 74
Traffic and parking, 43, 44, 52–53,
    55, 56, 61–62, 69–70, 73, 257
Trenton, N.J., 274

Union Carbide Corp., 153, 174
United funds, 20, 40, 75, 78–91, 94,
    110, 303, 311; see also Philan-
    thropy, corporate; Management
    community activity
U.S. Hoffman Machinery Corp., 282,
    284, 314
United States Steel Corp., 169, 277
    Fairless Works, 287–288
University of Houston, 136
University of Miami, 66
University of Pittsburgh
    Law School, 61
Urban renewal, 43–51, 55–61, 67–69,
    73; see also Slums and Location
    of industry
    Community action committee, 127

Utica, N.Y., 119, 127–128, 151, 244,
    250, 265
    Community Action Committee,
    127
    Utica College (Syracuse Univer-
    sity), 128

Vocational education, 114–146
    work-study, 139–142
Vocational guidance, 136–142, 149,
    151–152

Wagner, Edward, 246
Wampler, Cloud, 15, 20, 38
Washington, D.C., 175
Washington University, 146
Waste; see Pollution
Western Oil & Gas Association, 173
Westinghouse Electric Corp., 100,
    285–286
Williams, Mennan, Governor, 268
Will and Baumer Candle Co., 312–
    313
Wilson, Robert E., 10
Women Voters, League of, 48, 50,
    162, 184
Woody, Kennerly, 5
Worcester, Mass., 37

Yonkers, N.Y., 64, 282–284
Young, Ben, 82
Youngstown, O., 37, 128–130, 166
Youth programs, 10, 39, 40, 71

Zoning, 26, 61–62, 71, 72–73, 295;
    see also Location of industrial
    parks

Date Due